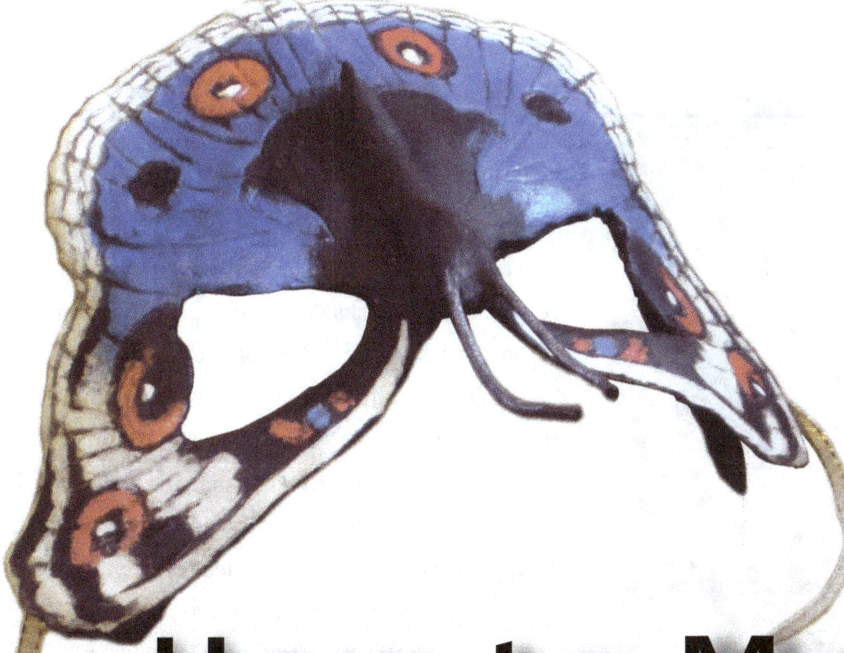

How to Make
Masks!

EASY NEW WAY TO MAKE A MASK
FOR MASQUERADE, HALLOWEEN AND
DRESS-UP FUN, WITH JUST TWO LAYERS OF
FAST-SETTING PAPER MACHE

BY JONNI GOOD

WET CAT BOOKS, LA GRANDE, OREGON

ABOUT THE AUTHOR

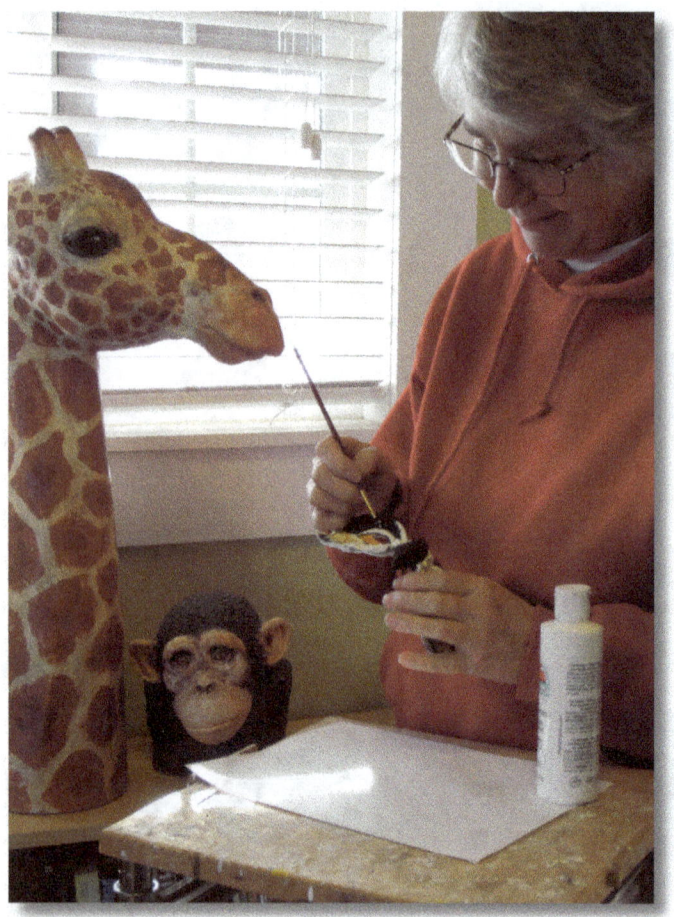

Jonni Good has worked with a variety of artistic media all her life—but she always comes back to paper mache. She currently lives in eastern Oregon with 6 real critters and a menagerie of paper mache animal sculptures and masks. She ~~works~~ plays full time as a sculptor, author and web publisher.

You'll find a lively community of paper mache fanatics on the author's blog. If you have any questions at all about the methods in this book, about paper mache in general—or if you just want to talk about whatever—drop by and leave a comment. And be sure to show off your new masks, at:

http://UltimatePaperMache.com

ALSO BY JONNI GOOD

Make Animal Sculptures with Paper Mache Clay:
How to Create Stunning Wildlife Art Using Patterns and My Easy-to-Make, No-Mess Paper Mache Recipe

Published by Wet Cat Books
1311 V Ave
La Grande, or 97850
http://WetCatBooks.com

ISBN: 978-0-9741065-4-0
Library of Congress Control Number: 2012931178

Contents

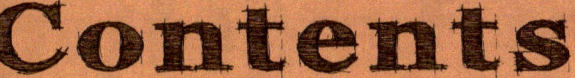

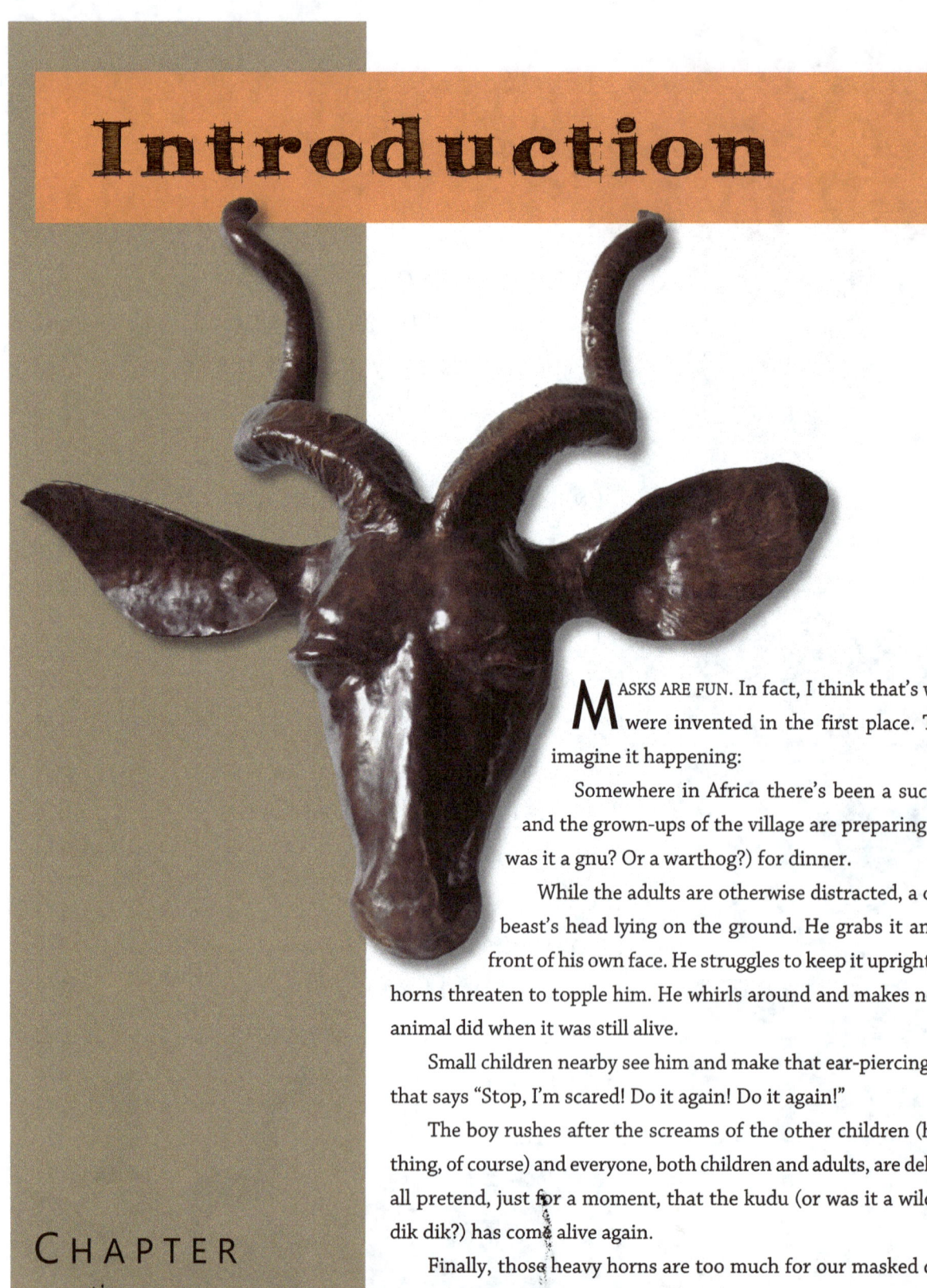

Introduction

MASKS ARE FUN. In fact, I think that's why masks were invented in the first place. This is how I imagine it happening:

Somewhere in Africa there's been a successful hunt, and the grown-ups of the village are preparing the kudu (or was it a gnu? Or a warthog?) for dinner.

While the adults are otherwise distracted, a child sees the beast's head lying on the ground. He grabs it and holds it in front of his own face. He struggles to keep it upright as the heavy horns threaten to topple him. He whirls around and makes noises like the animal did when it was still alive.

Small children nearby see him and make that ear-piercing play screech that says "Stop, I'm scared! Do it again! Do it again!"

The boy rushes after the screams of the other children (he can't see a thing, of course) and everyone, both children and adults, are delighted. They all pretend, just for a moment, that the kudu (or was it a wildebeest? or a dik dik?) has come alive again.

Finally, those heavy horns are too much for our masked clown and he plummets head first into the dust. Everyone roars with laughter.

When the kid grows up and becomes an accomplished craftsman, he remembers that day and says to himself "that would work a lot better if there were holes for the eyes. If I carved it from wood, it would be lighter and it could last almost forever. And with a bit of paint, a little fur..."

Every mask that has ever been worn was first created by an artist or craftsperson—or a child. It's this creative process that allows all the magic of masks to happen.

That magic is also why the history of masks is rather complicated. Although children are perfectly comfortable with magic, it makes older people a little nervous.

So, (in my invented version of things), sometime after that first child picked up the kudu's head and scared his delighted siblings and cousins, masks moved into the serious (and mysterious) world of religion, mythology and sacrament.

Masks create the same kind of magic that happens in a movie theater or at a good play, where actors make an entire audience see the same story—and even feel the same emotions—while at the same time every person there knows that somebody just made it all up.

With the help of music, dancing, and ceremony, the magic of masks can even bring the spirit world to life

In Africa, where the mask-making tradition undoubtedly began, mask-makers use abstract and sophisticated artistic forms to indicate the otherness of the spirit world their masks represent. You can find similar mask-making traditions associated with the spirit plane in communities all across the world, and these traditional masks often take on fantastic, and sometimes even monstrous, forms.

But that's not all we use masks for. Masks have also been used in the theater, most notably the Noh plays of Japan and Commedia dell'arte in Italy, where the masks cover the wearers' natural expression so the actors must use body language and movement to bring the stories to life.

Masks are sometimes used to disguise the faces of the people wearing them. This is one of the reasons for masquerade masks, of the type now used at carnivals and fancy-dress balls. These masks allow the wearer to let loose a bit and have more fun than they normally do when they're wearing their own faces.

Using a mask to hide one's identity was once a major cultural event in Vienna, when women were required to wear a male-faced mask when they went to the theater (often one like the Bauta mask found in Chapter 9), citizens had to wear them to maintain their anonymity when casting votes, professional men wore them to disguise themselves when they went to somewhat shady gambling spots in the city, and young noblemen wore them when they wanted to do something naughty (or even illegal) without getting caught. Today, Venetian-style masks are still fun to wear at events like Mardi Gras and Fat Tuesday celebrations. (I show you how to make some of the most popular styles in this book).

Halloween masks might be considered disguises, too—although this probably wasn't their primary purpose when the holiday first began in the distant past. Historians believe Halloween originated with the ancient Celtic festival of Samhain. Back then, the costumes and masks may have helped to ward off ghosts who come out on

Although it doesn't fit my story very well, archeologists think the oldest masks made by modern humans looked like this one, which was made of stone around 7,000 BCE. Recently, a bone mask made by Neanderthals was discovered on the banks of the Loire in France, and is estimated to be about 35,000 years old. It, too, has a human face (sort of).

Of course, lots of animal bones have been found around ancient human settlements. There's no way to know if kids played with them or not.

Photo courtesy Wikipedia.com

that particular night—October 31st is the official beginning of the "dark half" of the year.

Today, however, the Halloween mask brings us back to what was, in my opinion, the first reason for masks—to have fun.

Most of us don't wear masks very often—we seem to need an excuse like Halloween or a masquerade ball to give us "permission" to wear one. But even if we can't wear a mask to school or while we shop at the mall, we shouldn't let that stop us from making them. Making masks is just as much fun as wearing them. After all, the act of artistic creation is also a form of magic.

When you make your masks you also have a chance to experience some of the magical versatility of paper mache: it can be made to look like fur or feathers, antique gold, ancient bone, rusted iron, and even carved and highly polished African wood, like the Kudu display mask at the beginning of this chapter (you'll see how to make him in Chapter 17).

WHY MAKE MASKS?

Making a mask really does feel just as magical as wearing one. And remember—masks aren't just for wearing. They make great wall art, too. With just a few inexpensive materials and a few hours of "work," you can

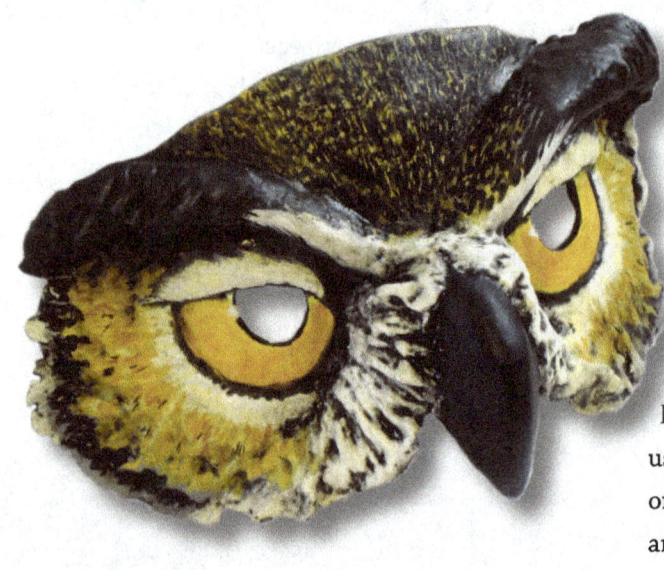

populate the walls of your home (or your costume chest) with brand new personalities, creatures, and beasts.

Even more exciting, think of this—just by making a mask of your own creation, you're following in the footsteps of a tradition that goes back at least 35,000 years, to the days when Neanderthals still lived on earth. I think that's pretty amazing, don't you?

I actually started making masks because I ran out of room for my life-sized paper mache animal sculptures in my small house—I wanted to make sculptures for my walls, and animal masks don't make me think of the Great White Hunter the way a sculpted trophy mount would. It's also fun to have a few masks in the toy box when my grandson comes to visit (the Plague Doctor mask in Chapter 10 is his favorite, I think. Although he likes the Duck Hat, too).

Although I have experimented with many different methods for making paper mache masks, I really started having fun with them when I began using positive molds. This is a traditional method of making paper mache sculptures of all kinds, and for good reason.

The mold lets us do all the sculpting with modeling clay, which is a much more intuitive sculptural medium than paper mache. And, in the spirit of starving artists everywhere, I like the fact that I can use my modeling clay again and again to make new masks. (I like using Super Sculpey® for this purpose, but I don't bake it. I just like using a soft clay for my masks, and it's the only soft modeling clay available in my small town.)

Because the molds are only used once, each mask made by this process is a one-of-a-kind original.

Once the paper mache has been applied to the mold and it dries hard enough to stand on its own, it's lifted off the mold. With the special plaster/glue paste I use, this only takes a few hours if I set the mask in front of a fan. Then it can be popped into a warm oven for another hour or so to make sure it's dry all the way through. It is actually possible to start a mask in the morning and wear it that evening, but it's definitely a good idea to give yourself a bit more time. (Why do paper mache artists always seem to be in a hurry? Halloween sneaks up on us, somehow—how does that happen?)

Although making paper mache masks using positive molds is a time-honored tradition, you'll use some new materials to make the paper mache itself. Instead of making paste with white flour and water, you'll be using a mixture of white PVA glue (the most popular brand in the U.S. is Elmer's Glue-All®), which is mixed with ordinary plaster of Paris. For each mask you'll also be using a few sheets of strong, stretchy paper from a roll of Scott Shop Towels®. These products are sold at your local hardware store or the DIY section of WalMart, and they cost just a few cents per mask. Of course, if you give your masks as gifts or sell them at the local art fair, you don't have to tell people how little they cost to make.

You don't even need a big dedicated studio space for your projects. Every mask in this book was made on the top of a 14" square kitchen cart. (The kudu would have

been a bit easier to make on a larger table, but it still worked). I use the cart because it's high enough for me to work on comfortably while standing up. You don't need anything fancy to make paper mache.

ABOUT THE INSTRUCTIONS:

There's no need to make your masks in any particular order—just choose the one that appeals to you and jump right in*. However, since all of the masks are made with the same basic methods, I cover these basics in detail in Chapters 2 through 6. When we get to the chapters showing individual masks, I'll assume that you've read those chapters, since repeating the repetitious steps would become, well, repetitious.

Each chapter will show you the way to sculpt your modeling clay to make your mold, how to apply the paper mache over any challenging features, and how to finish your masks to look like the ones shown at the beginning of each chapter. Then, if you discover that you enjoy making masks as much as I do, you might want to use your new skills to copy a ceremonial mask from a museum collection, or create masks for your local theater group. In fact, you can use these methods to make any kind of mask you want—you are certainly not restricted to the projects I could fit into these pages.

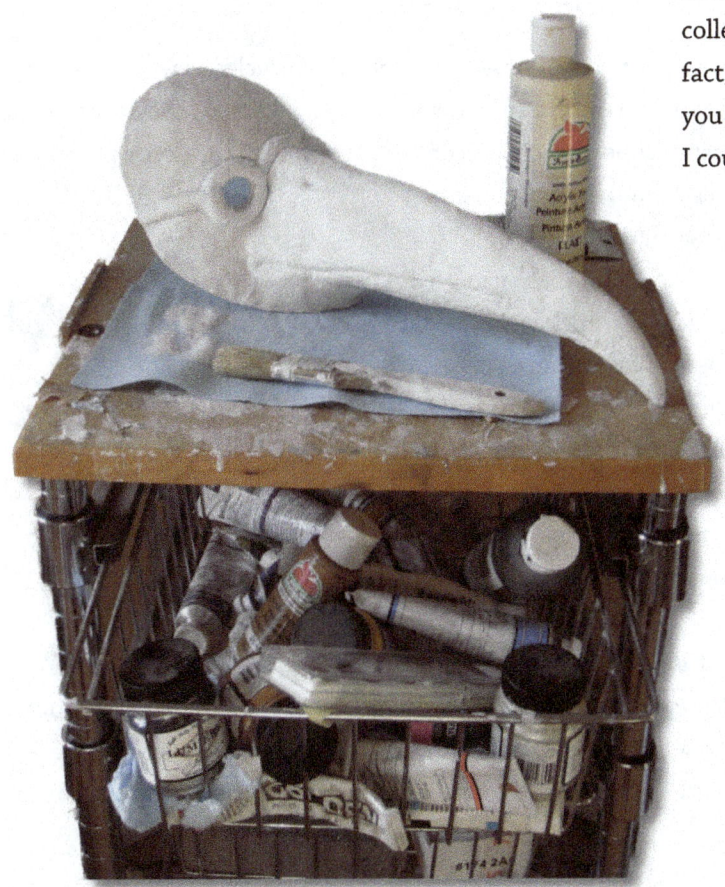

Since some of the masks are more challenging than others, you might want to start with the Volto mask first, just to get a feel for the materials.

5

Materials

THE PAPER

For the paper mache layers, you'll need a roll of Scott Shop Towels®, made by Kimberley-Clark. These exceptionally strong and absorbent blue paper towels are made for mechanics and craftsmen, so you should be able to find them in any American hardware store. A nice person at the Kimberley-Clark company told me you can also find their towels at Costco in the UK, and at Sam's Club and Walmart in Mexico. Unfortunately, they aren't available in all countries, so you may need to experiment with other brands.

These paper towels aren't free, like the recycled newspapers many paper mache artists like to use, but you only need a few sheets per mask. The strength and stretchiness of this paper makes the entire process so much easier, and the paper makes your masks incredibly strong..

The one drawback to using the towels is the thickness of the paper. The edges don't "melt" into the surface quite as well as thinner paper does, so you can sometimes see where the pieces join together.

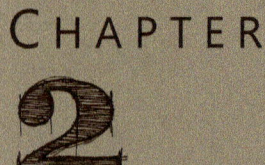

However, this isn't as much of a problem as you might think. The stretchiness of the paper lets us use much larger pieces, for fewer edges. Then, any bumps or ridges that remain in the dried paper mache are smoothed out with the easy finishing techniques I'll show you in Chapter 6.

CHAPTER

2

PLASTER-BASED PASTE

To make the paste, mix together:

- **1/4 cup (60 ml) white glue (Elmer's Glue-All® or any PVA glue)**
- **1 tablespoon (15 ml) cold water**
- **1 teaspoon (5 ml) vinegar (it slows down the plaster to give you more time to work)**

Then mix in:

- **1/4 cup (60 ml) plaster of Paris**

You can thin the paste with water, but that will make it take a bit longer before you can remove the mask from the mold. Be sure to use cold water—warm water makes plaster set up faster, and you need all the time you can get to spread the paste and apply the paper mache to your mold.

Because of the plaster, your paste might start to get too thick in the bowl or on your brushes before you're done applying the two layers of paper mache. In that case, just put the thickened paste in the garbage, rinse your bowl and brush (first in your bucket and then in the sink), and then make another batch. Never rush the process of adding the paper mache layers just because your paste is getting too thick—I've made that mistake a few times myself, and I always regret it.

PLASTER-BASED GESSO

Gesso will cover small imperfections in the paper mache, and will create a nice white ground for your paint. Traditional plaster gesso is made with hide glue, but that's hard to find and rather expensive. We'll use white glue instead—it works just fine. Mix your gesso just like the paste recipe.

- **1 tablespoon (15 ml) white glue**
- **2 teaspoons (10 ml) water**
- **2 tablespoon (30 ml) plaster of Paris**
- **¼ teaspoon (1 ml) vinegar**
- **Small dab of white craft paint (optional)**

Apply your gesso to the dry paper mache. You can sand between coats (use a mask when sanding) or you can use a damp sponge, paper towel or finger to polish the gesso. The gesso must be bone dry before sanding, but you can wet-polish it just a few minutes after applying, as soon as the surface is dry.

Use liquid craft paint if you want your gesso to be an opaque white (or any other color you prefer). Don't use acrylic artists' paint out of a tube—in my experiments the more expensive tube paint thickens the gesso to the texture of whipped cream, which is not terribly useful. Inexpensive craft paint works better in this recipe.

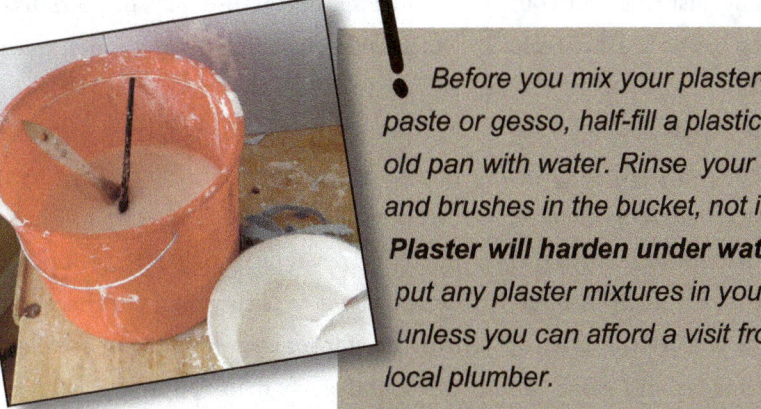

*Before you mix your plaster-based paste or gesso, half-fill a plastic bucket or old pan with water. Rinse your spoon, bowl and brushes in the bucket, not in your sink. **Plaster will harden under water**—so don't put any plaster mixtures in your pipes unless you can afford a visit from your local plumber.*

REALLY SMOOTH GESSO MIX

For some masks you may want a porcelain-smooth finish. The easy way to do that is to use one or two coats of the gesso recipe on the previous page, sanding or wet-polishing between coats. For the final coat of gesso, use this recipe:

- **1 tablespoon (15 ml) white glue**
- **½ teaspoon (2 ml) cold water**
- **¼ teaspoon (1 ml) vinegar**
- **½ tablespoon (7.5 ml) plaster of Paris**

You can double the recipe if you're making a larger mask. Don't make too much, or the gesso may thicken before you have time to use it all.

IMPORTANT THINGS TO KNOW ABOUT PLASTER

You can find plaster of Paris in hardware stores and art stores. When water is added (or, in this case, white glue and water) plaster turns solid, but for our purposes we don't want it to get hard too quickly. To slow it down a bit we add just a touch of vinegar to our paste and gesso mixtures. This will give you from 10 to 20 minutes to work.

You may notice that the gesso in your brush starts to get hard before the gesso in your bowl. Dried plaster paste on the surface of the paper mache will cause the gesso in the brush to harden faster (I don't know why it happens, but it does). If you see this happening, just rinse out your brush, or use a fresh one. I use cheap bristle brushes from the paint store, which cost about 49¢.

Plaster will harden underwater (that's why I keep saying that you shouldn't dump left-over paste or gesso into your sink) but it never gets rock-hard like concrete. That means that your paper mache surface will always stay slightly water-soluble, so you can use a damp sponge, paper towel or even a damp finger to polish the surface of your masks even after the paper mache and gesso are completely dry. This is much easier and less messy than sanding. However, since they aren't watertight, your masks must be protected from moisture with a final coat of varnish, both inside and out. I prefer to use a matte or satin acrylic varnish if the masks will be used inside. For display masks, you can also use wax varnish or paste wax, which gives the work a soft, warm finish. For outside use, you'll want to use a polyurethane varnish or marine varnish from the hardware store.

Since powdered plaster attracts water, even from the air, always keep your bucket tightly closed.

Plaster sets up through a mysterious chemical action, which will usually make your paper mache masks strong enough to lift off their molds in a few hours if you set them in front of a fan. However, they still won't be dry all the way through. You can finish drying them in a warm oven (not over 200°F or 93°C) after they've been lifted from the mold (but never put modeling clay or plastic in your oven). Or you could be patient and put them in a warm place, in front of a fan, or just on a table where the cat won't disturb them, and let them dry naturally.

OTHER MATERIALS YOU'LL NEED

MODELING CLAY

The clay is used to create the positive mold that you'll make for your masks. I like using a soft modeling clay, because it allows me to work quickly, and the soft clay is easy to pull out of the mask after it's lifted off the mold.

PLASTIC MASK FORM

The clay is applied over a mask form that gives the inside of your mask room for your nose and eyes. Plastic forms are inexpensive, and can be purchased online. Unfortunately, most plastic forms seem to be made for children, so it's difficult to find one that will fit older kids or adults.

HOME-MADE MASK FORM

If you find a plastic mask form that fits, that's great. Go ahead and use it. However, if you can't find one, don't worry—I'll show you how to make one that will work just fine.

ACRYLIC PAINT

You can use either liquid craft paint or artist's paint from a tube. I also used Metallic Paint for several masks, and Puffy Paint for raised designs.

ACRYLIC GLAZING LIQUID

I use the Golden brand glazing liquid, which I purchase online from http://www.dickblick.com. You may be able to find it at your local store.

INSTANT IRON AND INSTANT RUST

Used only for the Iron Celtic Helmet in Chapter 16.

CHARCOAL STICK

This is used only one time in this book, to soften the shadows on the Neanderthal skull.

ACRYLIC OR POLYURETHANE VARNISH

Acrylic varnish can be purchased from any art store. For most masks, I prefer the matte finish, but this is just a personal preference. If you intend to wear the mask outside in the rain you may want to use a water-based polyurethane finish from the hardware store.

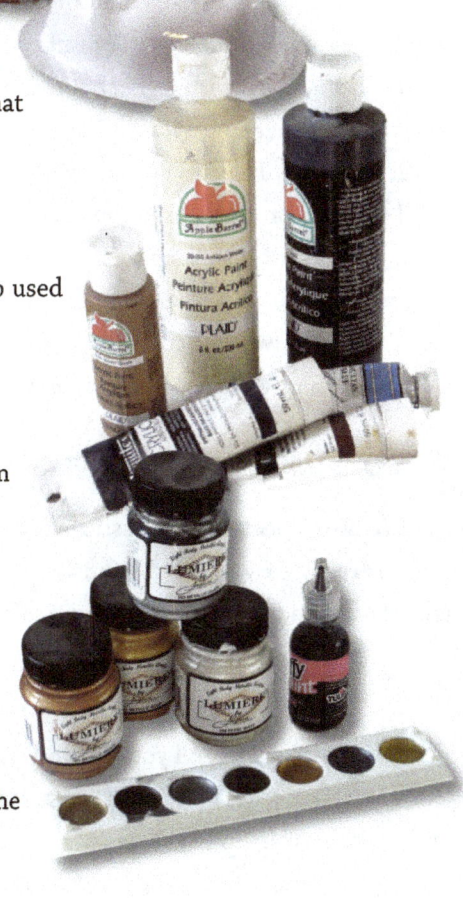

KRYLON MATTE FINISH

I use this product to seal the masks before adding a glaze. This prevents the dark glaze from being absorbed unevenly. You could use the brush-on acrylic varnish for this purpose, instead. If the previous paint layers appear to have sealed the mask enough, you won't need to use either product.

PLASTER CLOTH

We use plaster-impregnated gauze only for the home-made mask form. If you will be using a plastic form, the plaster cloth is not needed.

DUCT TAPE

This is also used only for the home-made form.

JOINT COMPOUND

This is a product that's used in the construction industry, for taping the joints between two sheets of drywall on new walls. It looks like plaster that has already been mixed with water, but it doesn't harden as quickly as plaster. If you don't already have some, it isn't absolutely necessary to run to the hardware store to get some, but I always keep it on hand.

I use this product for my masks only when my paper mache comes out really bumpy (usually because I was in too much of a hurry to do a good job during the pasting process), and it's used to create the veins on the Butterfly mask. Any brand will work. It comes in a plastic tub. If the lid is kept tightly closed, one bucket would last you for a very long time.

PETROLEUM JELLY AND THIN PLASTIC SHEET

We use a sheet of thin plastic over our home-made mask forms to make it really easy to lift the finished mask off the form. The petroleum jelly is used under the plastic to keep it from slipping around.

ALUMINUM FOIL

Use the cheapest foil you can find. We use it for the home-made mask form, and to pad areas, like big beaks or noses, so we don't need to use so much modeling clay. The foil is left inside the horns on the Unicorn and Kudu masks.

HOT GLUE GUN

This is used to attach the stick to the owl mask, and to attach a hanger to display masks. If you prefer, you can use a two-part epoxy cement instead. You may also want to attach the ribbon or cord with a hot glue gun.

TOOLS

YOU ALSO NEED TO HAVE THESE ITEMS ON HAND:

- **Small Bowl, Measuring Spoons and Measuring Cup** (for the paste and gesso)

- **Cheap Bristle Paint Brush** (for spreading the paste and gesso)

- **Artist's Brushes** in your favorite sizes

- **Modeling Tools and a Knife** (for working with the clay)

- **Sandpaper** (for smoothing the edges of the mask after the excess paper has been cut away.

- **Kitchen Sponge** (for wet-polishing the gesso to get it smooth. You can also use a paper towel for this purpose)

- **Small Plastic Bucket or Old Pan** (for rinsing your bowls, spoons and brushes so the plaster doesn't end up in your sink)

- **Scissors**

- **Ruler or Tape Measure**

- **Craft Knife or Razor Knife** (for trimming dried paper mache)

- **Small Fan** (optional)

SAFETY ISSUES:

Plaster of Paris is dusty, and the very fine particles don't belong in your lungs. Wear a face mask when mixing plaster (you can find them at the hardware store, often in the same section where you buy your plaster.) You'll also want to use that face mask when you sand your masks—or just wet-polish them, instead.

Plaster can dry out your hands. If this becomes a problem for you, get yourself a box of cheap plastic gloves from the hardware store.

If you're working with younger children, you'll want to use craft paints with a non-toxic rating on the label, and don't use the Instant Iron and Instant Rust to make the Celtic Helmet, because it's toxic. Gray and orange paint would be a safer alternative.

Since knives are sharp, use caution when cutting the paper mache with your craft knives.

Mask Forms

All of the masks in this book, except the Kudu display mask, are built over a basic form that creates the shape of the inside of your mask. The inside shape is important—there's nothing more irritating than feeling your nose or eyelashes constantly rubbing up against the inside of your mask. Of course, you won't need this chapter if you make masks to use as wall art.

Using a pre-made form is obviously a time-saver, and they usually cost just a few dollars. You can find them online or at hobby and art stores. Unfortunately, most plastic mask forms fit a child's face, so if you want to make masks for older kids or adults you will probably need to make your own form. You don't need to make an exact duplicate of your own face, and your form doesn't need to look nice—you just need to make sure there's room inside the mask so you'll be comfortable wearing it. At the end of this chapter I'll also show you how to turn your basic mask form, either store-bought or home-made, into a form that will let you make helmet-style masks that fit over your head.

YOU WILL NEED:

- Plaster-Based Paste
- Scott Shop Towels
- Sandpaper
- Aluminum foil

- Wide and narrow duct tape
- Plaster cloth
- Petroleum jelly
- Mirror

Cut your duct tape into pieces 4" to 6" (10 cm to 15 cm) long and stick them to the edge of your work table. You'll need the narrow ones to start with. If you can't find narrow duct tape, cut your wide tape lengthwise into strips about 1" (2.5 cm) wide.

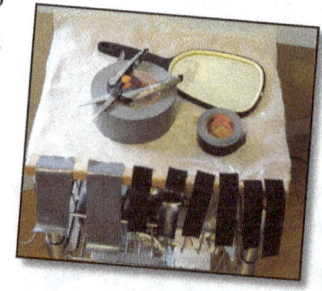

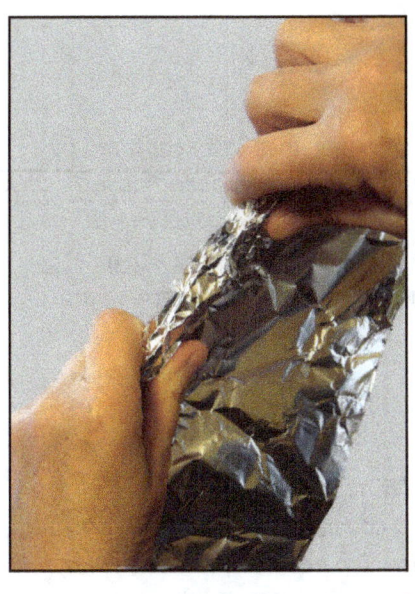

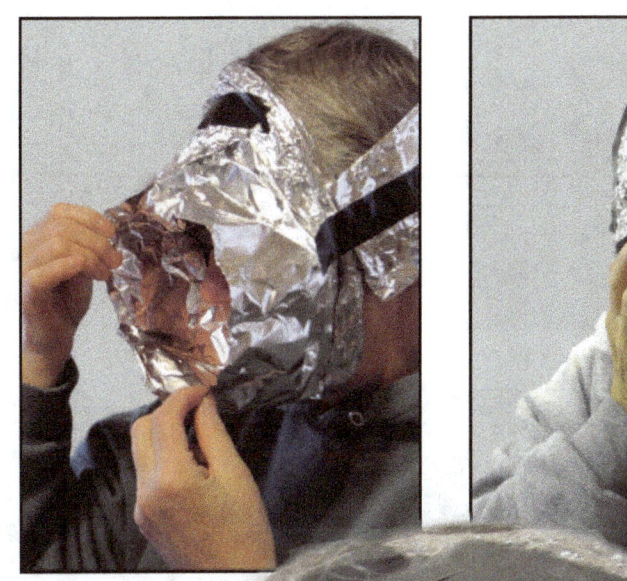

1 Tear off a piece of foil that's long enough to go around your face, and then roll and crumple one long edge, as shown. Leave about 6" (15 cm) uncrumpled.

2 Wrap the crumpled edge around your face and tape the ends together. Use another piece of foil or a piece of paper as a strap around the back of your head, to keep the foil in place on your face.

3 Carefully press the foil to your face. Fold the edges of the foil outward so you don't poke yourself in the eye with one of the sharp points, and try to avoid catching your hair in any of the tape.

4 Add smaller pieces of foil to fill the empty spaces, and tape them on with your narrow duct tape. Continue to carefully flatten the foil against your face to make the inside as smooth as possible.

5 Carefully tape the area between the eyes and across the top of the nose with the narrow tape. Then switch to the wider tape and cover the foil with at least two layers. Keep pushing the foil up against your face as you work.

6 When the form is completely covered with several layers of tape, you should be able to carefully remove it from your head, making sure you don't bend the outside edge even if you accidentally caught a few hairs in the tape. (It kind of hurts...)

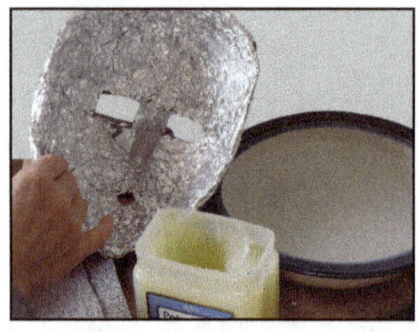

ADD PLASTER CLOTH

1 Now that the basic shapes of your face have been captured by the foil and tape, you're ready to make a permanent mask form. Begin by applying a thin layer of petroleum jelly to the inside of the shape you've just made. This helps the plaster strips stay in place while you work—they slide around too much on bare foil.

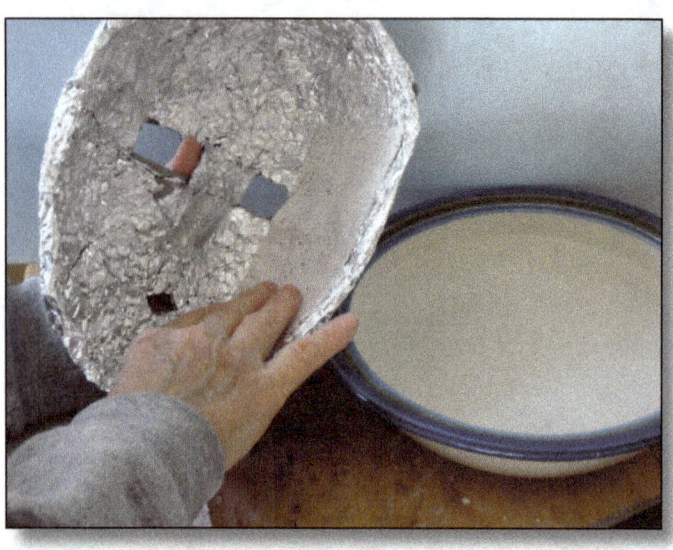

2 Cut your plaster cloth (available at all hobby shops) into strips about 2" (5 cm) wide and 6" (15 cm) long. You'll need enough to cover the inside of the form at least twice. Dip each strip in cold water, allow the excess water to drip back into the bowl, and then lay the strip over the foil. Carefully push the plaster strips into the indentation of the nose, and cover the eyes and mouth. Rub the wet plaster with your fingers to spread the plaster out over the spaces in the cloth.

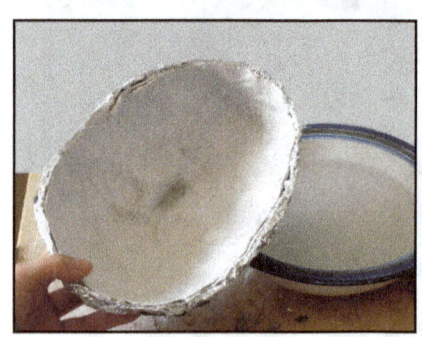

3 Continue to add strips until you have at least two layers covering the foil. Fold the ends of the strips back into the inside of the form so you'll end up with a smooth, reinforced edge. Your form will probably feel quite solid at this point, and can now be set down on the table, nose side up.

4 When the form is solid enough to safely work on it, use your scissors to cut away the foil and tape. The plaster form will be weirdly bumpy, but don't worry about it—we'll fix that in the next steps. Allow the plaster to dry for at least two more hours, in front of a fan, if possible.

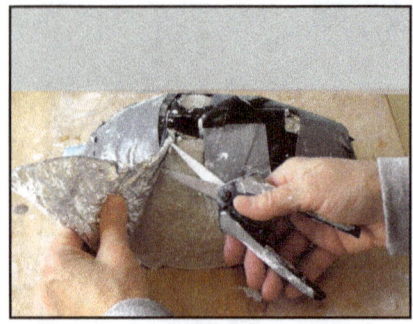
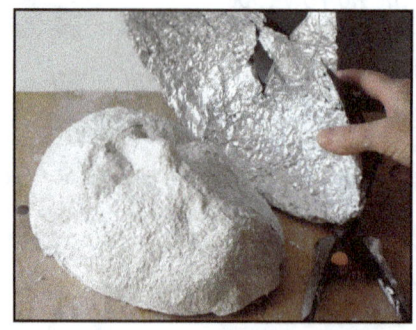
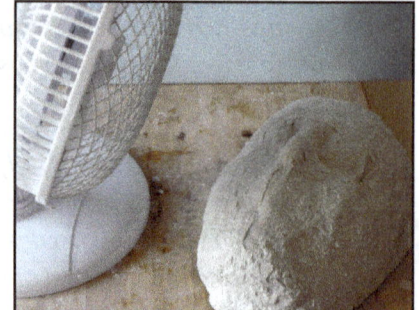

SMOOTHING IT OUT WITH PAPER MACHE

Your mask form should now be dry, but it still needs some work. Use some fine sandpaper to knock off the top of the biggest bumps, but don't worry too much about getting it "perfect." The paper mache layer will even things out enough to make it work just fine.

For this step you'll need one blue paper shop towel, edges removed and torn in half, plus a few smaller pieces to fill in areas that the first two pieces don't cover. (Dampen the towels, then wring out as much water as you can.) You'll also need one batch of plaster-based paste. The recipe is on page 7.

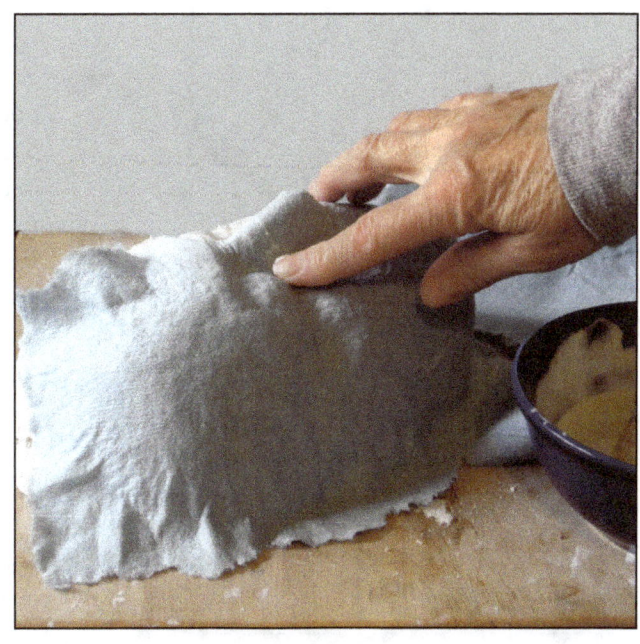

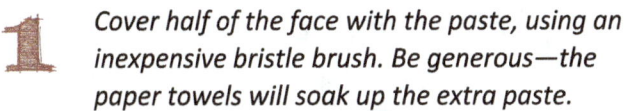 **1** *Cover half of the face with the paste, using an inexpensive bristle brush. Be generous—the paper towels will soak up the extra paste.*

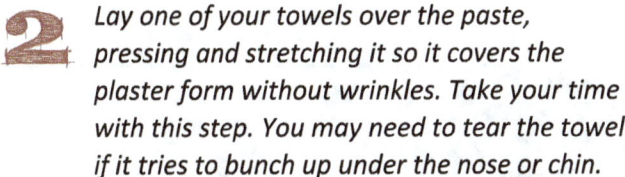 **2** *Lay one of your towels over the paste, pressing and stretching it so it covers the plaster form without wrinkles. Take your time with this step. You may need to tear the towel if it tries to bunch up under the nose or chin.*

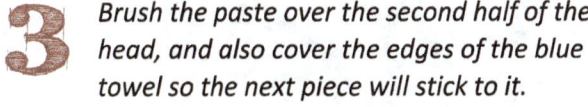 **3** *Brush the paste over the second half of the head, and also cover the edges of the blue towel so the next piece will stick to it.*

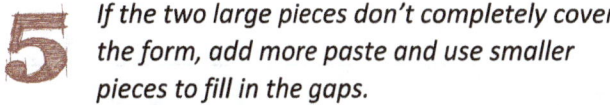 **4** *Lay the second half of the shop towel over the new paste, smoothing and stretching as you did before.*

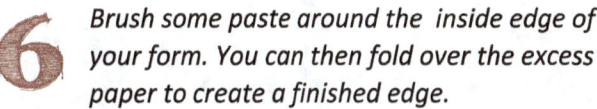 **5** *If the two large pieces don't completely cover the form, add more paste and use smaller pieces to fill in the gaps.*

6 *Brush some paste around the inside edge of your form. You can then fold over the excess paper to create a finished edge.*

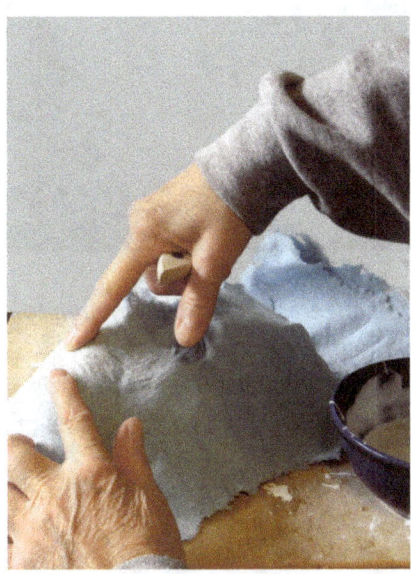
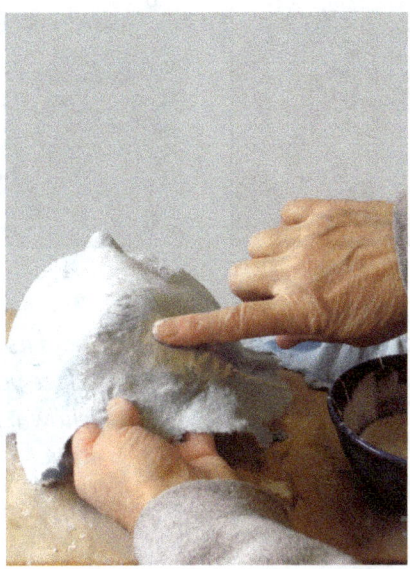
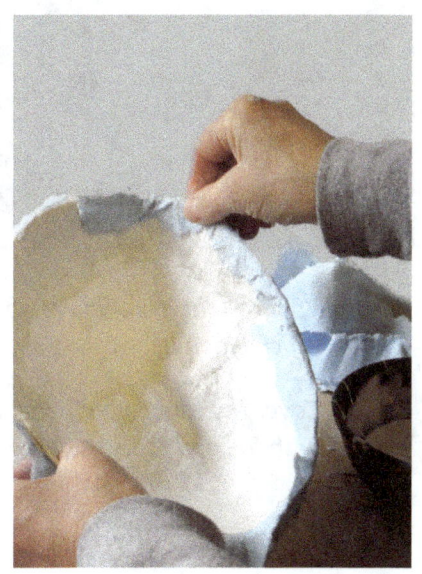

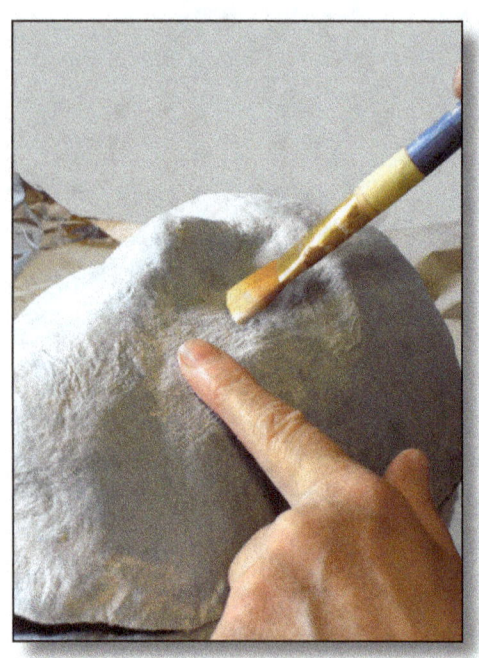

7 *When the plaster is completely covered with one layer of paper mache, use a soft wide brush to lay a thin layer of paste over the paper toweling. If there are still any wrinkles in the paper, use your finger to smooth them out. Set the form in front of a fan or in a warm place to dry for several hours or, preferably, overnight. You can use the form as soon as it's dry, or you can make it even smoother by adding a layer or two of gesso, sanding between each layer, (see page 7). As soon as it's dry you can make your first mask.*

Your form may still look a bit weird and bumpy, but as long as you have room for your nose, it really doesn't matter. You're the only one who will ever see it.

MAKING A FULL-HEAD FORM FOR HELMET-STYLE MASKS

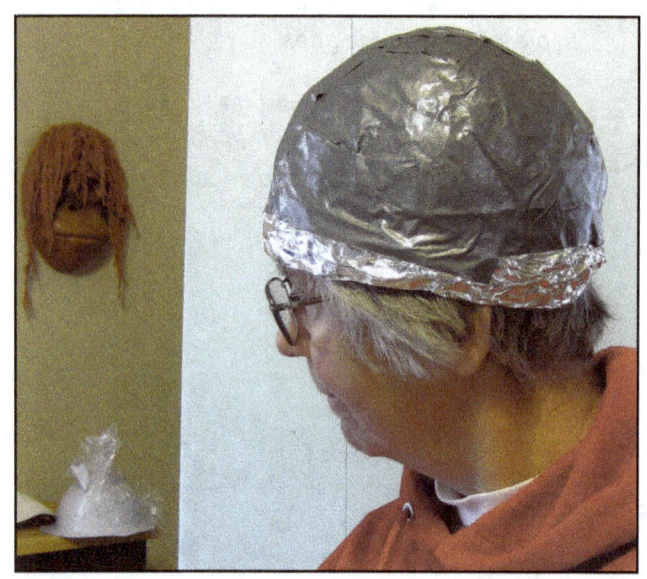
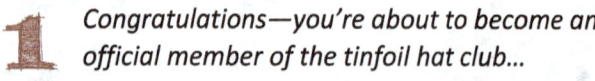

1 *Congratulations—you're about to become an official member of the tinfoil hat club...*

Cover the top of your head, above your ears, with foil and tape, as described on page 13.

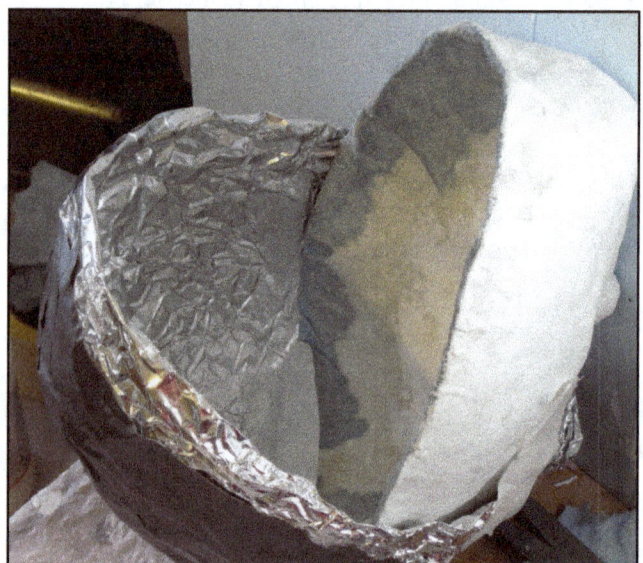

2 *When the tape-covered foil is solid enough to hold its shape, remove it from your head. Place your face form inside the foil shape, as shown, holding it in place with a few pieces of tape.*

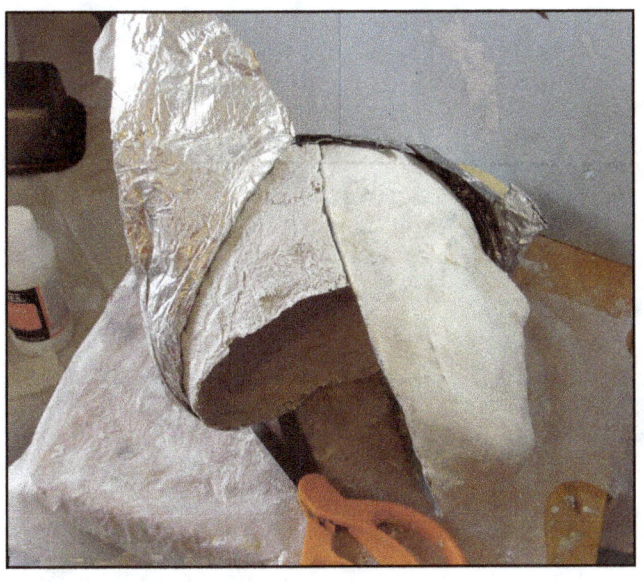

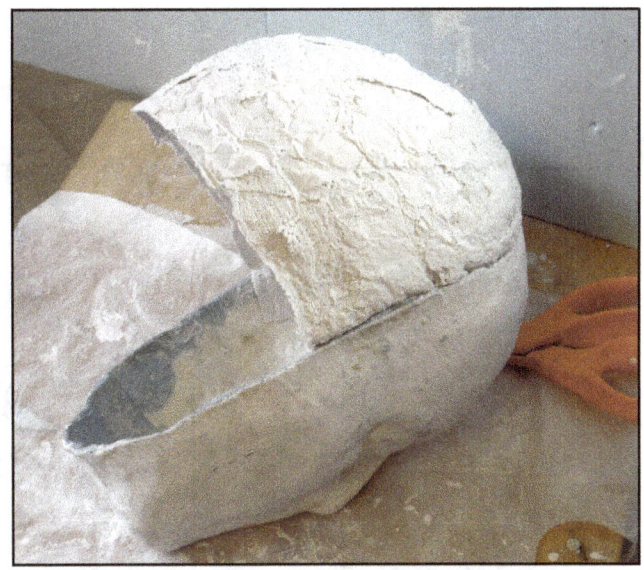

3 *Cover the foil with plaster cloth, as described on page 14. Be sure to overlap the seam so there's a good solid connection*

When the plaster is hard, cut away the foil and tape.

4 *Leave the mask form to dry completely.*

5 *When the plaster is dry, you can attach the form to a make-shift stand, as shown. I used a clay flower pot, which I filled with plaster. Choose something that is heavy enough to make the form stable while you're working on it.*

First, stuff the inside of the top portion of the form with newspaper, and cover the paper with masking tape. Then tape the form to your stand, or use plaster cloth, as I did. You can then cover the form with a layer of paper mache, as shown on page 15.

If your form seems way too lumpy, like mine die, you can smooth it out with joint compound (see page 29).

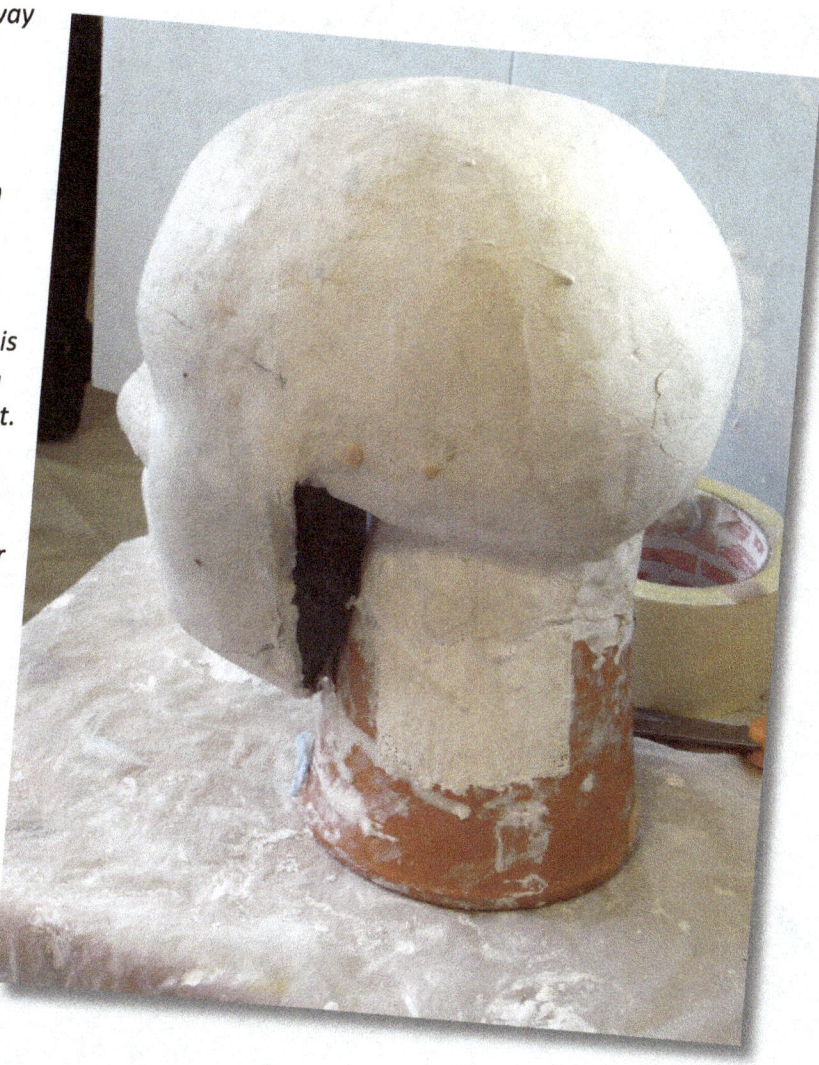

The Clay Molds

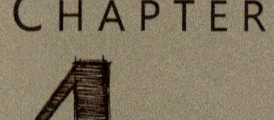

THE POSITIVE MOLDS are made with modeling clay (and sometimes light cardboard or aluminum foil). The features are sculpted over the basic mask form, which I discussed in the last chapter.

It's easier to create the features with modeling clay instead of building up features with more paper mache, and the masks are lighter and more comfortable to wear. I use Super Sculpey™ for modeling, because I like working with it and it's available here in my small town—but any oil-based modeling clay will work just fine. Many of the masks in this book can be made with just one pound of modeling clay, but the larger masks will need more.

I almost always put a sheet of plastic over my custom-made form before I begin modeling features with clay. The plastic sheet makes it easy to lift your mask from the mold without distorting its shape or using tools to pry the mask away from the clay, which can damage the inside of the mask.

It is possible to remove a mask from a mold even if you don't use the plastic, but you'll need to let the paper mache dry at least overnight, instead of taking it off the mold in just a few hours. You'll also need to use plenty of petroleum jelly to make sure the mask doesn't stick to the form, and you'll probably need a long tool to dig under the mask to pry the clay away from the form. Using the plastic is much easier, and there's less chance of ruining your work.

If you use a plastic mask form, the plastic sheet isn't absolutely needed.

CHAPTER

4

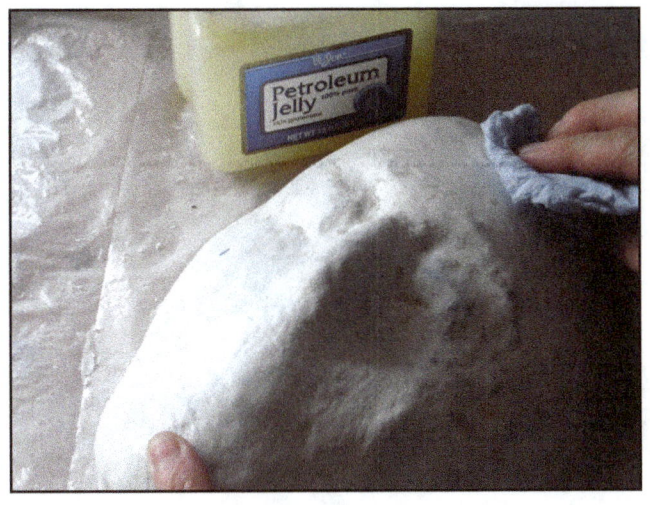

PUTTING PLASTIC OVER THE MASK FORM

1 *Use a paper towel or your fingers to rub a thin layer of petroleum jelly over your mask form. The petroleum jelly will make the plastic cling to the form and follow all its contours.*

2 *Lay a sheet of thin plastic over the form, and smooth it out as much as possible. If the plastic doesn't want to stay where it belongs, use a bit more petroleum jelly. Be sure to push the plastic down into the eye areas first.*

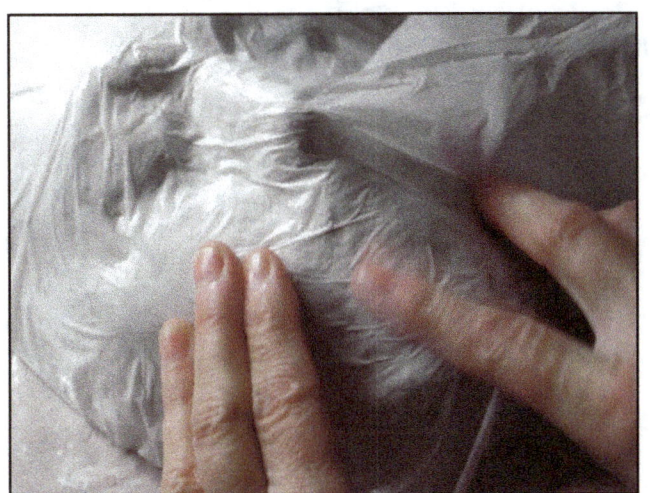

3 *To keep it from folding too much under the nose, cut the plastic from the chin to the point of the nose. Smooth one flap over the form, then cover it with petroleum jelly so the second flap will stick to it. Smooth everything down as well as you can. (If your fingers have oil on them, they will probably stick to the plastic. It may be easier to press the plastic over the form with a brush, instead.)*

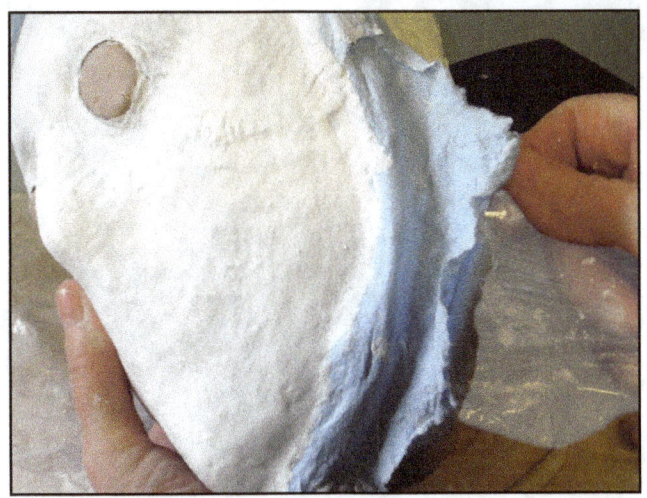

You can use thin plastic wrap for masks that have very little clay on the molds. The thin plastic will cause fewer wrinkles to show in the paper mache. However, the plastic wrap is pretty flimsy, so whenever possible you'll want to use heavier plastic so it doesn't tear when you lift the mask off the mold. A piece of plastic from a garbage bag or grocery bag works better.

When it's time to remove the mask from the form, pull the plastic down and sideways to break the attachment between the plastic and the petroleum jelly. Do this all away around. The mask will then fall away from the form. Take your time with this step so you don't distort the shape of the mask, which is probably still a bit damp on the inside.

SCULPTING THE MOLDS

In each chapter I'll show you how the features are sculpted to make the masks. At any step you are certainly free to create features that fit your own creative impulses.

Because the clay we used to make the mold remains soft, we don't need to worry about undercuts. You can create any shape you like, as long as none of the clay will remain trapped inside the mask after the paper mache is dry. That's because modeling clay has oil in it—if the clay stays inside the paper mache, the oil will eventually seep out and destroy the painted surface. It won't happen right away, but it *will* happen (I learned the hard way).

Remember that each bit of clay you add to the form changes both the outside *and* inside shape of the mask. If the form is completely covered with clay, the mask may no longer fit comfortably. For that reason, we will always leave some portion of the mask form bare when adding clay. In these photos of the Unicorn and Volto mask molds, the white plastic can be seen where no clay has been added. These non-covered areas allow the finished mask to fit.

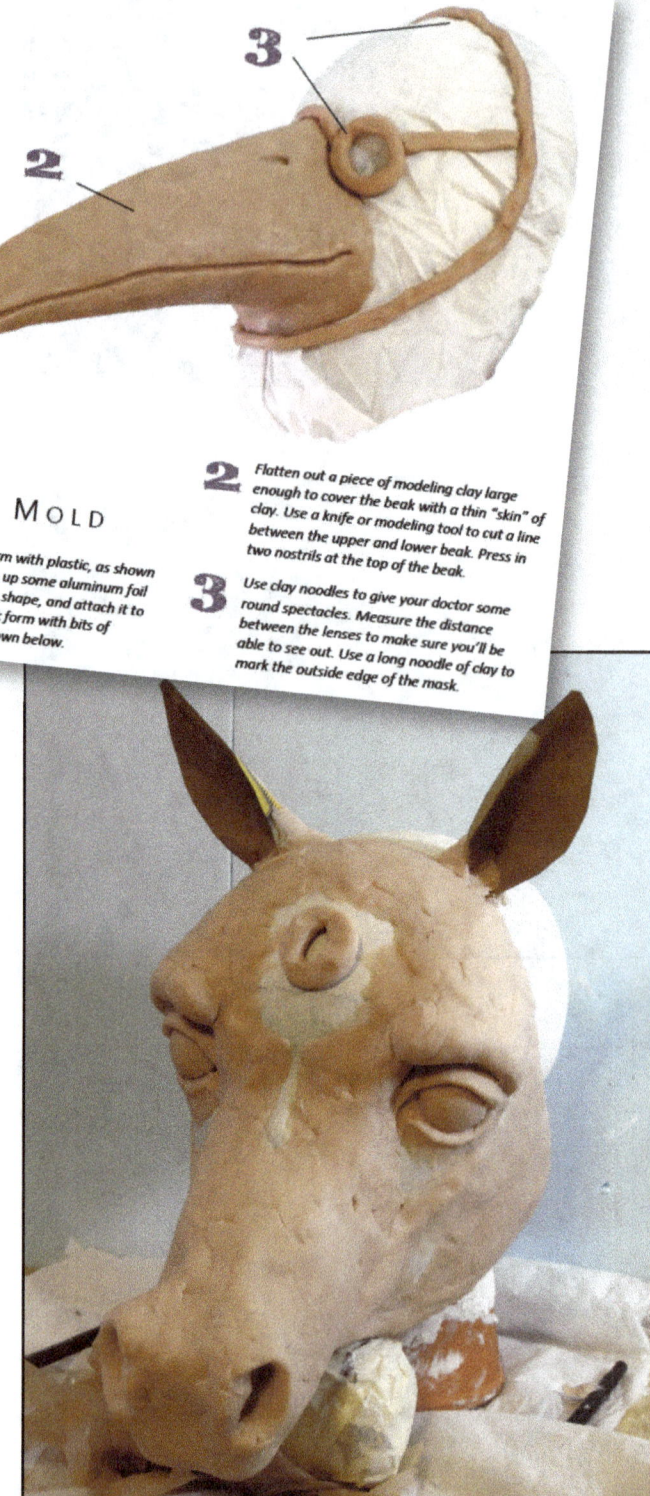

MAKE THE MOLD

1 Cover your mask form with plastic, as shown on page 18. Scrunch up some aluminum foil into a long beak-like shape, and attach it to the front of the mask form with bits of modeling clay, as shown below.

2 Flatten out a piece of modeling clay large enough to cover the beak with a thin "skin" of clay. Use a knife or modeling tool to cut a line between the upper and lower beak. Press in two nostrils at the top of the beak.

3 Use clay noodles to give your doctor some round spectacles. Measure the distance between the lenses to make sure you'll be able to see out. Use a long noodle of clay to mark the outside edge of the mask.

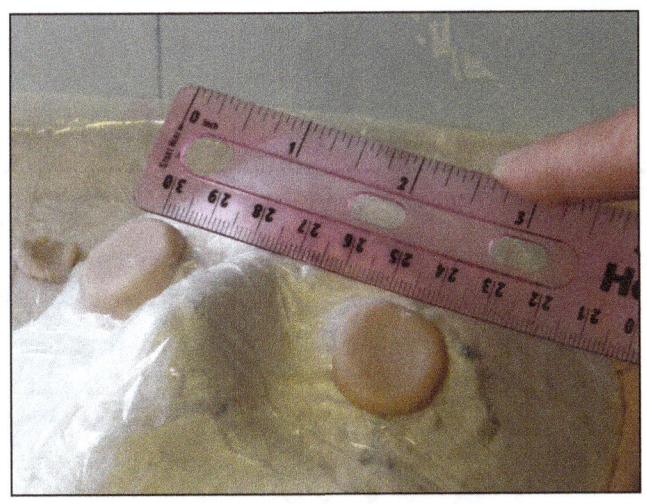

MAKE SURE YOU CAN SEE OUT OF YOUR MASK:

Measure the distance between the middle of your own eyes. Then use that measurement when placing eyes on your molds.

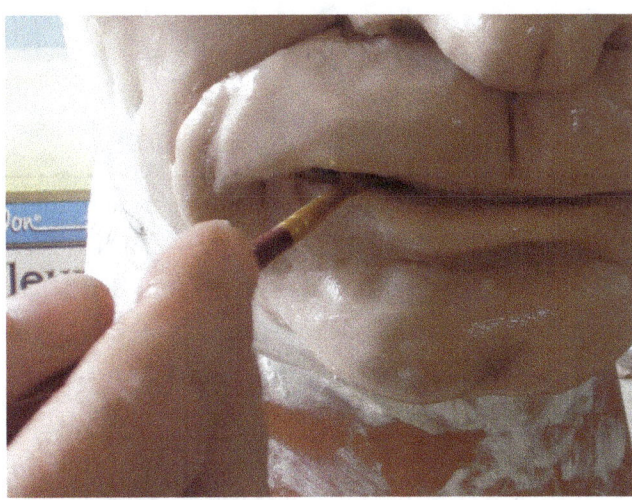

EXAGGERATE DETAILS

You'll be pasting two layers of thick paper over the positive mold. To make sure the paper mache doesn't hide the important details on your mask, go back over your clay mold and deepen any line that may get lost.

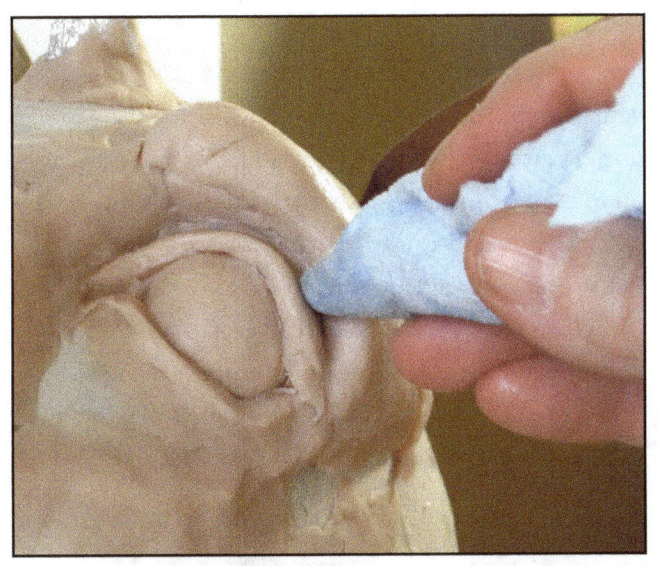

SMOOTH THE CLAY

Before you add your paper mache you'll want to smooth out the bumps and dips that happen naturally when you're working with modeling clay. Petroleum jelly really helps. For deep areas that are hard to reach, you can use a knife or modeling tool wrapped with a Scott Shop Towel that's been dipped in petroleum jelly, as shown smoothing out the eyelid on the Unicorn, above.

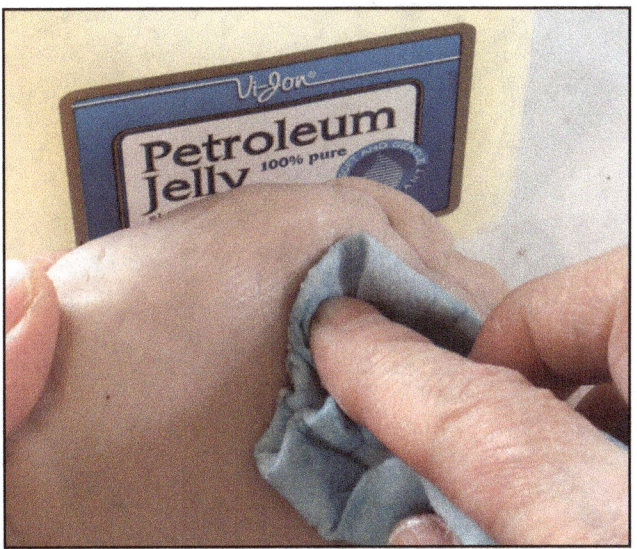

For more open places, put petroleum jelly on your Scott Shop Towel. Use just enough petroleum jelly to make the towel move easily over the clay. Press down with your fingers through the towel if you need to move a lot of clay or to even out a curve. For some spots you might want to use your fingers, instead.

Design Tips

Simplify, and Avoid Tiny Details

When you're sculpting your mold you need to think about the way the mask will look after the mold has been covered with two layers of paper mache. Tiny details will get lost under the paper. Be sure you exaggerate any thin lines, like the ones in the nose and mouth and around the eyes. It helps to use a soft modeling clay, which works best with this bolder style of sculpting.

After you make several masks from your own designs, will will be more comfortable with the idea of simplifying the shapes and features, and visualizing how the design will work with the paper mache.

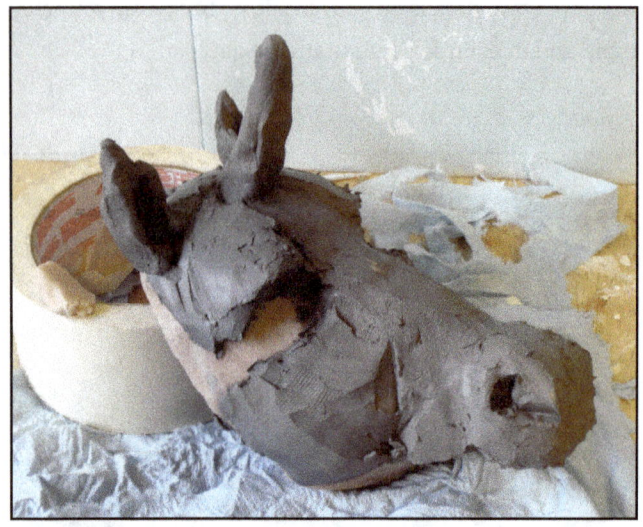

Consider Making a Small Clay Sketch:

Sculptors often create a small model, called a maquette, before attempting the full-sized sculpture. This is really helpful for mask-makers, too. It lets you determine in advance the best way to make the mask design fit the shape of your own face. (I made three small-sized models before I was happy with the Unicorn). A small clay sketch also gives you a chance to play with expressions.

To make this process easier for myself, I made a tiny mask form with Super Sculpey and baked it according to the package instructions. I used my life-sized mask form as the model for the little one. The miniature form isn't strictly necessary, but it is fun to use. Now, when I make a sketch on paper, I also make a quick sketch over my little mask form to see if the original design will translate well into three dimensions.

If you don't like the clay version as much as you liked your sketch, you can keep playing with the little model until it turns into something you like, or you can move on to a something else. Either way, you don't invest very much time on it because you don't have to go through the entire process of making a real mask.

When I started the cat mask, I played with the ears on a small clay sketch to decide which expression I liked best. I then used the maquette as a model when I sculpted the full-sized mold for the cat mask on page 64.

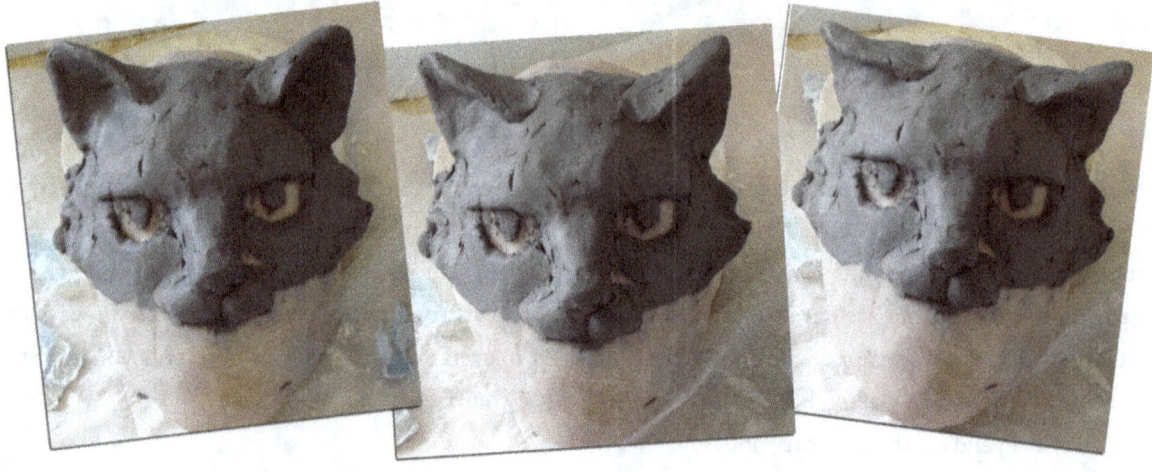

LIFTING THE MASK FROM THE MOLD

When the mask is dry enough to hold its shape, you can lift it off the mold and remove all the clay from inside the mask, as shown in the photo. At that point, the paper mache on the inside of the mask is probably still slightly damp. You can pop the mask in a warm oven if you want to finish drying it quickly.

Remember that you must never put the clay or the plastic-covered mask form in the oven.

If you leave the paper mache on the mold for several days while you work on another project, the modeling clay will tend to dry out and become a little stiff, which makes it a bit harder to remove. This happens most noticeably if you put it in a warm place, like over a heat register. If possible, remove the mask from the mold within 24 hours of applying the paper mache.

If you didn't use a plastic sheet over your mask form, as described on page 19, the clay holds onto the form, and the paper mache holds onto the clay, so a tool is needed

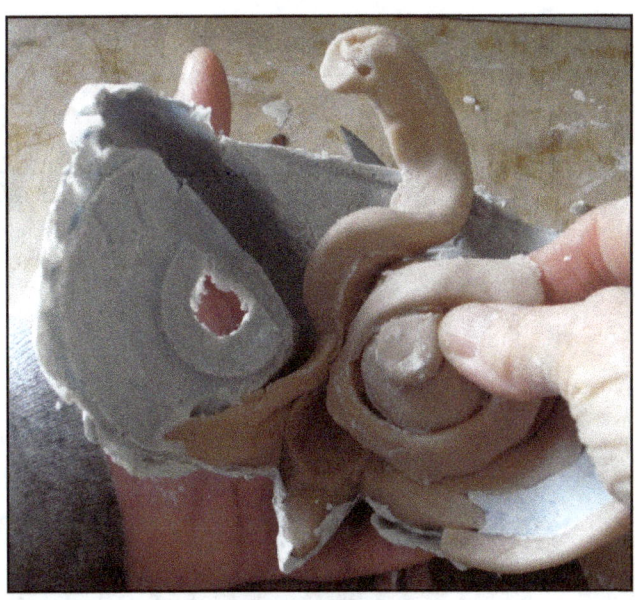

to pry them apart. Work carefully and take your time so you don't gouge the inside of the mask.

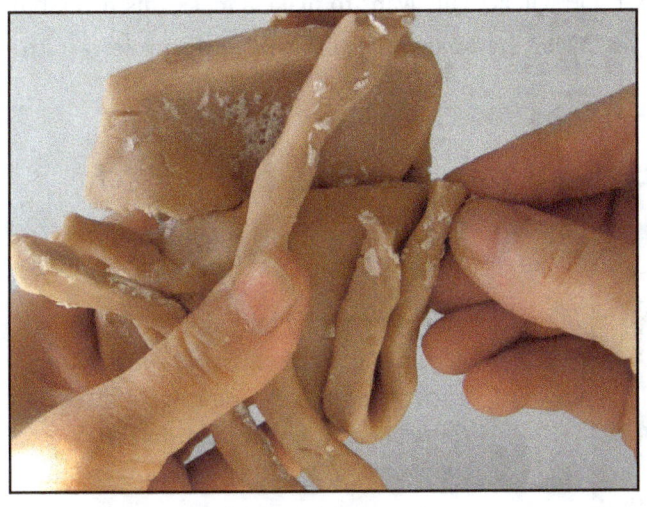

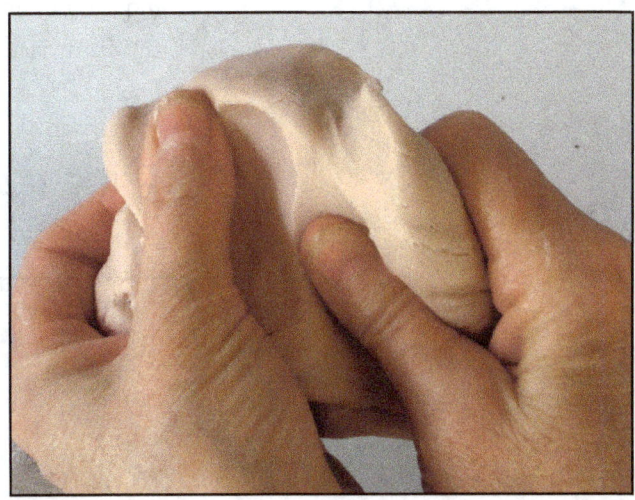

CLEANING PASTE OFF YOUR CLAY:

When you remove your masks from their molds, some of the dried paste will be stuck to the clay. You'll want to use your clay again to make more masks or sculptures. I clean off my Super Sculpey by running the clay under warm water to wash off as much of the paste as I can. I like to knead in just a bit of petroleum jelly to replace any moisture that may have been lost while the clay was being used. This method is probably not recommended by the clay manufacturers, but it seems to work just fine.

The Paper Mache

Y OUR SCOTT SHOP towels stretch when they're wet. It's the stretchiness and the wet strength of these towels that allow us to cover our masks with much larger pieces of paper than we could if we used newspaper. Simple molds like the one I'm using for this demonstration can be covered with just four large pieces of paper. Masks with protruding noses, deep chins or odd-shaped beaks may require smaller pieces and more patience, (see page 27), but always try to use the largest pieces that you can.

The mold shown in this chapter would create a paper mache copy of the ancient stone mask on page 3. (A stone mask replica would actually make a nice display for a science project). On such a simple mask, clay is only used to outline the edge of the mask and to define the holes for the eyes and mouth. I doubt that you will actually want to make a mask this plain, but the same basic paper mache methods will be used on all the projects in the book.

PREPARE YOUR PAPER

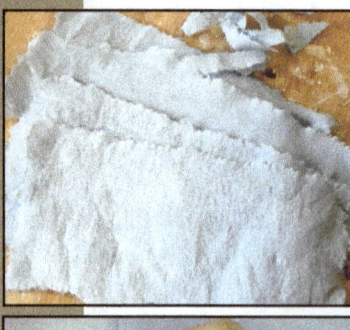

1 *Always start by tearing off all the edges of your towels, and then tear each sheet in half. The towels tear fairly straight if you start on the perforated edge.*

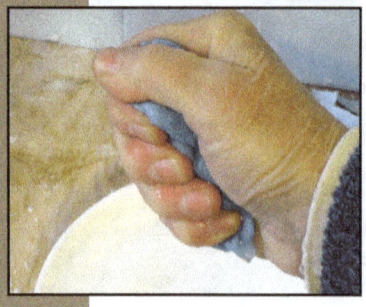

2 *Wet the towels, and then squeeze out as much water as you can. (This helps you get a nice smooth layer of paper mache. If the paper is used dry, it will wrinkle when it's dampened by the paste.) Then carefully separate the damp towels and lay them out flat on your work table, within easy reach.*

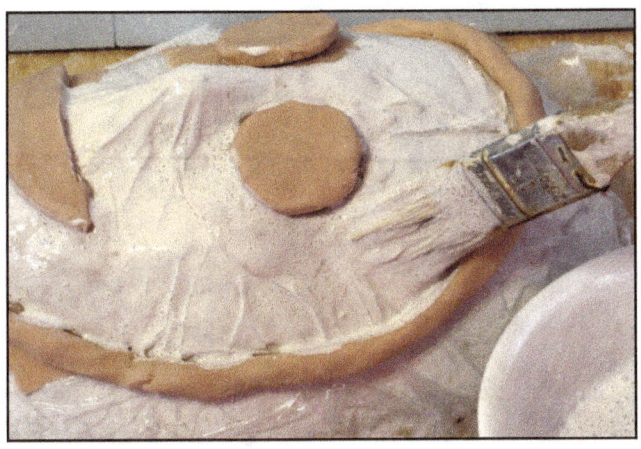

CHAPTER 5

3 Brush paste on a little more than half of the mold with a cheap brush. For the first layer, we'll cover the mask with two pieces that go from the chin to the forehead.

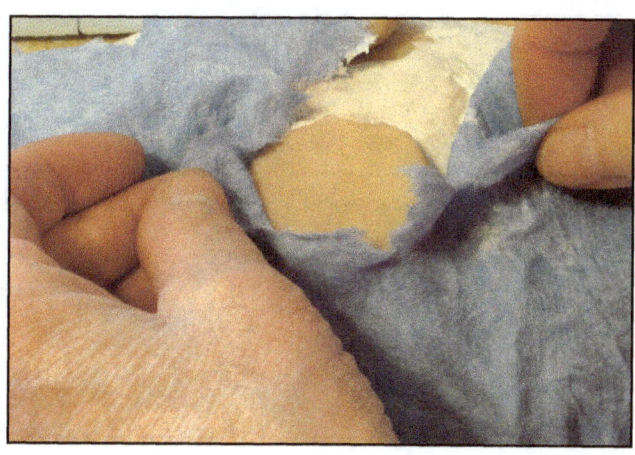

4 Lay a piece of damp paper towel over the paste. Tear the paper to expose the clay that defines the mouth and eye holes.

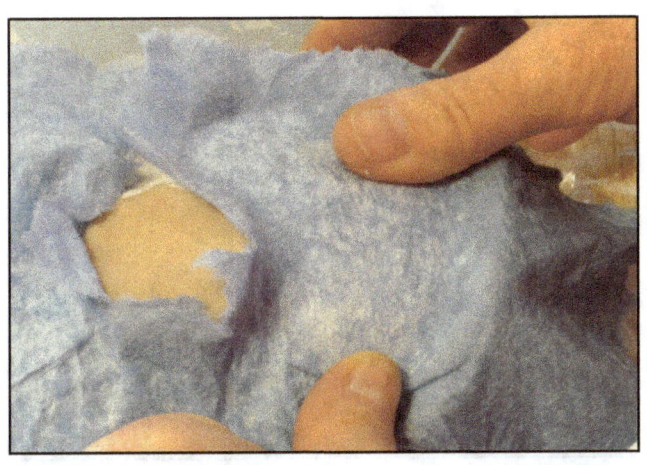

5 Use your fingers to stretch the paper over the mask's "skin." If any bubbles of air or paste form under the paper, use your fingers or the brush to chase them out.

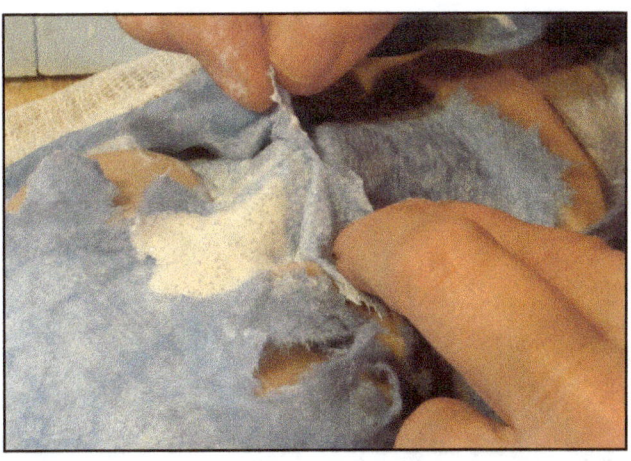

6 You may need to make tears in the paper to make it lie flat around the nose and chin, where the paper often tries to fold.

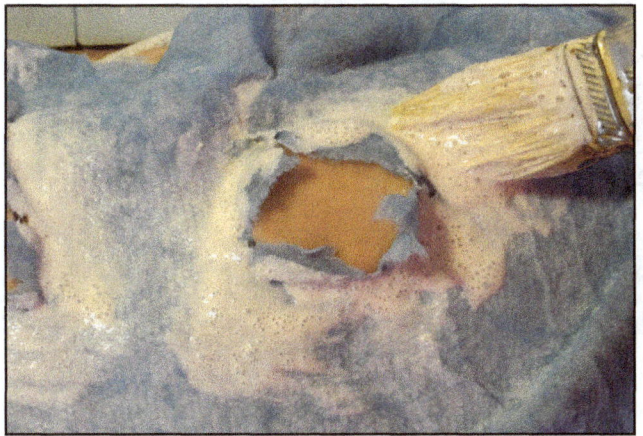

7 Brush paste around the eye and mouth so you can fold the extra paper down, forming the shape of the open spaces in the mask.

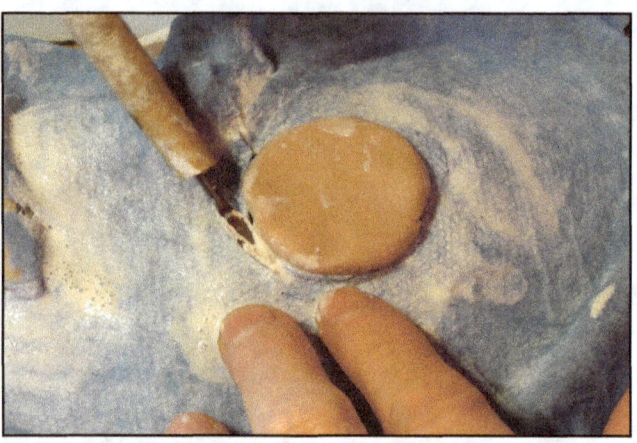

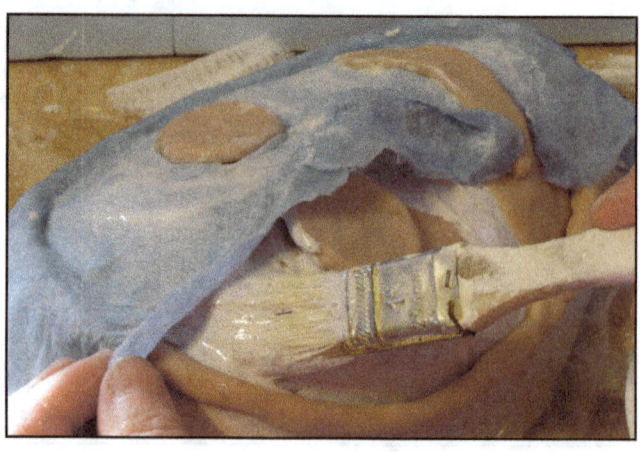

8 Press the extra paper down flat around the openings. You can use a tool to help. (Tools also help when you need to press the paper deep into nostrils and other deep features, and to emphasize lines.)

9 Turn the mask around so you can reach the other side. Check the edges of the paper to make sure it's all been pasted down. Then finish brushing paste on this side of the mask, and add the second piece.

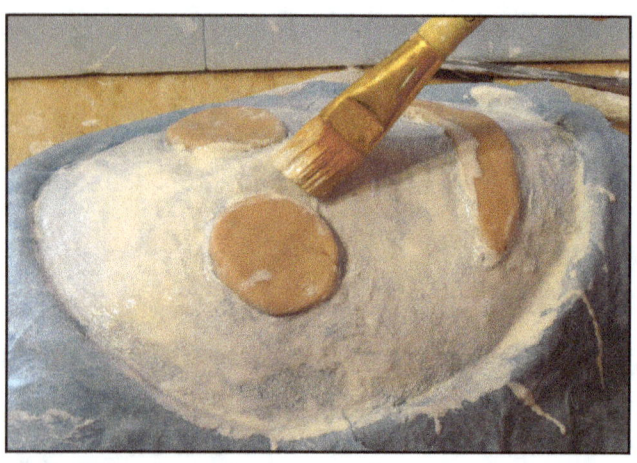

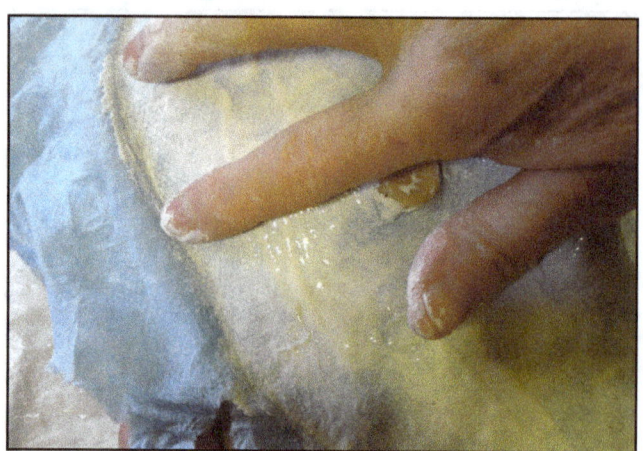

10 Add the second layer of paper mache, laying the paper crosswise so the seams on both layers won't overlap. Then use a soft brush to cover the final layer with a coat of paste.

11 Go back over all the details to make sure they are as crisp as you want them. Also, make a nice sharp crease at the outside edges of the mask, using a tool or your finger. Set your mask aside and let it dry.

! Don't try to dry your mask in the oven while it's still on the mold. If you used Super Sculpey for the mold, the oven would weld the paper mache to the clay—permanently. Oil-based modeling clay, plastic forms and plastic sheets will melt. In other words, your mask will be ruined. To speed up the drying, place your mask in front of a fan if you have one, or just put it in a warm place to dry. You can use a warm oven to finish the drying after the mask is lifted off the mold.

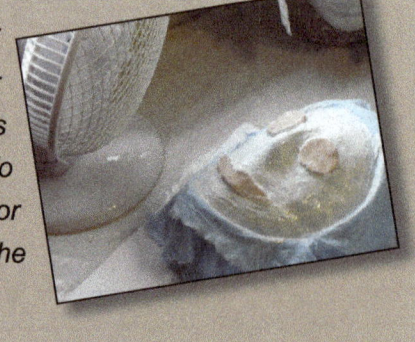

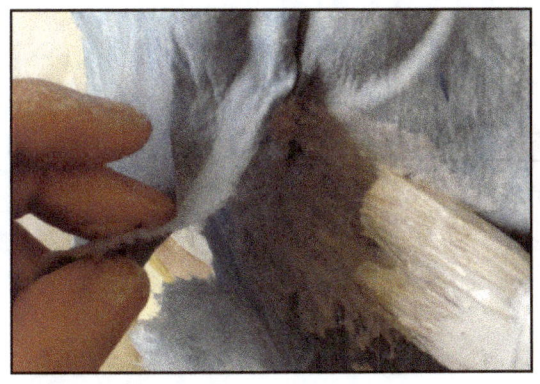

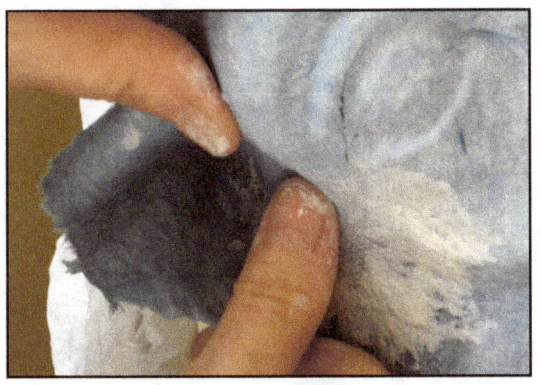

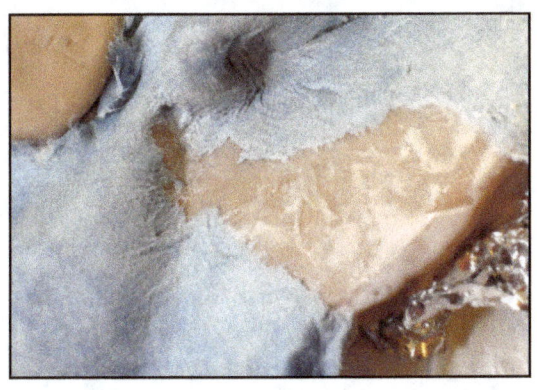

COVERING ODD SHAPES:

On more highly-detailed masks, the paper will often try to fold up in spots instead of laying down flat. In other places, the paper may not be able to stretch far enough to cover the area.

To prevent folds, tear the paper from the edge up to the spot where the fold begins. Stick one of the pieces to the paste that has already been brushed onto the mold, and then cover it with more paste. Carefully press the second piece over the first, and smooth out the edge where they overlap.

In spots where the paper can't stretch enough to cover the curve of the mask, tear the paper from the edge up to the place where it lies flat against the mold. Then press the new edges down onto the paste that covers the mold, leaving a gap. The uncovered spot can then be filled in with a smaller piece of paper. Use your brush or finger to smooth over the seams.

Try to avoid making a tear or leaving a fold over areas that need to be especially smooth, like the eyes, if they aren't going to be cut out.

DIPS AND VALLEYS

To make sure the paper mache doesn't make a bridge across dips and valleys, press the paper into the deepest parts of the design first. You may need to lift up on one edge of the paper and push the paper down into the dip with a tool or knife, as shown in the exaggerated example on the bottom left.

If there still isn't enough paper to go down into the dip, you will need to tear the paper like you see in the third photo on this page. Fill in any gaps with another piece of paper.

Don't rush this process—take as much time as you need to stretch, push, tear and smooth the paper over your mold. If you discover that your details are getting lost no matter how carefully you apply the paper mache, try to make your mold less highly detailed next time. After one or two masks you'll know how the finished paper mache will look when you're working with your clay.

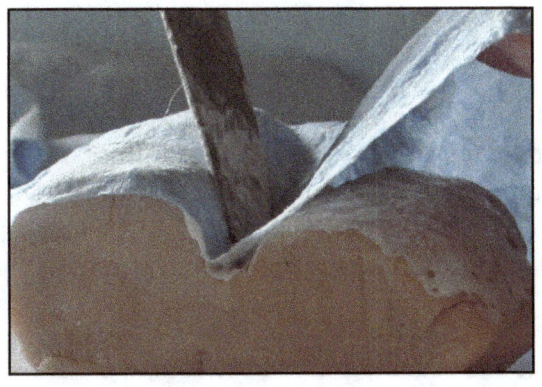

Finishing

THE SPECIFIC INSTRUCTIONS for finishing each mask will be found in the project chapters. Some basic methods will be used on all the masks, and I discuss those methods here.

Don't remove your mask from its mold before it's dry enough to stand up on its own. If you do, the shape will slump and you'll end up with a pancake with a face on it. (I learned the hard way).

PREPARE THE MASK FOR PAINTING

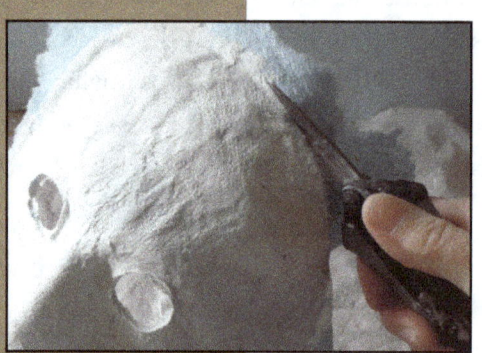

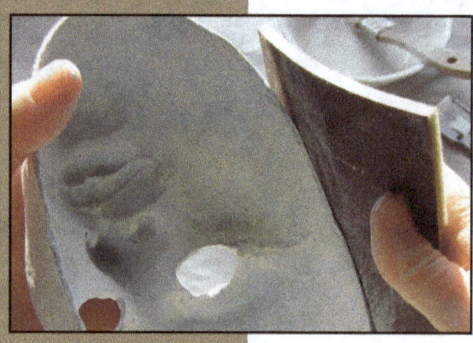

1 *When you lift your mask from the mold, use sharp scissors to cut away the extra paper that hangs over the edge. Then sand the edge smooth. I like to use the sanding pads that have a thin foam backing, because they curve easily around the masks and they don't crack or tear. I use the medium grit.*

Also go over the inside of the mask to feel if there are any pointy bits sticking out that would cause discomfort when the mask is worn. This is particularly important around the eyes. You might even want to hold the mask in front of your face as though you were wearing it, to make sure it's comfortable. Sand or cut away any sharp protrusions.

At this point you can give your mask a coat of gesso, inside and out. After one coat of gesso has been added, it will be obvious if there are any bumps or wrinkles that gesso can't cover.

CHAPTER

6

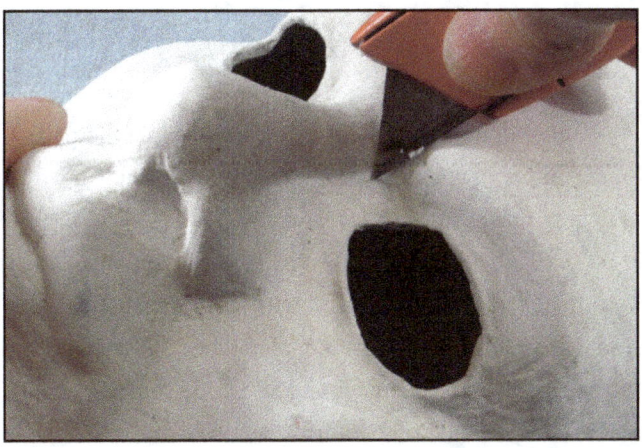

2 *Check the outside for unwanted bumps that formed when the paper mache was added, and cut them off (carefully!) with a craft knife.*

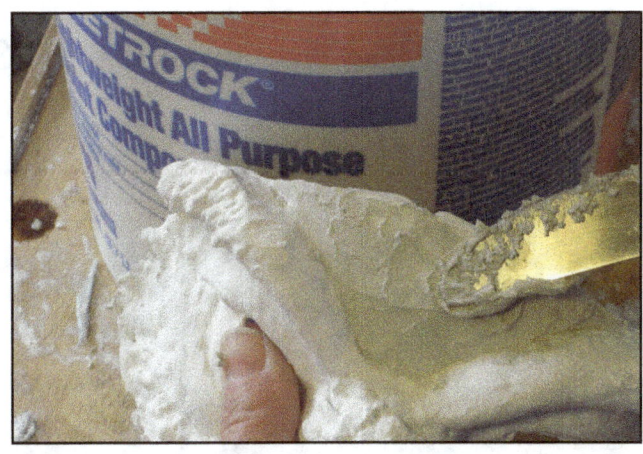

3 *If a part dips more than you like, fill it in with joint compound. Allow the joint compound to dry and then wet-polish it smooth.*

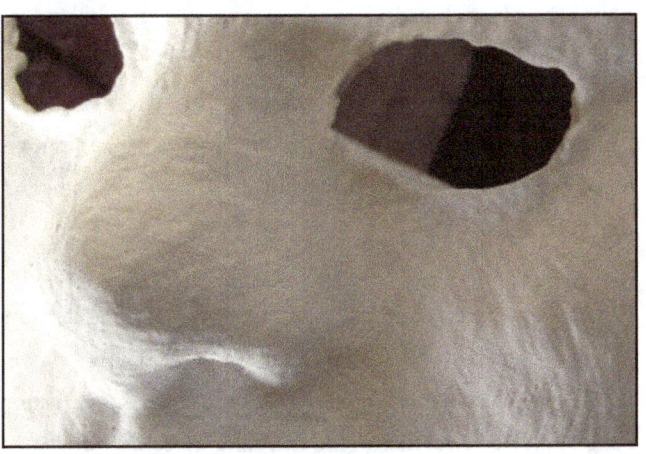

4 *Add one or more layers of home-made gesso. The photo above shows the Plaster-Based Gesso, page 7, applied with a large stiff brush.*

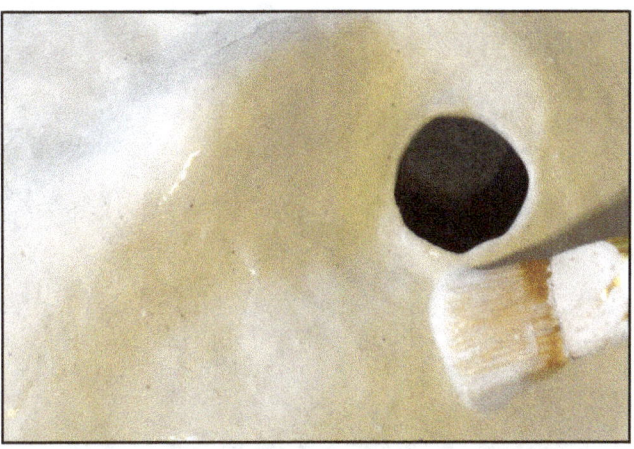

This photo shows the Really Smooth Gesso Mix, page 8. I often use the first recipe, wet-polish it, and finish with a coat of the second recipe.

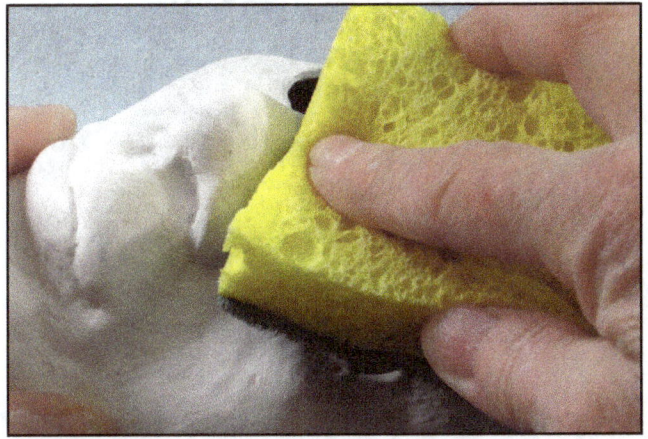

5 *Wet-polishing is easier and faster than sanding. Use a slightly damp sponge or shop towel.*

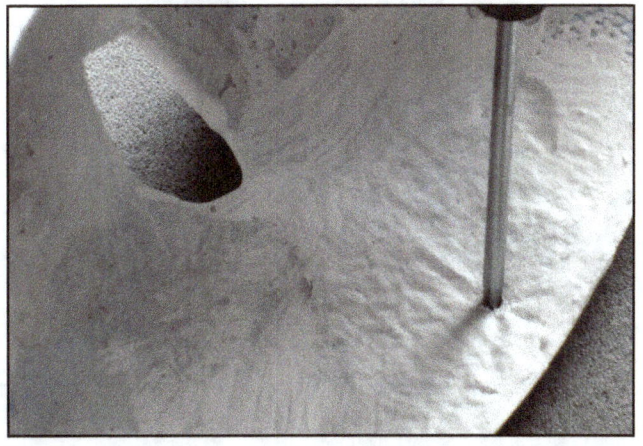

6 *Use a sharp pointy tool or craft knife to make a hole for the cord, ½ inch or more from the edge—unless you're using a hot glue gun.*

PAINTING THE MASKS

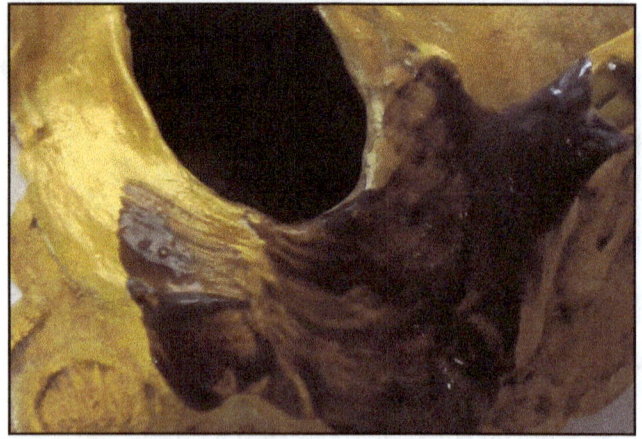

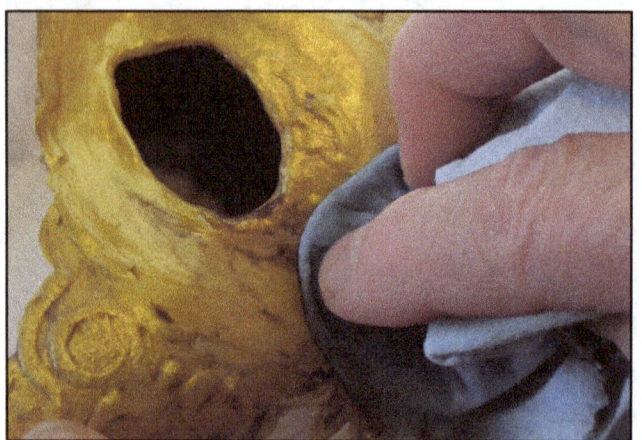

You will be painting your masks with acrylic paints, and you can use any colors you like—you don't need to copy my masks unless you want to.

To bring out details after the paint is dry, I like to use Acrylic Glazing Liquid mixed with dark paint. I use this product by first painting it over a fairly small area on the mask, and then either wiping it off or dabbing it off, depending on how much of the dark color I wish to leave on the finished mask. Although I like the way this makes the masks look, it's certainly optional.

Before you use the glazing liquid, always have two paper towels on hand. One of these towels should be dry, and the other one should be slightly damp. The dry towel will leave dark color in the creases and crevices, and the glaze will just lightly color the rest of the mask. To remove all of the glaze from any area that gets too dark, use your damp towel.

The result can be subtle, like it is on the gold sections of the Volt mask, or it can be rather dramatic, as it is on the owl's feathers, (before and after shown below).

The glaze must dry completely before adding another coat of paint or varnish. This can take up to 24 hours.

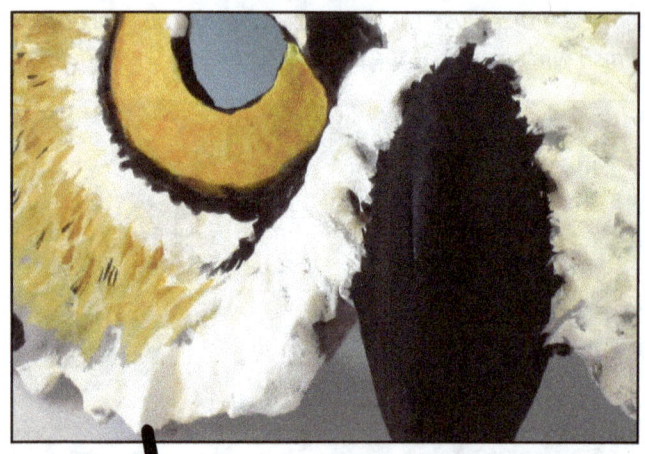

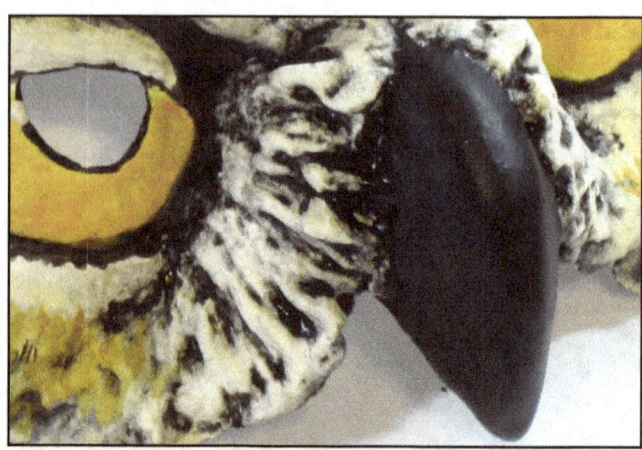

Always make sure the gesso has been sealed by the paint layers before adding glaze. If the gesso has not been sealed, the dark glaze will be absorbed and it will make the mask too dark. To make absolutely sure, you can spray the mask with Krylon Matte Finish or brush on a coat of matte acrylic varnish before you use the glazing liquid.

ADDING A CORD

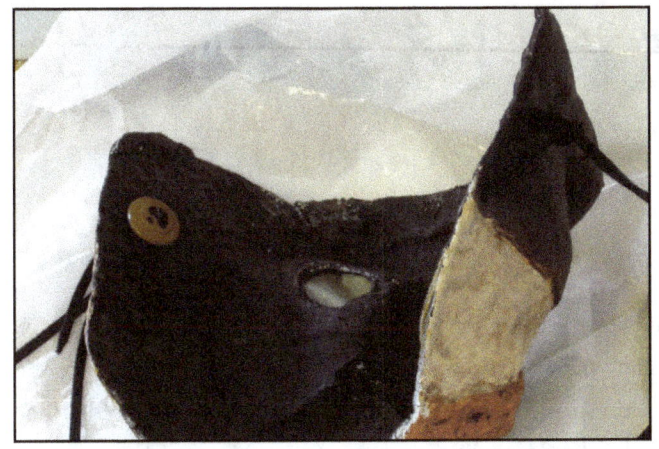

Some people prefer to attach elastic or a strong ribbon or cord to the mask with a hot glue gun, so no hole is needed.

If you don't use hot glue, make a hole in the mask as shown on page 29. If you first pass the cord through a wide flat button your cord will be less likely to pull through the paper mache wall. Pull both ends out through the mask, and tie on the outside. Keep ribbon ends from fraying with a drop of white glue.

ADDING A HANGER OR STICK

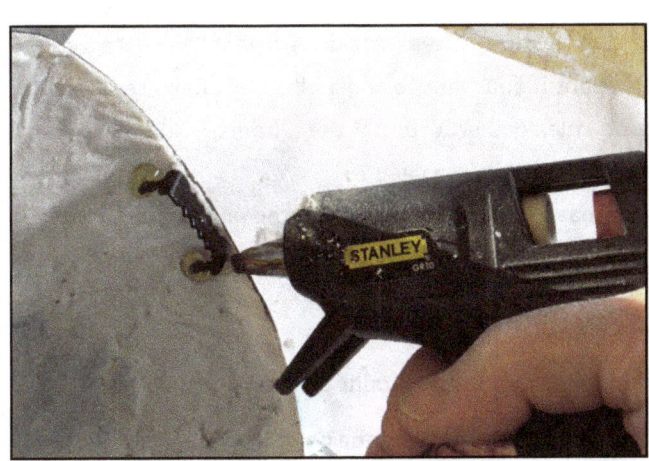

You can attach a small metal hanger to a display mask with a hot glue gun. You can find these hangers anywhere that picture hanging supplies are sold.

You can also use a glue gun to attach a stick to stick-held masks, like the owl mask in Chapter 14.

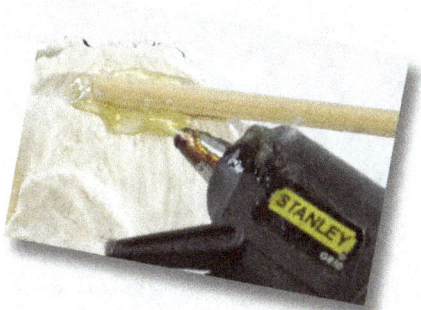

PADDING HELMET-STYLE MASKS

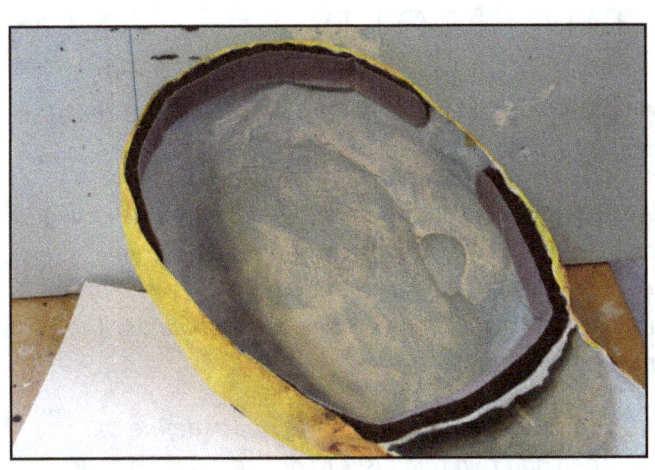

I make my helmet-style masks, like the Duck Hat on page 74, slightly larger than the mask form. Then I pad the inside using stick-on foam strips made for bicycle helmets. You could also use the foam strips that are made for insulating doors and windows, which you can find in any DIY store. The foam makes the hard paper mache much more comfortable to wear. It also lets you make helmet-style masks for a child even if you don't have the exact head measurements.

Stick-on foam is a modern invention, of course, but ancient metal helmets were also padded, usually with wool.

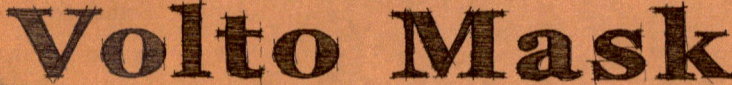

Volto Mask

T HE VOLTO MASK is one of the most popular Venetian designs for carnivals and masked balls. It's almost always painted white (that's why it's sometimes called the Ghost Mask). It may be decorated either elaborately or plainly, depending on your tastes. Many of these masks have raised gold lace designs, like the one in the photo.

If you have a plastic mask form with well-defined features, you could just cover it with paper mache and skip any additional sculpting (but then you'd miss out on half the fun!). These masks traditionally show a generic male or female face, but if you want to add a bit more character to yours, there's certainly no rule against it. If you use a home-made mask form, cover it with a sheet of plastic (see page 19).

To finish your mask to look like the one in the photo, you'll need:

- Acrylic Paint

- Puffy Paint (for the raised design)

- Metallic Gold Acrylic Paint (and Metallic Bronze, optional)

- Acrylic Glazing Liquid (for antiquing the gold)

- Satin Acrylic Varnish

MAKE THE MOLD

1 *Add clay to the tip of the nose and the nostrils to give the nose the shape you want.*

2 *Sculpt the lips, as shown in the small photos on the next page. (For good lip models, do a Google image search for your favorite actor.) Emphasize the crease behind the wing of the nose and between the lips so they don't get lost under the paper mache.*

3 *If needed, add some classic cheekbones and redefine the eyebrows. Then add two thin disks to define where the eye holes will go. You can give the eye holes any shape you want.*

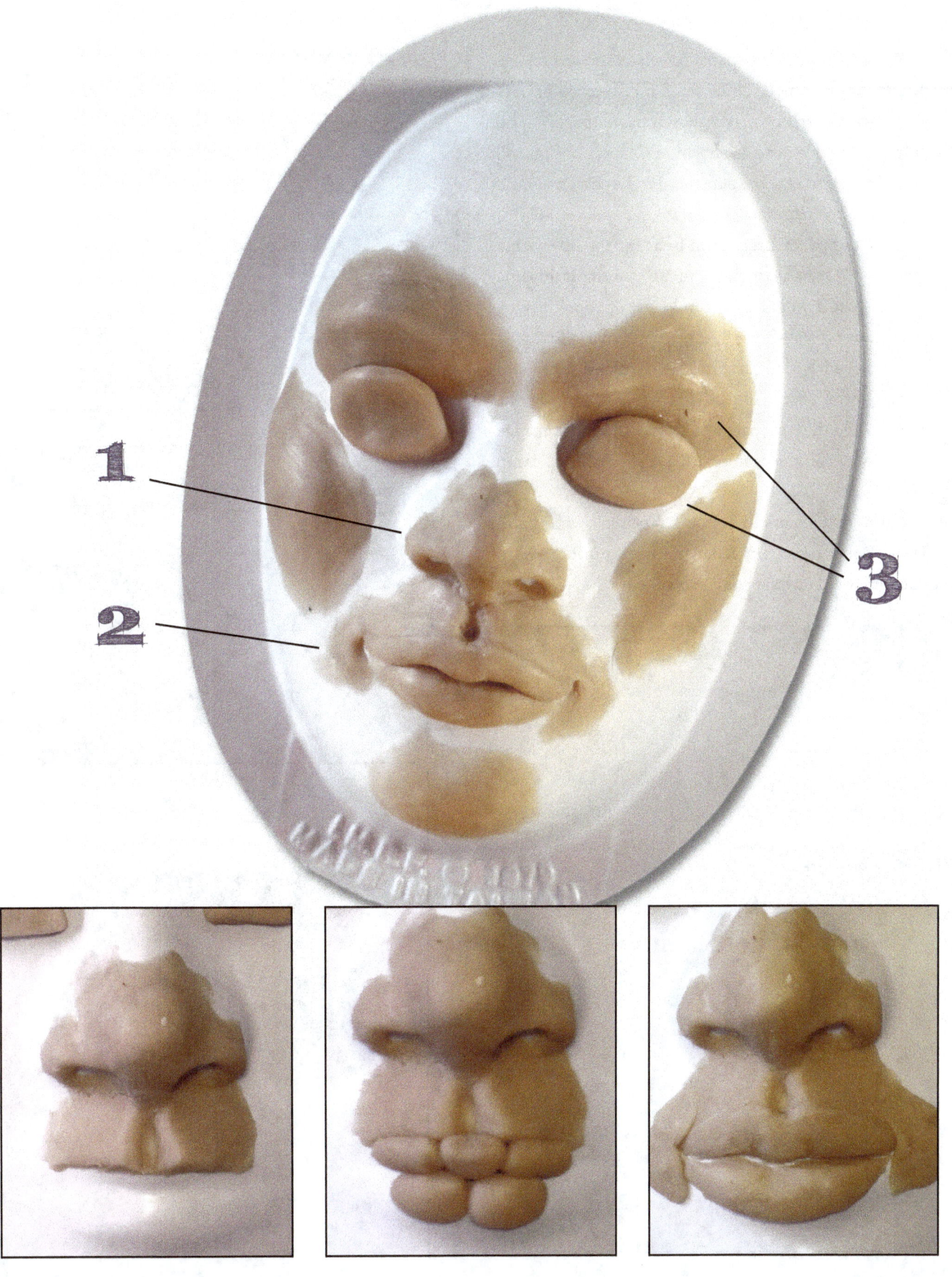

CHAPTER 7

ADD THE PAPER MACHE

Prepare two or three paper towels as shown on page 24. You may also need some small pieces to fill in bare spots. Mix a batch of plaster-based paste (page 7) and apply the paper mache as shown in Chapter 5. You will probably need to tear the paper under the chin, nose and temples, so the paper will lie flat.

Push the paper deep down between the lips with a modeling tool or the tip of a knife. If you think this line might be lost if you add a second layer of paper mache, you can put just one layer over the lips. Cover the rest of the mask with the second layer, smoothing and stretching the paper to make it as smooth as possible. After you add the last coat of paste over the paper mache, smooth down all the seams with a soft brush or a damp finger.

Then set the mask in front of a fan or in a warm place to dry. Don't remove it from the form until it's hard enough to hold its shape on its own.

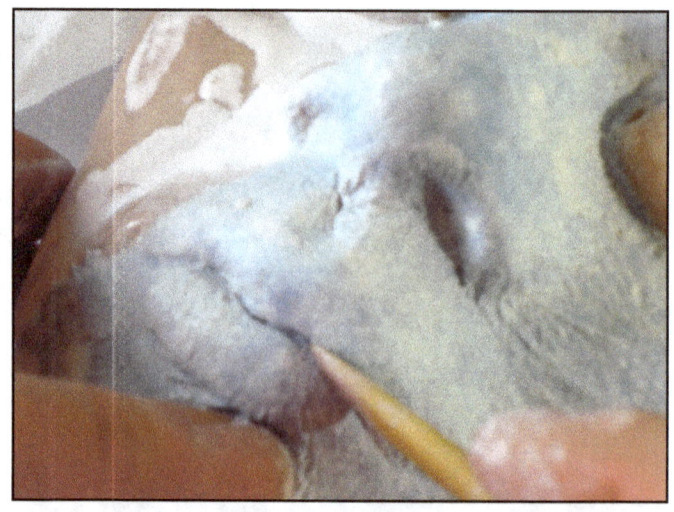

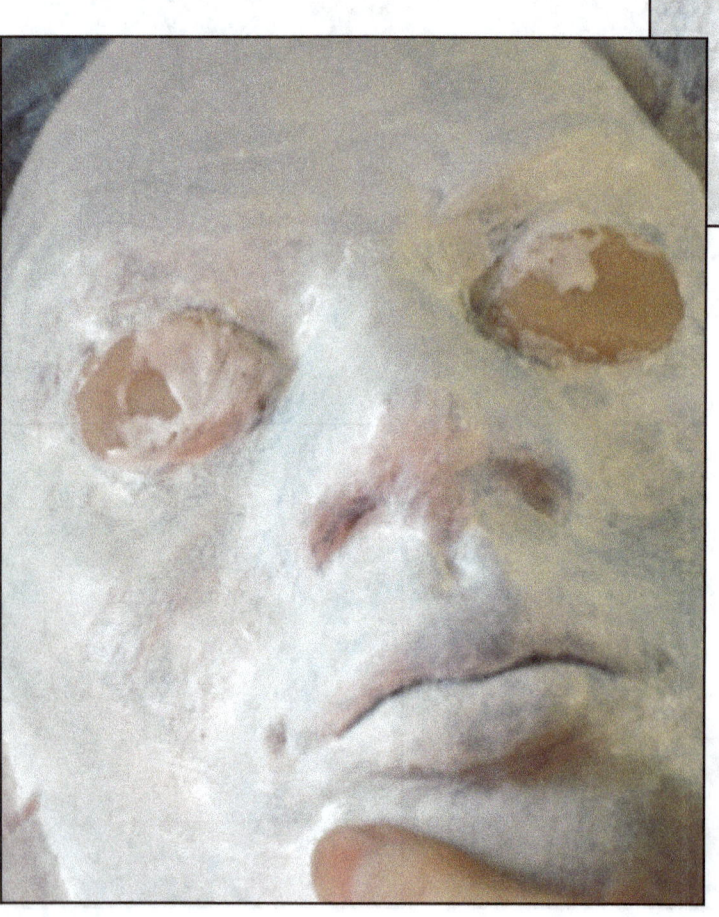

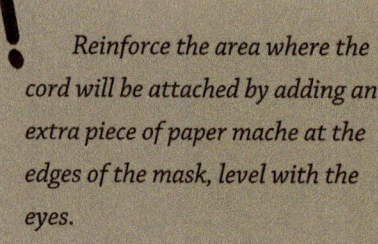

Reinforce the area where the cord will be attached by adding an extra piece of paper mache at the edges of the mask, level with the eyes.

PREPARE THE MASK FOR PAINTING

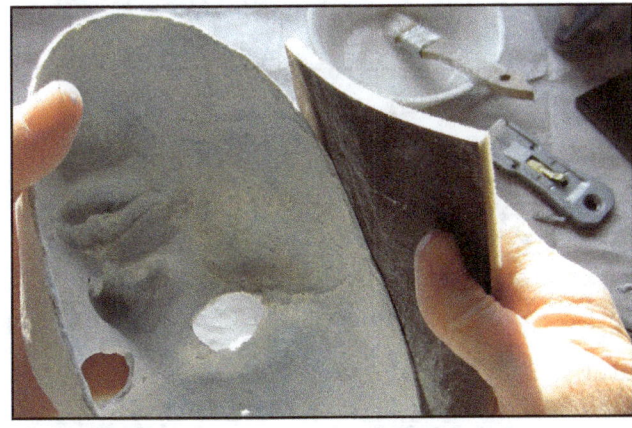

1 Cut off the excess paper and sand the edges.

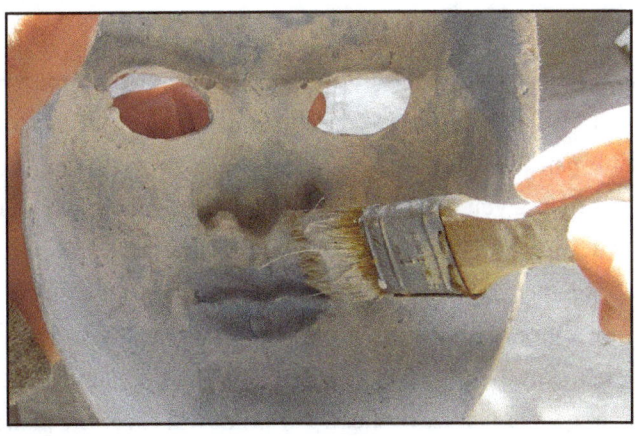

2 If there's only one layer of paper mache on the lips, reinforce them on the inside with a small piece of paper, using gesso for paste.

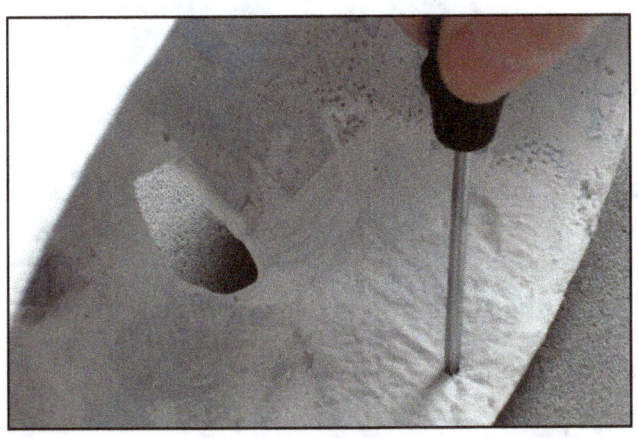

3 Punch or drill a hole for the cord or ribbon, and then apply a coat of gesso to the inside.

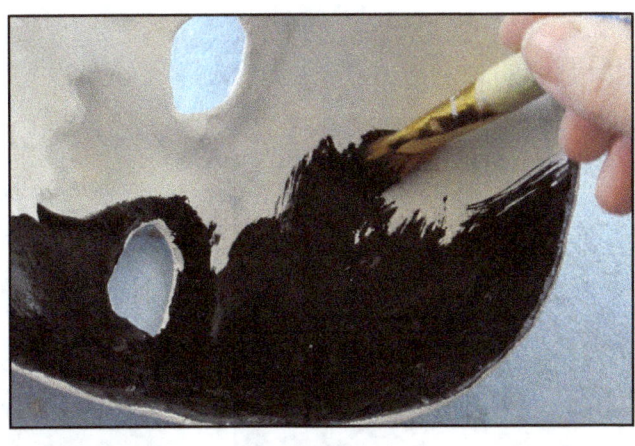

4 If desired, finish the inside with a coat of black acrylic paint.

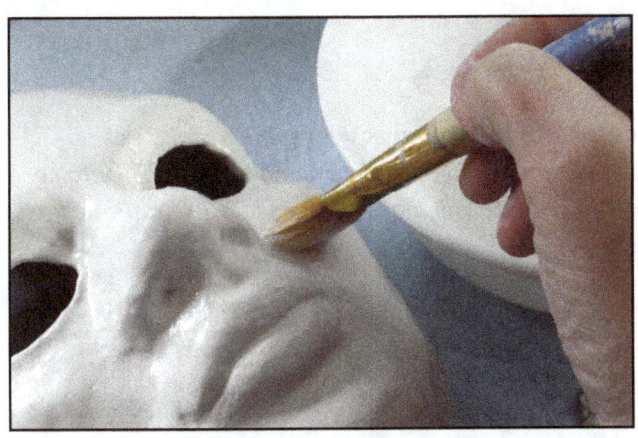

5 Apply gesso to the front and sand or wet-polish. Use Really Smooth Gesso mix for the top coat (page 8. Allow the gesso to dry.

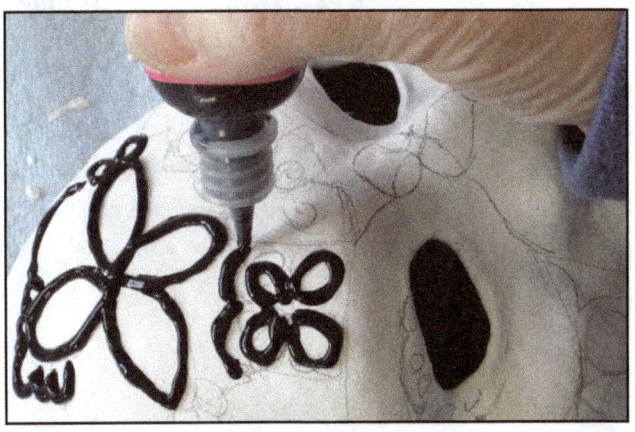

6 Draw a lace design with pencil, and trace over the lines with Puff Paint. (Or see page 86 for an alternate method using gesso.)

FINISH YOUR MASK

Be sure to give the Puff Paint plenty of time to dry. You'll be painting over the raised design, so it doesn't matter what color of puff paint you use.

Before you draw the lace design on your mask, it really helps if you can take a digital photo of your blank mask and print it out on copy paper. Try out a variety of designs in pencil on the printed mask first. Once you have one you like, you can then draw it onto the mask itself. Any penciled mistakes can be easily removed with a damp sponge—or just leave them. The paint will cover the pencil lines.

Since many traditional Volto masks are embellished with gilded lace, I did a Google image search for "tatting" (a type of lace), and then simplified and combined several of the designs.

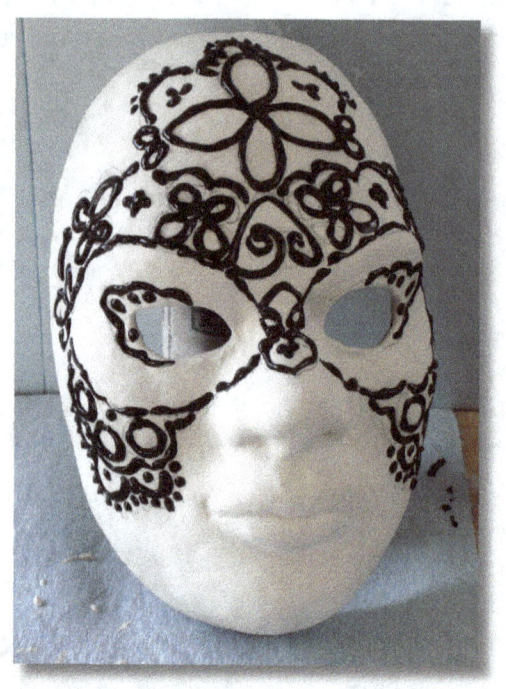

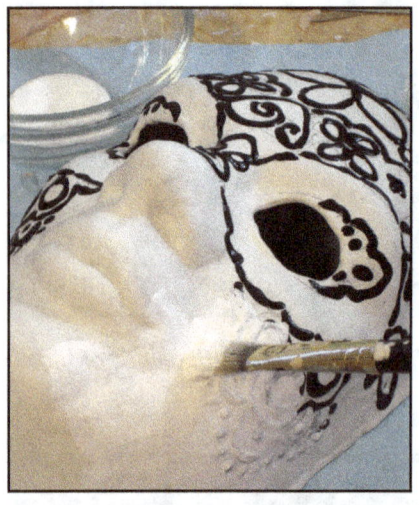

1 *When the Puff Paint is dry (it can take four hours or more) cover the mask, including the lace design, with several coats of white paint.*

2 *Paint just the lace pattern with Metallic Gold.*

3 *Before moving to the next step, be sure you have two paper towels on hand. One towel should be dry, and the other one should be slightly damp.*

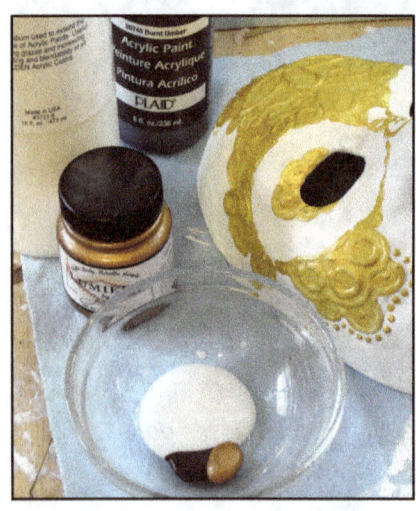

4 *Mix a small amount of Burnt Umber with some Acrylic Glazing Liquid. If you have some, you can add a small amount of Metallic Bronze, as I did. The glaze will make the lace look like antique gold.*

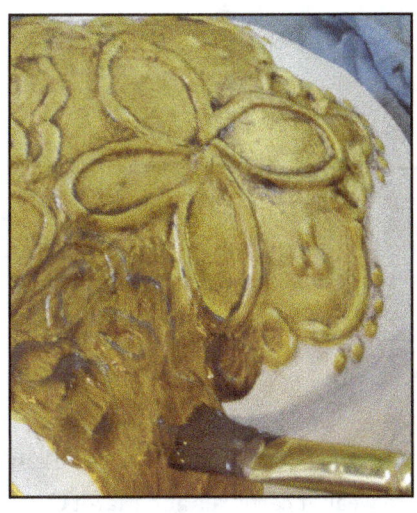

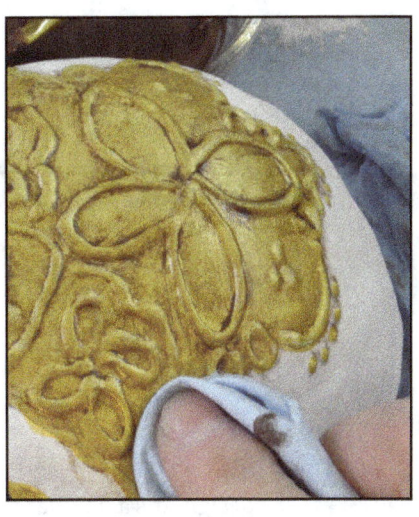

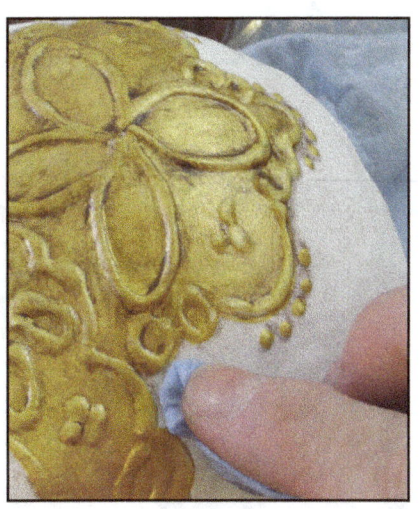

5 Lightly brush the glaze over the gold portion of the mask, using a small soft brush.

6 Use the dry paper towel to remove most of the glaze, leaving just enough to help define your raised lace pattern.

7 Use the damp paper towel to go back and remove the glaze from the white parts of the mask. If you want, you can, brush a small amount of glaze over the lips and nostrils, and the valley between the lips and nose. (It's called the philtral dimple, for you trivia buffs). Use your damp towel to remove most of this glaze, leaving just a hint to bring out the features.

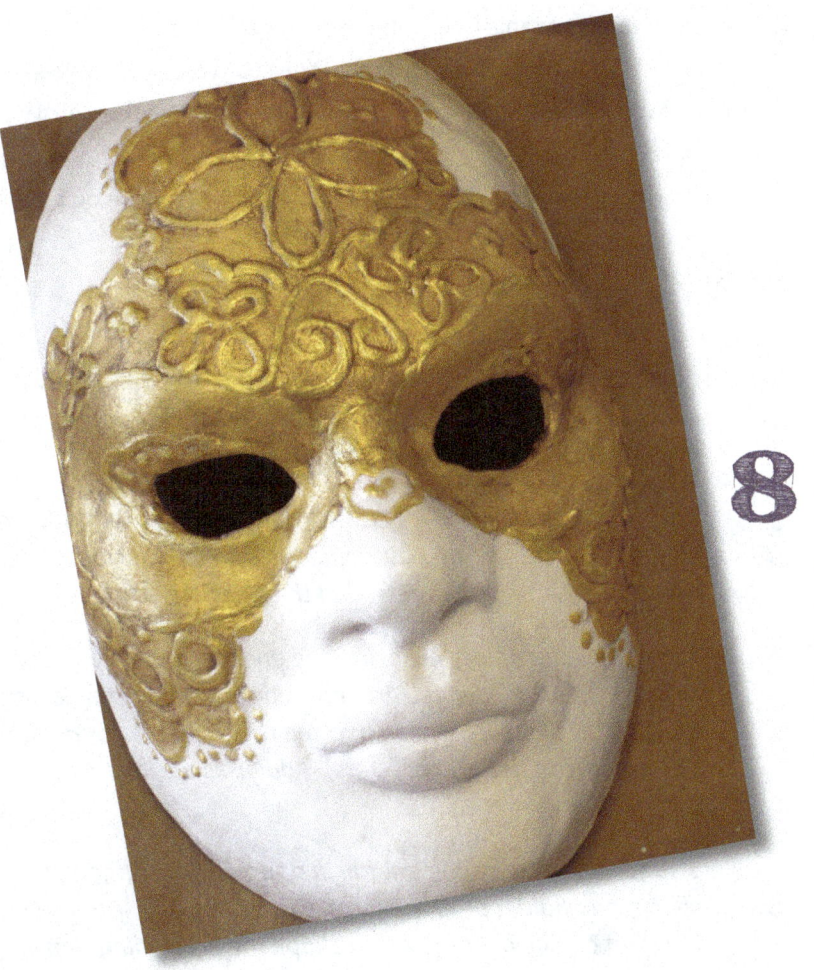

8 Let your mask dry completely, (the glaze can take up to 24 hours to dry). Then give the white portion of the mask two or three coats of satin acrylic varnish mixed with a small touch of white or antique white craft paint. This will give your mask the look of glazed porcelain. When the varnish is dry, tie on the cord or ribbon, and enjoy!

Bauta Mask

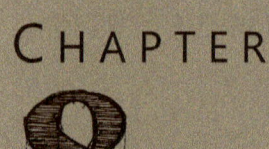

THIS SLIGHTLY STRANGE-LOOKING mask is a traditional Venetian design. It's a popular mask to wear at carnivals and Mardi Gras. The protruding upper lip allows the wearer to talk and drink without removing the mask. This mask was traditionally worn with a black tri-cornered hat and a long black coat.

If you leave off the lower lip (step 4 below) your mask will look like those used in traditional Commedia dell'arte masked theater.

I used Lumiere® brand Pearl White and Bronze paints by Jaquard to finish my Bauta mask. You might prefer to use gold paint, or blue, or any other color that suits your fancy. You could also add a raised gold or silver lace pattern for the upper half of the mask, like the Volto mask in the last chapter.

Remember to cover your mask form with plastic as shown on page 19.

MAKE THE MOLD

1 *Begin by modeling the eyebrows, which arch dramatically and almost meet in the middle. Then add a bit of clay above the eyebrows to square off the forehead.*

2 *Add prominent cheeks. Add a long noodle of clay to mark the edges of the mask. The Bauta mask is traditionally quite square on the upper corners, and the sides are straight.*

3 *Sculpt the long pointy nose, like the one shown. (If you decided to make a Commedia dell'arte mask by leaving off the lower lip, do a bit of online research to see the different noses that represent traditional characters). Add disks of clay to mark the opening for your eyes.*

4 *Scrunch up some aluminum foil in a somewhat triangular shape, and hold it onto the form with bits of clay. Then place a thin skin of clay over the foil to shape the protruding upper lip, as shown.*

CHAPTER

8

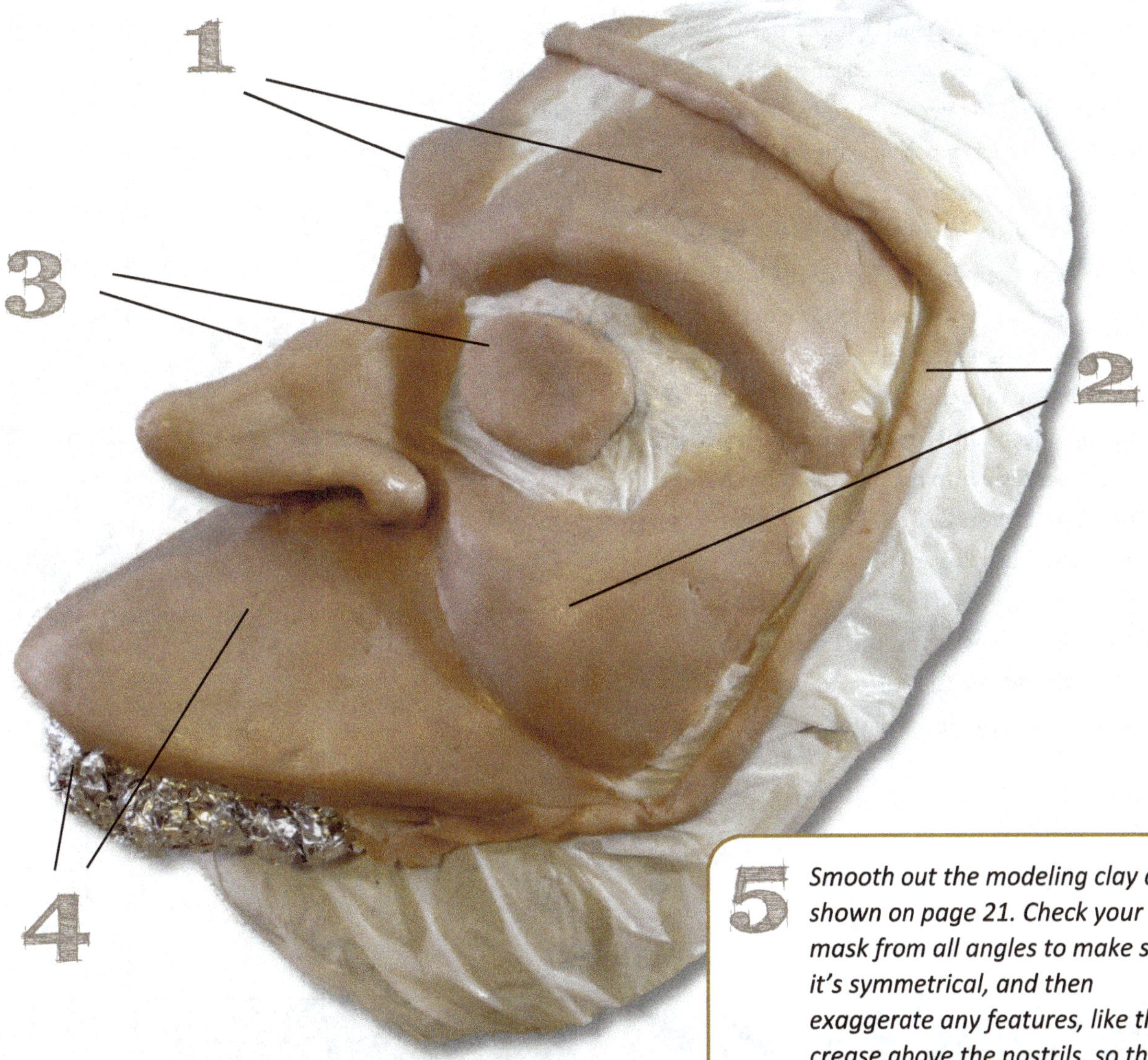

1

3

2

4

5 Smooth out the modeling clay as shown on page 21. Check your mask from all angles to make sure it's symmetrical, and then exaggerate any features, like the crease above the nostrils, so they won't be hidden under the two layers of paper mache.

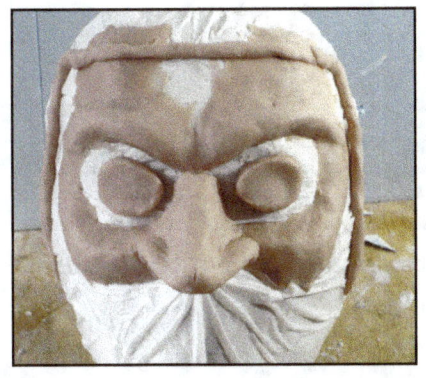
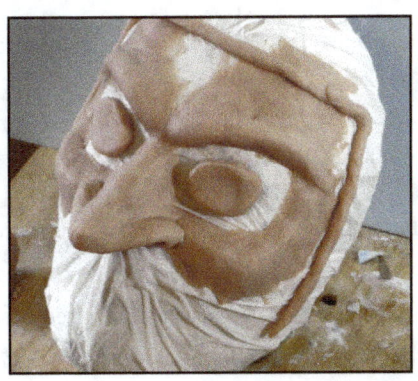
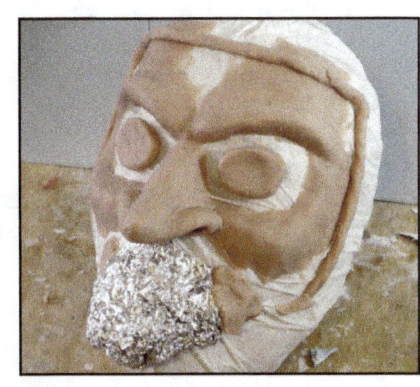

ADD THE PAPER MACHE

Prepare three sheets of Scott Shop Towels, as shown in Chapter 5. Then mix up a batch of plaster-based paste and add two layers of paper mache. Take your time, because the long, thin nose is a challenging feature to cover. Be sure to stretch the damp paper over the paste so it's as smooth as you can make it.

Tear the paper whenever it tries to fold instead of laying flat (this almost always happens under a big nose). You may also need to tear the paper if it tries to bridge the space between the cheek and upper lip, as shown in the small photo below. Fill in any gaps with smaller pieces of paper.

Use a knife or modeling tool to smooth the area where paper has been turned back around the eyes, and to push the paper deep into the nostrils and the crease behind the wings of the nose. Don't cover the underside of that weird shelf-like upper lip.

If you go slowly, as you should, your paste may get too thick in the bowl or on the brush. If this happens, just throw out the stiffened paste and make another batch. Don't hurry this process.

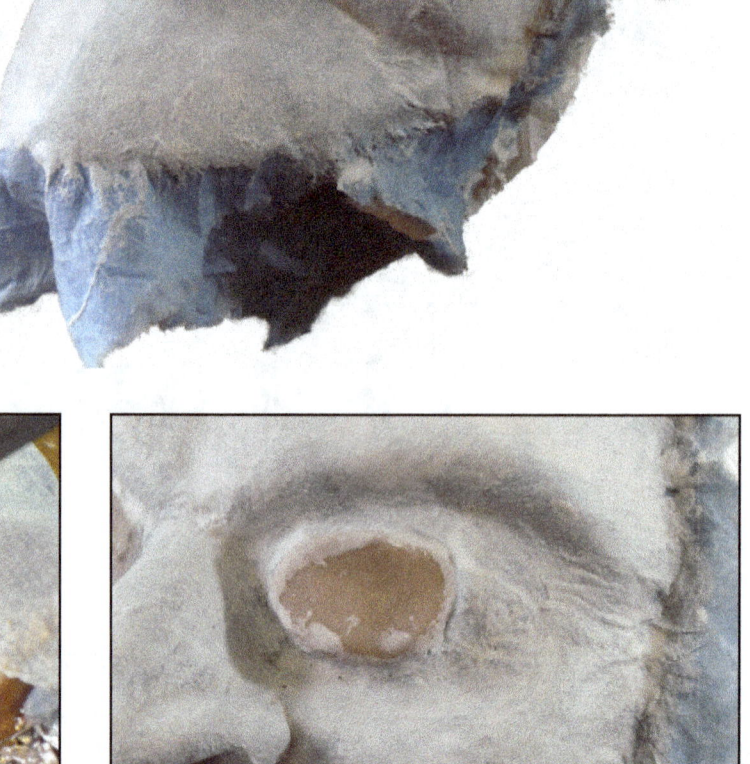

Tear the paper where needed to make it lie flat. Use a tool to sharpen details.

Fold the paper around the eye and press flat. Make a nice crisp edge so it will be easy to see where to cut when the mask is lifted off the mold.

PREPARE THE MASK FOR PAINTING

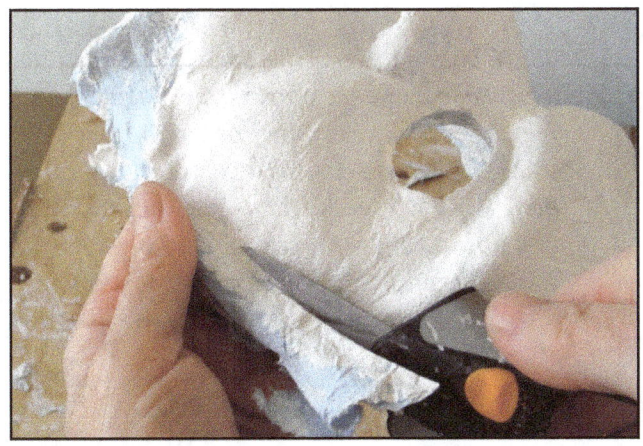

1 Cut off the extra paper around the edges.

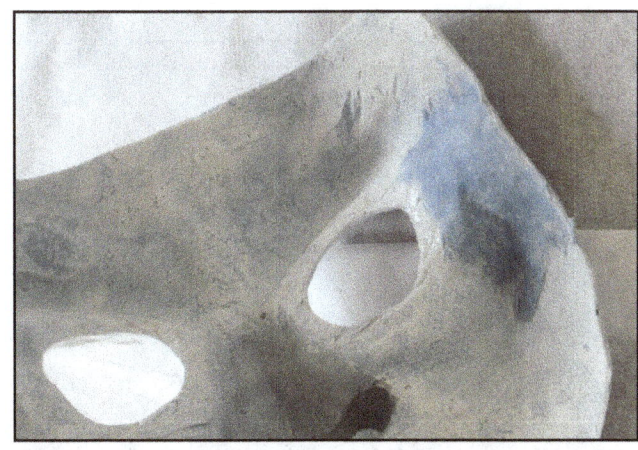

2 If needed, reinforce the spot where the cord will be attached, using gesso as paste.

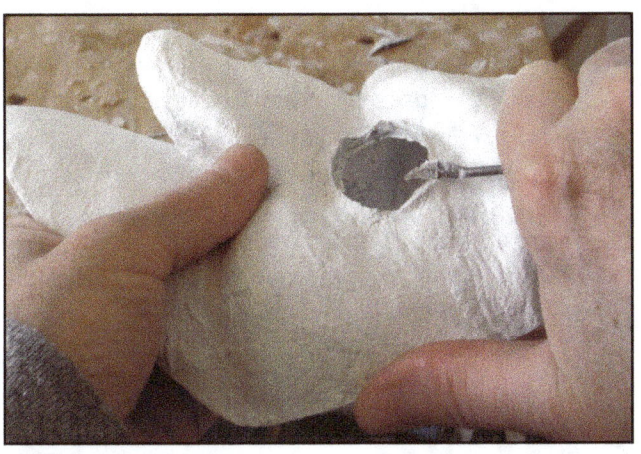

3 Use a knife or modeling tool to remove excess paste around the eyes.

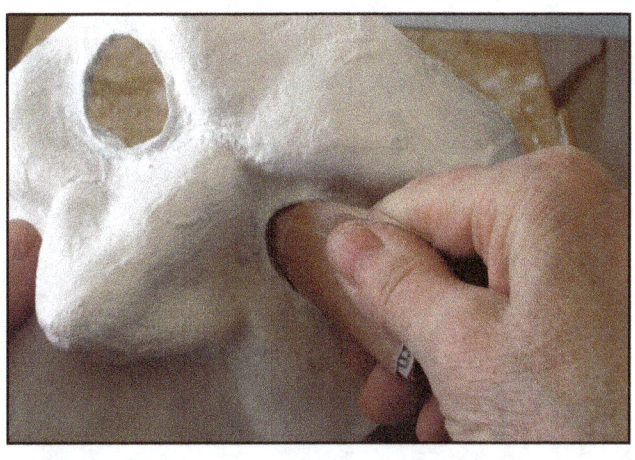

4 Sand the edges of the mask, the eye holes, and any rough spots inside and out.

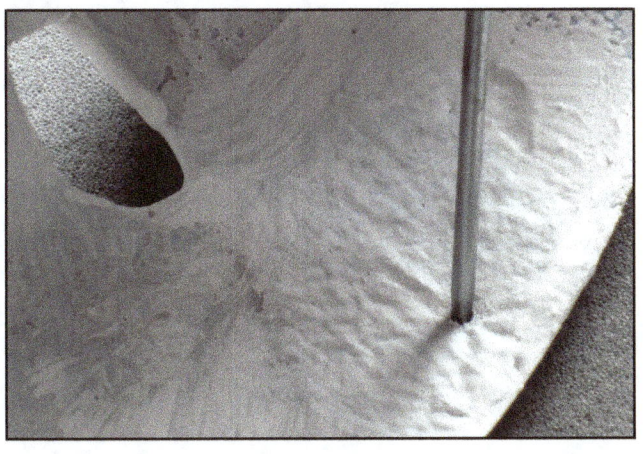

5 Punch or drill the hole for the ribbon.

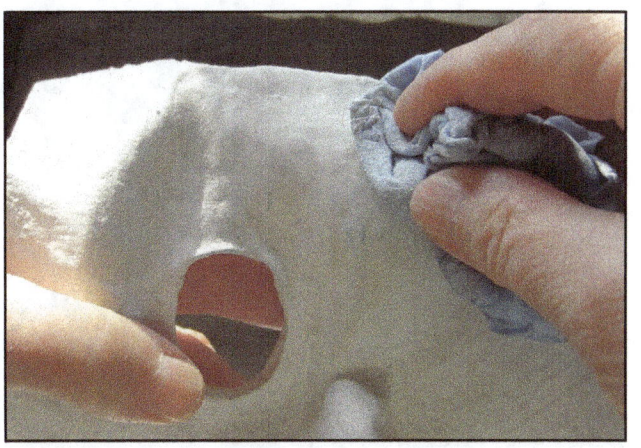

6 Apply one or two coats of gesso, sanding or wet-polishing between coats.

FINISH YOUR MASK

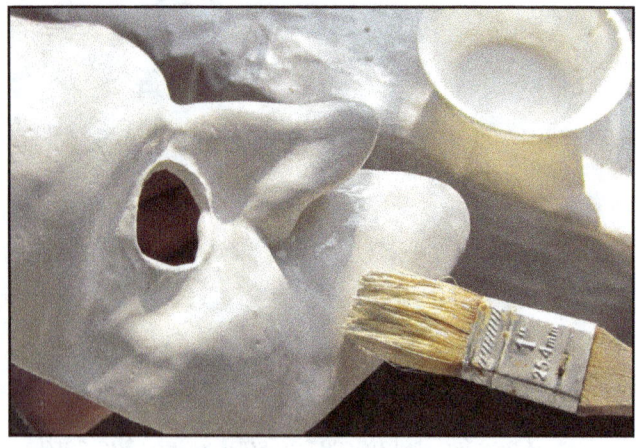

1 If you intend to finish the back of the mask, do it now and allow the paint to dry. Then apply a final layer of gesso to the front of the mask, using the Really Smooth Gesso Mix recipe on Page 8. Let it flow smoothly over the mask, and don't brush into the areas that are beginning to dry, because that will leave brush marks.

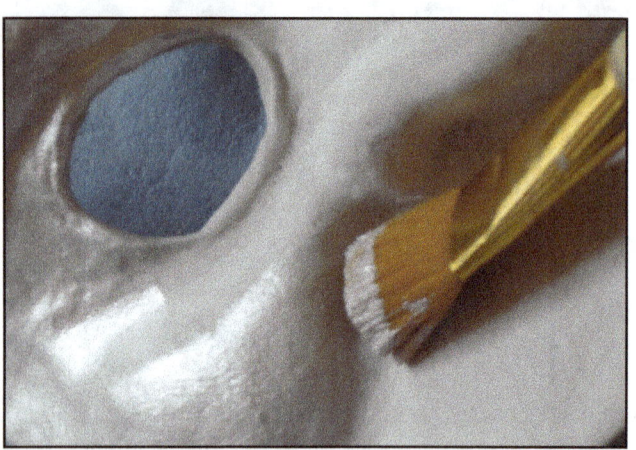

2 When the last layer of gesso is bone dry, you can give mask a nice pearly glow by applying a coat of **Pearl White** paint with a very soft brush. (Of course, you can paint your mask any color you like).

If you want, you can leave your mask this nice pearly color, without adding the glaze shown in the following steps.

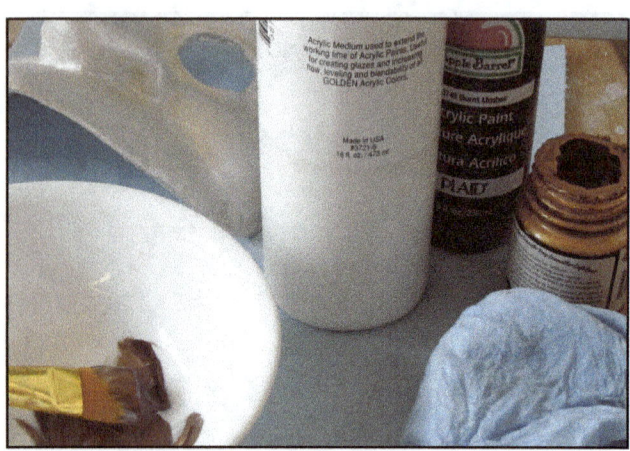

3 Allow the white paint to dry completely. Then mix together a small amount of **Burnt Umber**, a tiny amount of **Metallic Bronze**, and some **Acrylic Glazing Liquid**. You will also need two paper towels. One towel should be dry, and the other one should be slightly damp. Make sure you have these towels on hand before you begin the next step.

4 *Liberally apply the glaze with a wide soft brush. Do a fairly small area at a time. The glazing liquid keeps the acrylic paint from drying too fast so you have plenty of time for the next step.*

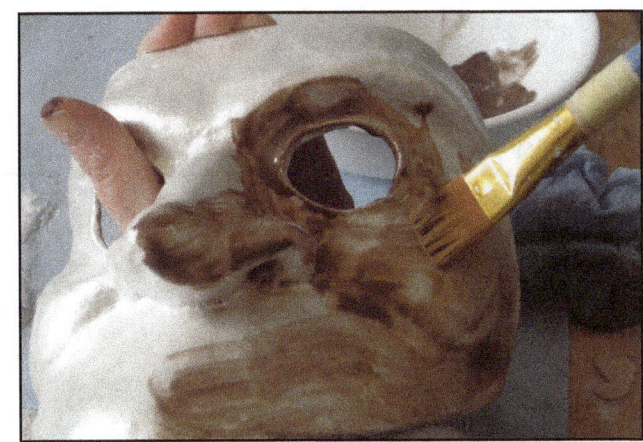

5 *Wipe off almost all of the glaze with the dry paper towel, allowing the glaze to remain in the deeper crevices. If too much glaze remains in a place where you prefer the mask to be lighter, use the damp paper towel to remove the glaze completely.*

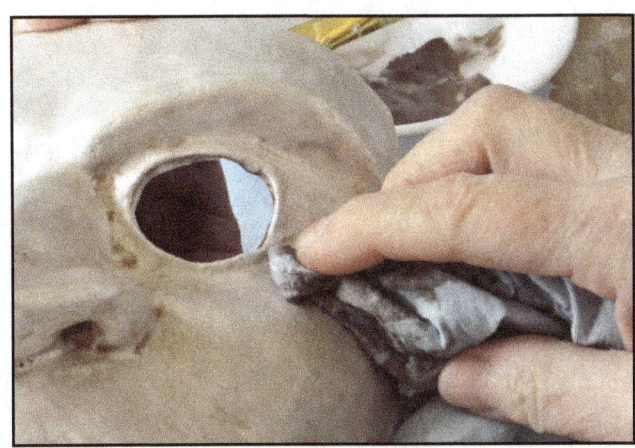

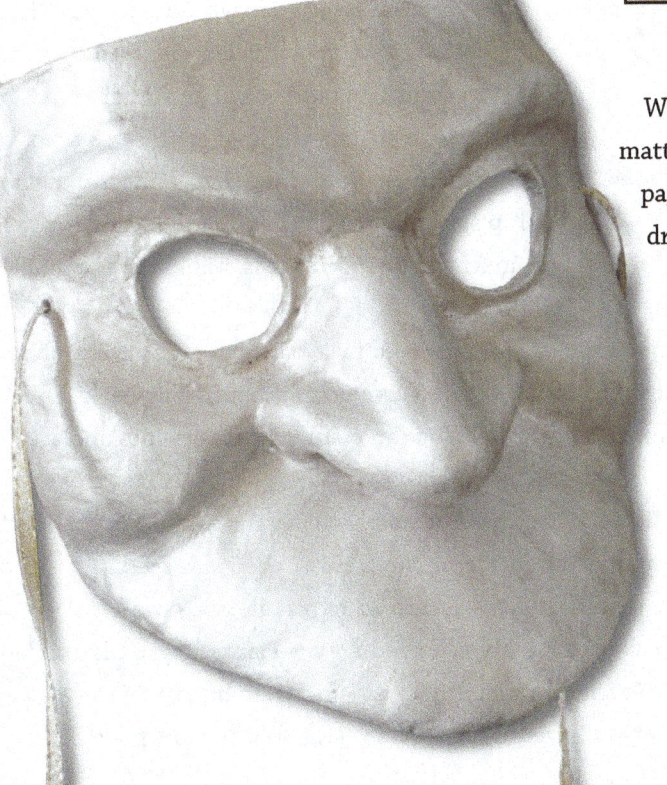

When the paint is dry you can add a protective finish of matte acrylic varnish and attach the ribbons or cords (see page 31). You're now ready for a masquerade ball or that dream trip to New Orleans for Mardi Gras!

Plague Doctor

T HE PLAGUE DOCTOR mask was worn during the seventeenth and eighteenth centuries by doctors—and some untrained, unemployed people who were willing to act as doctors. These brave (or perhaps just desperate) souls were hired by cities to treat victims of the bubonic plague. This is now a popular mask to wear at carnivals, but its original purpose was rather grim—to help doctors survive their close association with sick people. The long beak was hollow and filled with medicinal herbs.

During an outbreak of an air-born illness (like the flu, for instance) it makes sense to cover one's face to help prevent infection. Unfortunately, the bubonic plague is spread by fleas, so the costume probably didn't do much good. This mask is said to have originated in Paris in the early 1600's.

This mask has been interpreted by artists in a wide variety of ways. I thought it would be fun to use a common European long-beaked bird, the painted stork, as my model. You can paint your mask white or black if you prefer more conventional colors.

Traditionally, the glasses would have red lenses, but I made do with a red ring around the inside of the frames. You can see the rest of the traditional costume that was worn with this mask on page 47.

To finish your mask you'll need Acrylic Paint, Acrylic Glazing Liquid, and Matte Acrylic Varnish. If you have some on hand, you can also add a glaze of Metallic Silver to the spectacles, as shown in the photo.

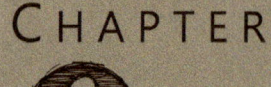

C H A P T E R

9

44

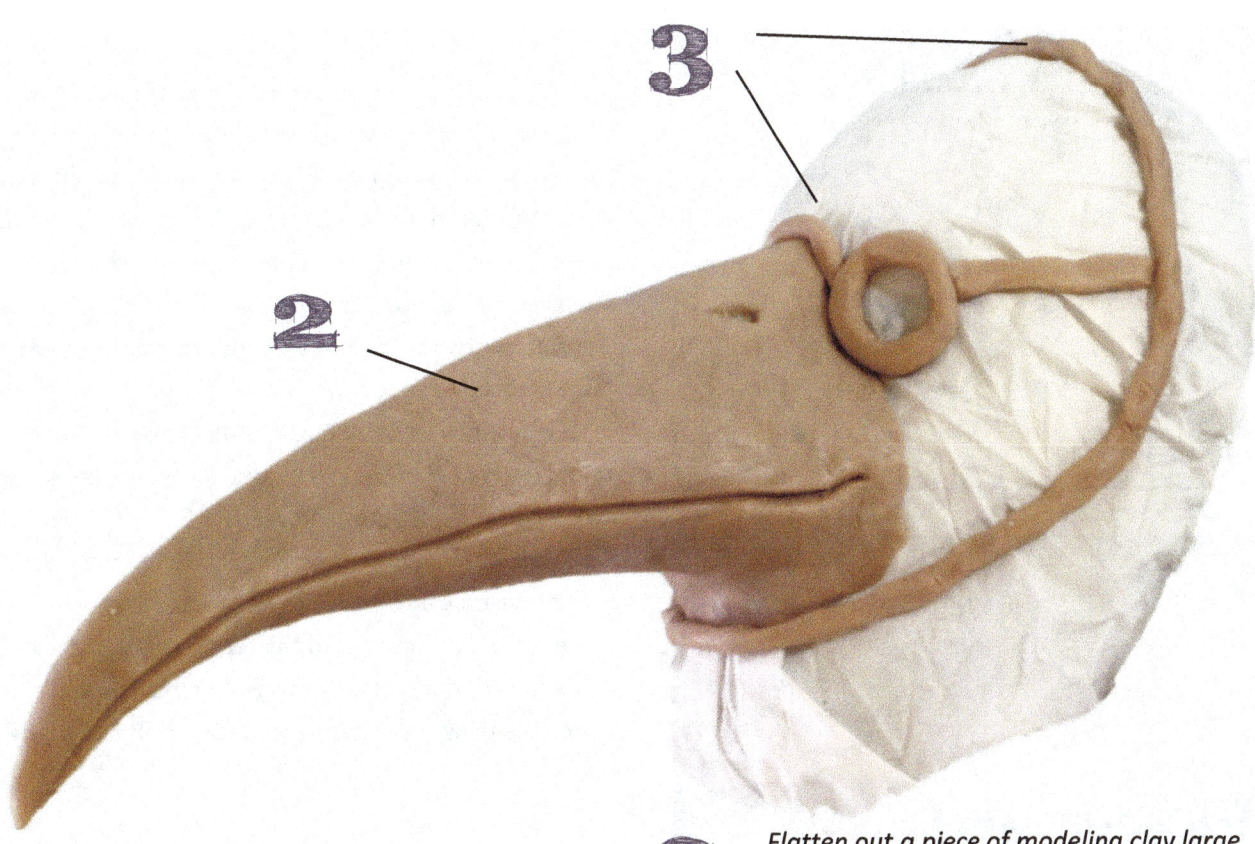

MAKE THE MOLD

1 *Cover your mask form with plastic, as shown on page 19. Scrunch up some aluminum foil into a long beak-like shape, and attach it to the front of the mask form with bits of modeling clay, as shown below.*

2 *Flatten out a piece of modeling clay large enough to cover the beak with a thin "skin" of clay. Use a knife or modeling tool to cut a line between the upper and lower beak. Press in two nostrils at the top of the beak.*

3 *Use clay noodles to give your doctor some round spectacles. Measure the distance between the lenses to make sure you'll be able to see out. Use a long noodle of clay to mark the outside edge of the mask.*

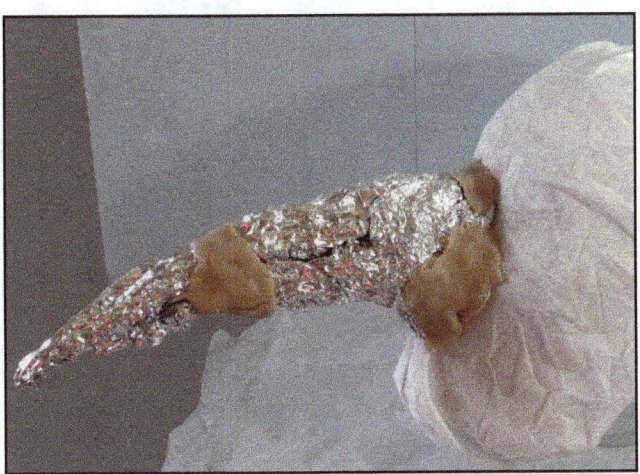

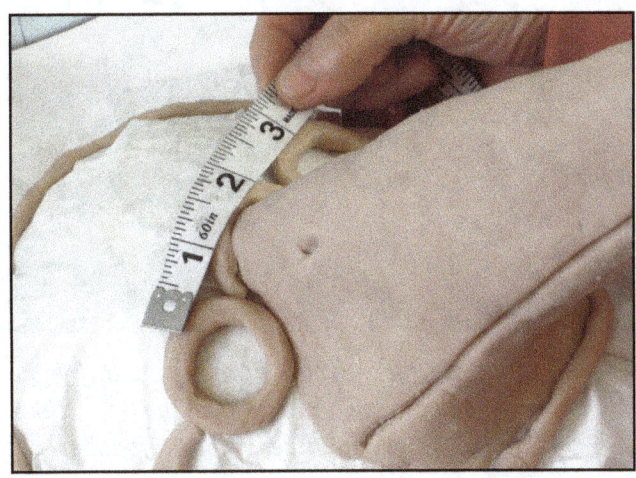

45

ADD THE PAPER MACHE

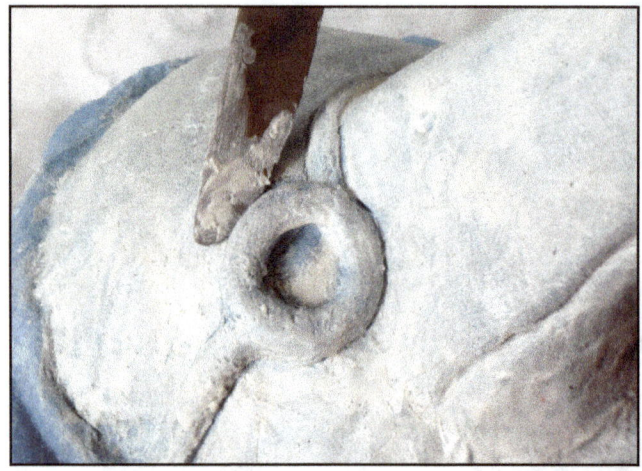

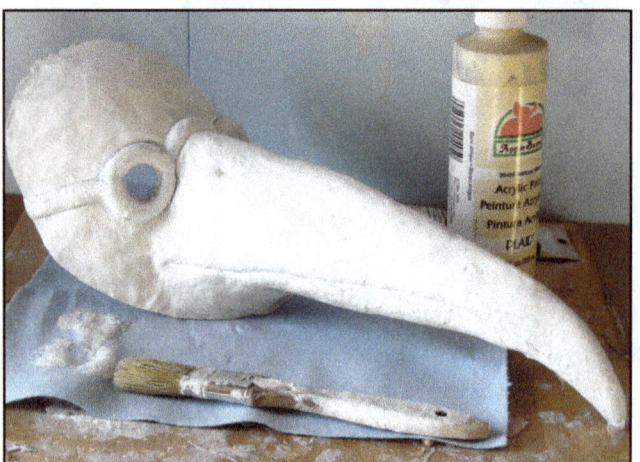

Prepare three or four paper towels, as shown on page 24. Mix up a batch of plaster-based paste, and apply two layers of paper mache to the mask. The challenge in this project is covering the beak smoothly—I wound some long thin pieces of paper around the beak, but you my want to do it differently. Be sure to smooth out the many edges where pieces overlap.

Use a knife or modeling tool to make a crisp line around the frames of the glasses, and down the separating line between the upper and lower beak.

The beak is quite heavy, so be sure to support the mask so it won't tip over while you work.

Leave an empty space in the center of the spectacles so you can see out when the mask is worn. You can trim any overhanging paper mache in this area after the mask is dry.

PREPARE THE MASK FOR PAINTING

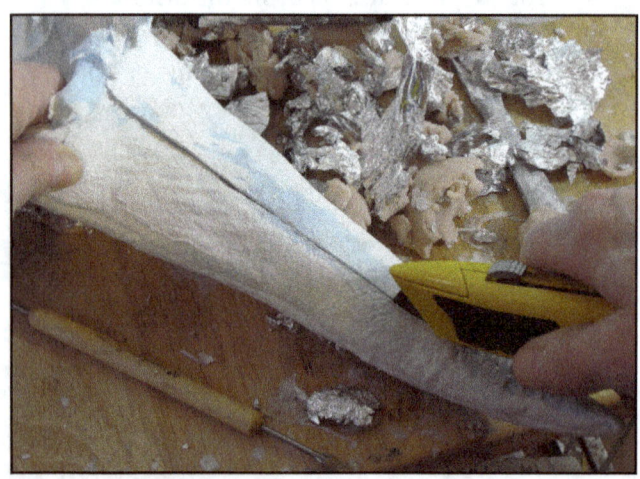

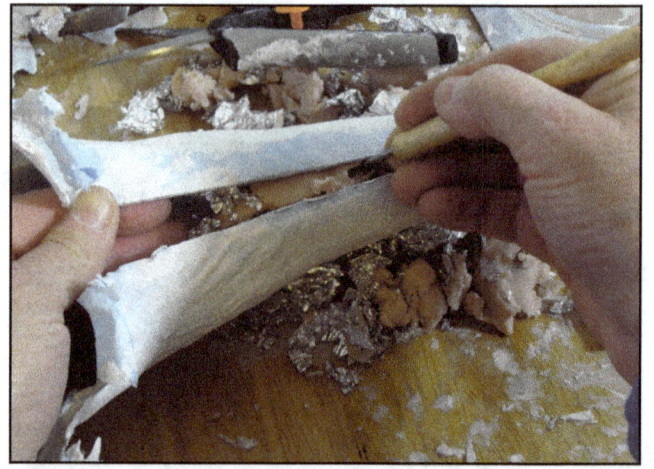

1 *When dry, lift the mask from the mold. If you can't pull the foil and clay from the beak, cut a line down the underside with a craft knife.*

2 *Use a tool to pry the foil and clay out of the beak. (This process is a little messy, as you can see.)*

46

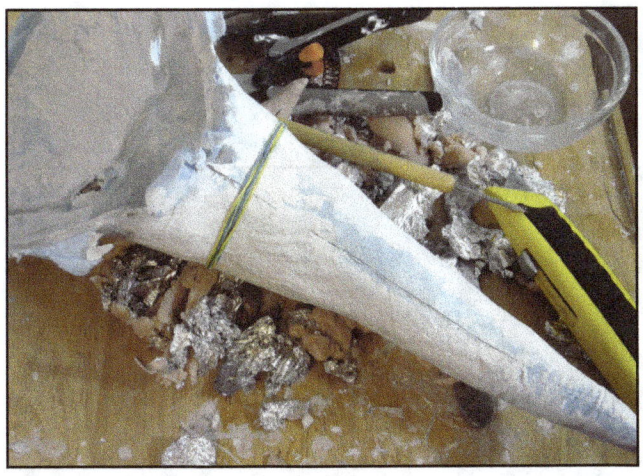

3 *When the beak is empty, hold the two sides back together with rubber bands.*

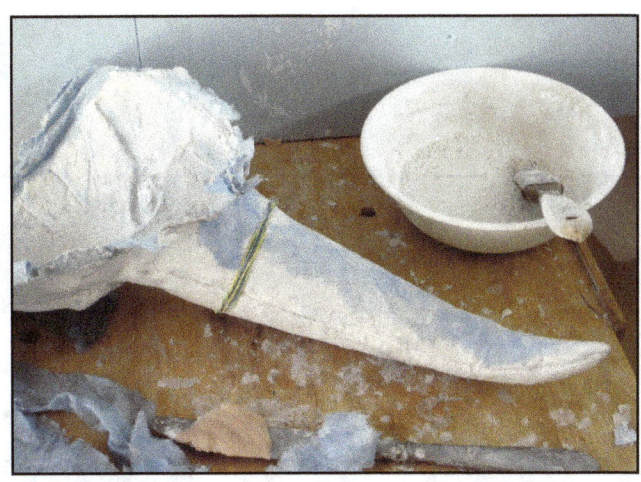

4 *Mix up a ½ batch of paste and repair the wound with two layers of paper mache. Don't remove the rubber bands until the paper mache is dry.*

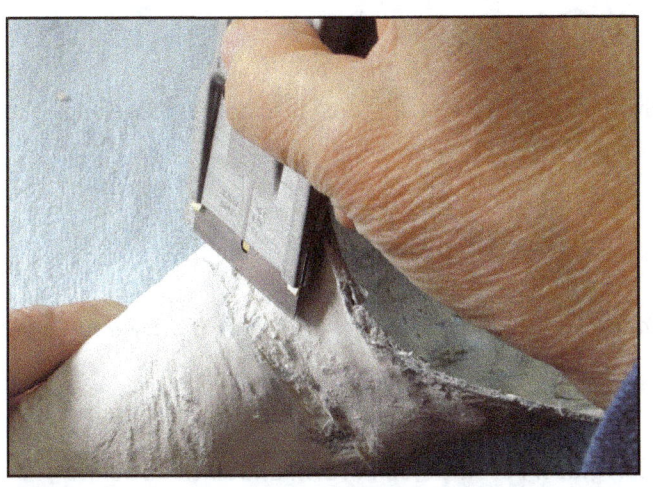

5 *Remove the rubber bands and trim the extra paper from around the edges of the mask. Use a craft knife or razor knife to smooth the ridges left by the paste where the rubber bands held the beak together.*

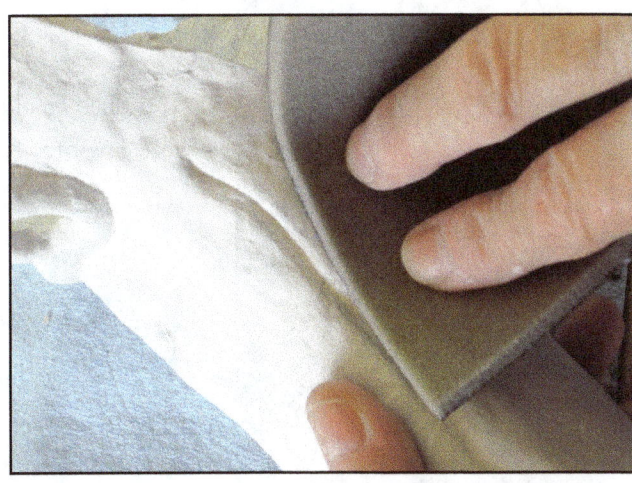

6 *Sand the edges, punch or drill a hole for the ribbon, and apply one or two layers of plaster-based gesso. Sand or wet-polish the gesso, and apply one last layer of Really Smooth Gesso Mix, page 8.*

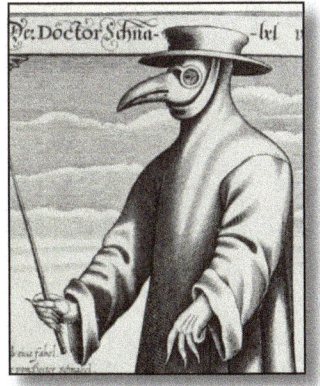

While you're waiting for the gesso to dry, you can take a few minutes to decide how you'll finish your mask. There are a number of old paintings and engravings of doctors wearing this mask, like the one shown here. You can find them doing an Internet image search using the term "plague doctor mask" in the search bar. That will also show you many of the ways that modern artists have interpreted this mask.

Or, you can follow the instructions on the following pages, and make your mask look like the one at the beginning of this chapter. The colors aren't very conventional, but I think they're more fun than plain black and white.

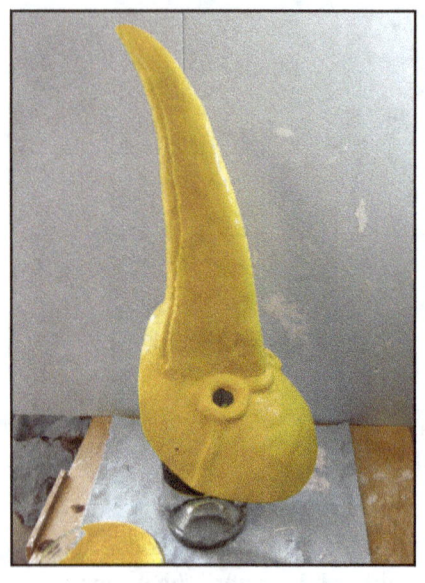
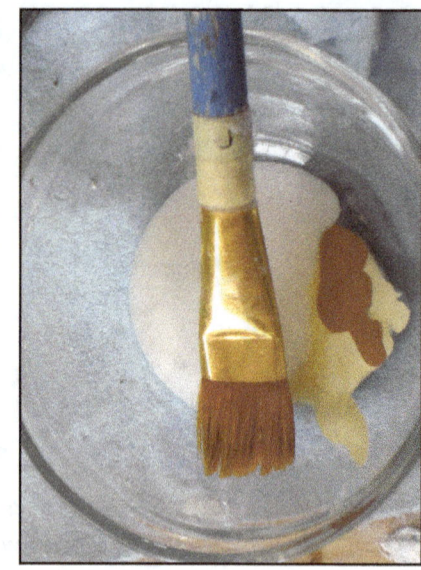
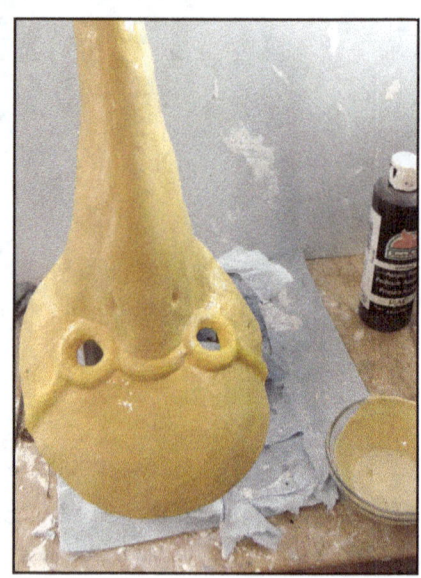

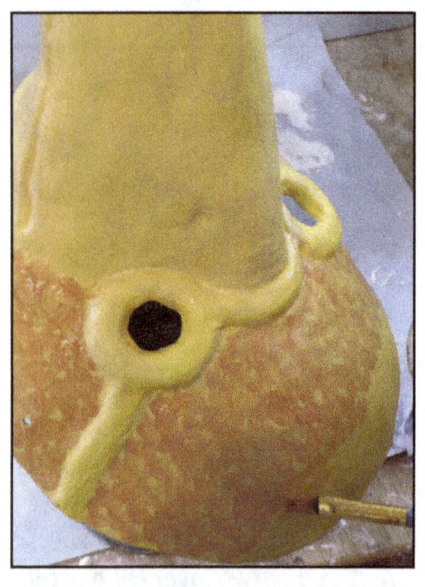

FINISH YOUR MASK

I filled an old wine bottle with water and used it to hold my mask upright while I painted it.

1 *Paint your mask yellow—I used Cadmium Yellow Light. Allow the paint to dry.*

2 *Mix a light tan glaze. I used Golden Brown and Antique White acrylic craft paint, mixed with Acrylic Glazing Liquid. Paint this over the yellow. The original yellow will still show through, but the tan will mellow out the color a bit, and make it more interesting.*

3 *When the tan glaze is dry, mix red and yellow paint to make a reddish orange. Mix in some Acrylic Glazing Liquid or water to make the paint transparent. Use a small flat brush to make some scalloped "feathers" on the stork's head.*

4 *Mix a bright red to go around the inside of the frames.*

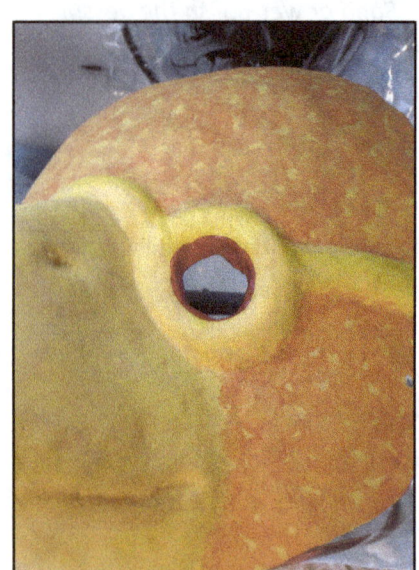

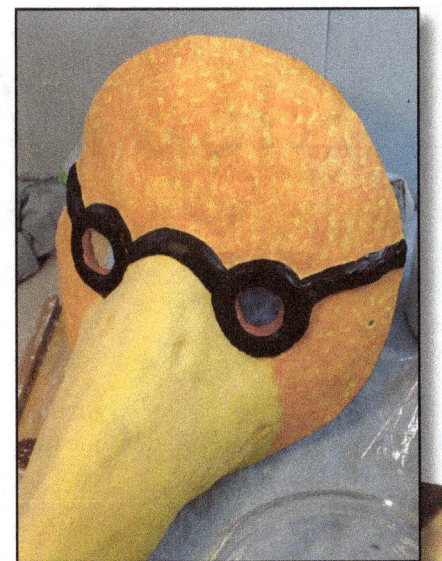

5 *When the red is dry, paint the spectacles black.*

6 *Mix a very thin glaze, using just a small dab of Burnt Umber with Acrylic Glazing Liquid. Make sure you have two paper towels, one dry and one slightly damp, before applying the glaze over the mask, one small area at a time. Brush the glaze on, then wipe off almost all of it (see page 29). Leave just enough of the dark brown to give the mask an antique look, and to bring out the line between the top and bottom of the beak.*

Since I had some Metallic Silver on hand, I mixed it with a little water and brushed a thin wash over the frames after the black paint was dry. It makes the spectacles sparkly, but this is definitely too much "fun" for a conventional Plague Doctor mask. (I like it, anyway.)

Finish your mask with Matte Acrylic Varnish, and attach your ribbon.

Neanderthal Skull

T HIS PARTICULAR SKULL was inspired by one that once belonged to a Neanderthal who has been dead for at least 35,000 years. That's about as dead as you can get, so it would make a perfect mask for Halloween.

I simplified the bone structure quite a lot so it would be easier to make the mask. A real skull has bones that bridge open space (the mandible and zygomatic bones, or what we would call the lower jaw and cheek bones). If you want an anatomically correct skull to take to a science fair, those bones should be formed over aluminum foil, so no modeling clay gets trapped inside the paper mache. If creepy is your aim, I think the simplified version works just fine.

MAKE YOUR MOLD

1 *Begin by using your clay to outline the bony eye socket. The distinguishing feature of a Neanderthal is the overhanging brow. This also causes the forehead to slope much more than yours probably does.*

2 *Add the bony portion of the nose and the cheek bones. Place two flat disks of clay for the eye holes—be sure to measure to make sure they're placed so you will be able to see out.*

3 *Add the muzzle, where the teeth go. Draw in the teeth with a sharp tool. Use your modeling tool to make each tooth stand out. Remember to exaggerate the dividing lines so they aren't lost under two layers of paper mache. You may also open the mouth, if desired. Leave all the teeth, or remove a few, as I did.*

4 *Add the lower jaw bone, which extends from the bony structure that holds the teeth and up towards the ear. Smooth the clay, as shown on page 21.*

CHAPTER

10

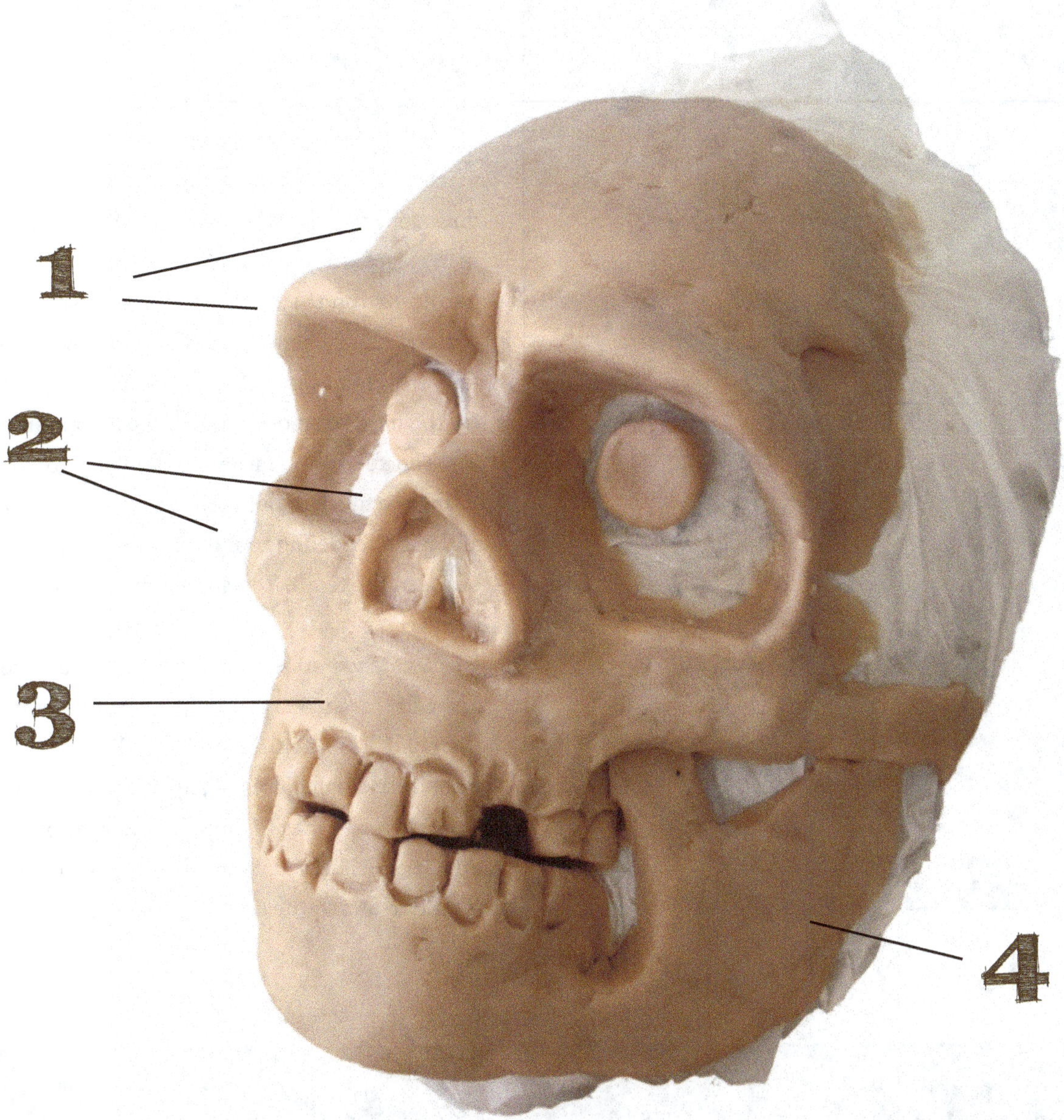

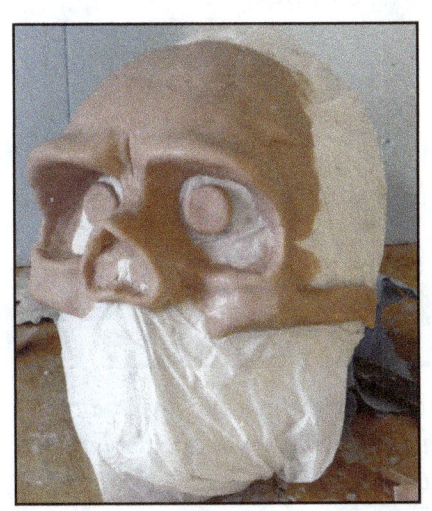
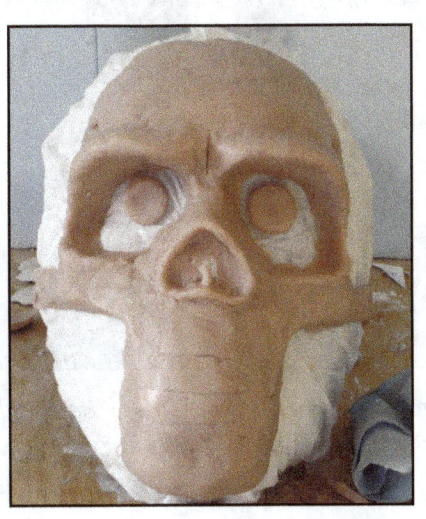
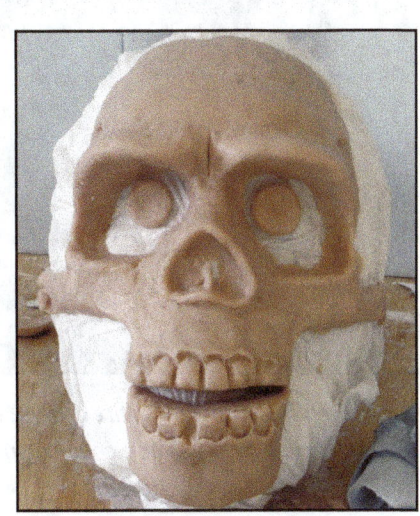

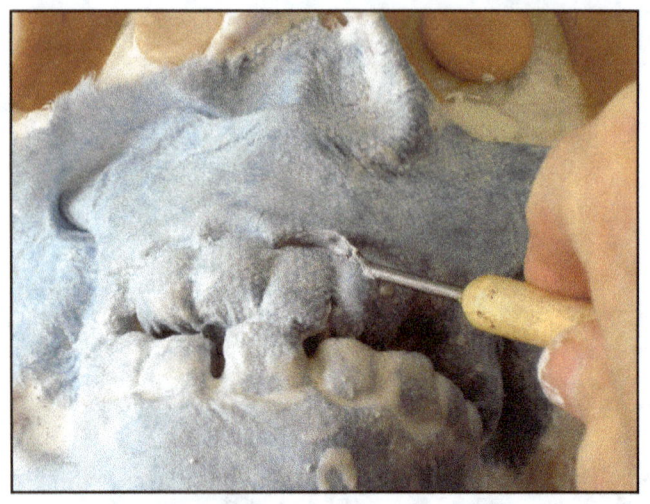

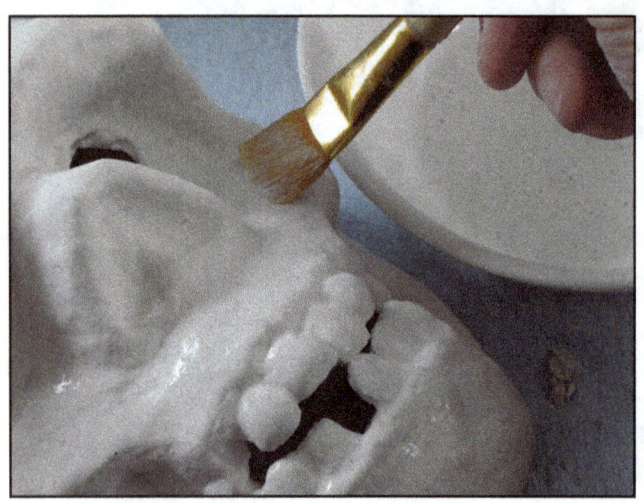

ADD THE PAPER MACHE

Take plenty of time to cover your mask with paper mache. There are a lot of dips and bulges and changes in direction, so you'll probably need to tear the paper in many places to get it to lay smoothly over the skull. If your paste gets too thick before you're finished, just throw it out and make some more. But I will confess—since this fellow spent at least 35,000 years in the ground, I didn't try too hard to smooth out all the bumps and ridges.

The teeth are rather challenging to cover without losing too much detail. Add the first layer of paper mache and use a modeling tool to press the paper into the lines between the teeth. You should be able to tell at that time if you can get away with another layer of paper mache. If you decide to put only one layer over the teeth, be sure to allow the mask to dry completely before removing it from the mold. Then reinforce the teeth from the back of the mask with small pieces of paper, pasted on with gesso.

When the mask is dry, add a layer or two of gesso. Punch or drill the hole for the cord or ribbon unless you intend to attach the cord with a hot glue gun.

FINISH YOUR MASK

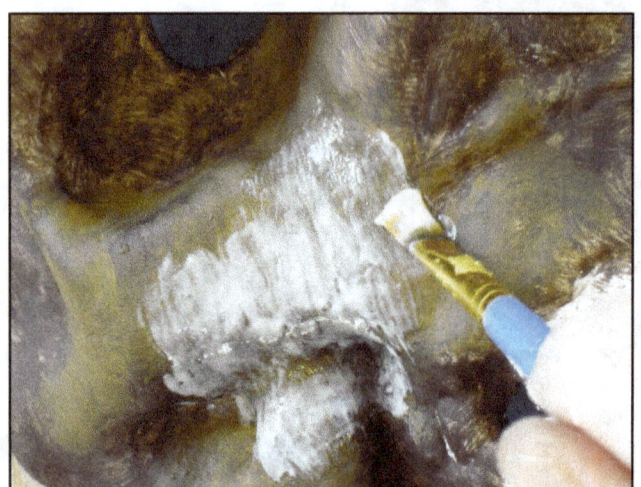

1 Paint your mask dirt brown, and allow the paint to dry. Then cover a small area of the mask with white glue.

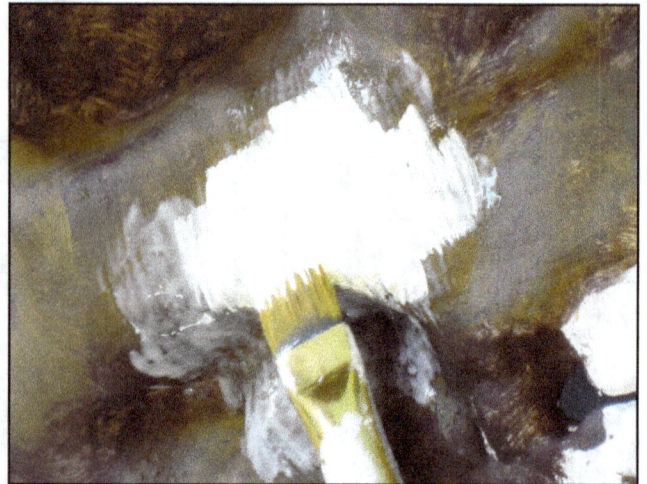

2 Before the glue has a chance to dry, paint over it with warm white liquid craft paint. I used Antique White.

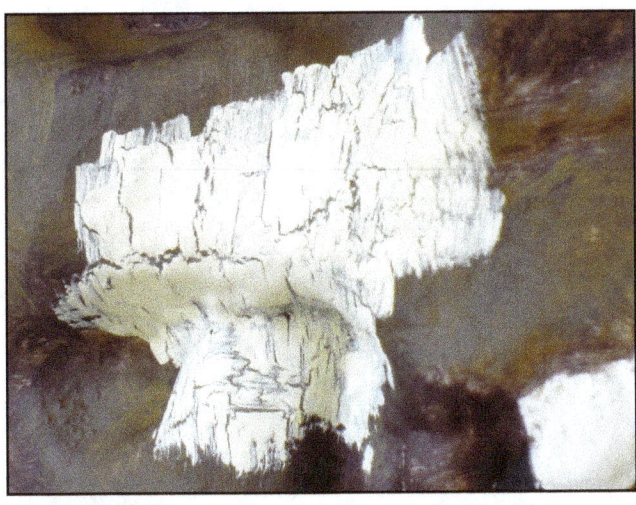

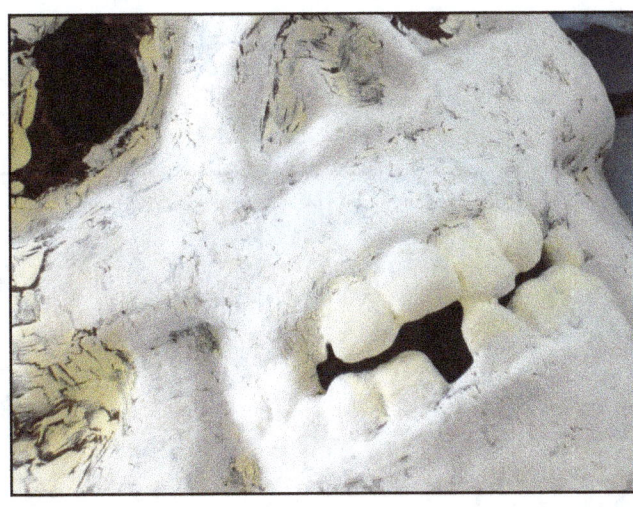

3 Continue to cover the skull with glue and craft paint. It will crackle as it dries, as shown in the photo above.

4 Apply a coat of Light Gray over the dried crackled paint. Use an almost dry brush so much of the randomly-spaced cracks and dark spots show underneath.

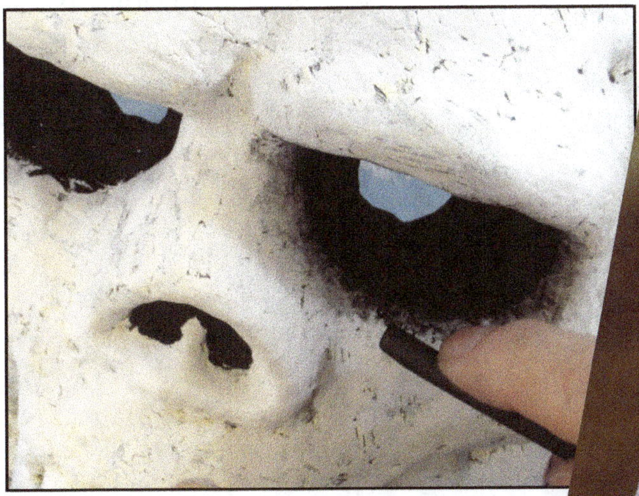

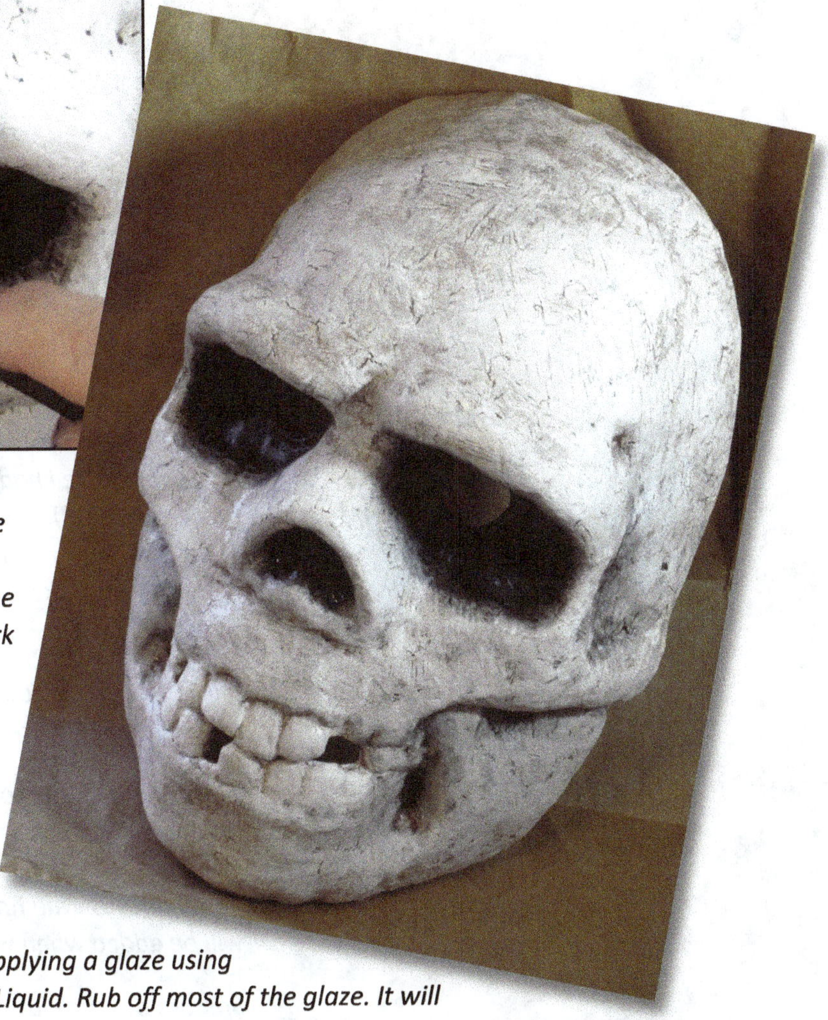

5 Use Black paint to darken the eye sockets and the hollow area of the nose. Blend the black paint at the edges, using a dry brush. When the paint is dry, you can blend the dark areas a bit more naturally by rubbing a piece of charcoal over the edges, and then smudging it with your finger. You can also add a shadow for some of the bones with your charcoal. Spray the charcoal with a fixative.

6 Add one last layer of grunge by applying a glaze using Burnt Umber and Acrylic Glazing Liquid. Rub off most of the glaze. It will settle into the cracks made by the glue and white paint. Use a damp paper towel to remove the glaze from the teeth. Finish with Matte Acrylic Varnish.

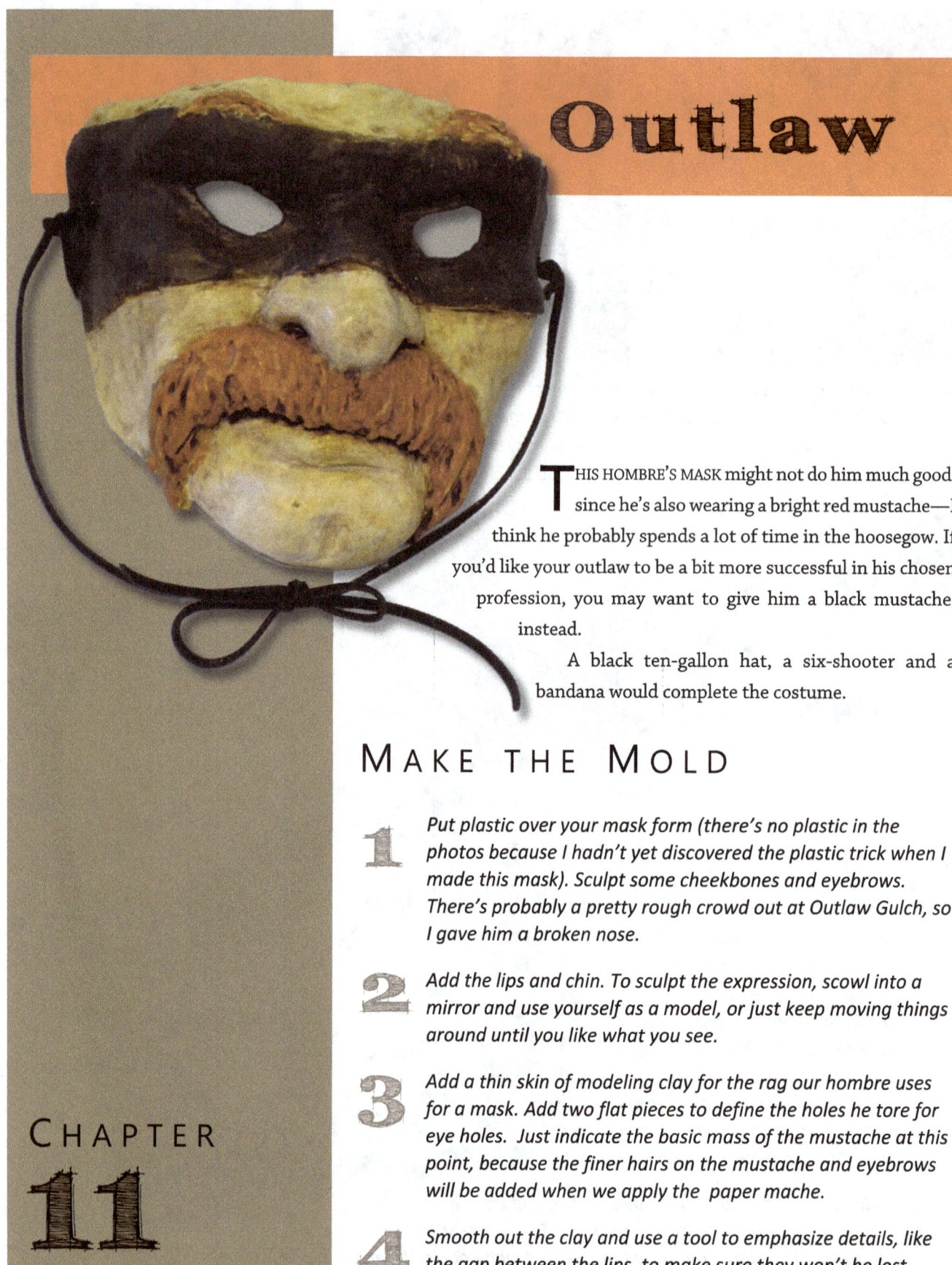

Outlaw

THIS HOMBRE'S MASK might not do him much good, since he's also wearing a bright red mustache—I think he probably spends a lot of time in the hoosegow. If you'd like your outlaw to be a bit more successful in his chosen profession, you may want to give him a black mustache, instead.

A black ten-gallon hat, a six-shooter and a bandana would complete the costume.

MAKE THE MOLD

1. Put plastic over your mask form (there's no plastic in the photos because I hadn't yet discovered the plastic trick when I made this mask). Sculpt some cheekbones and eyebrows. There's probably a pretty rough crowd out at Outlaw Gulch, so I gave him a broken nose.

2. Add the lips and chin. To sculpt the expression, scowl into a mirror and use yourself as a model, or just keep moving things around until you like what you see.

3. Add a thin skin of modeling clay for the rag our hombre uses for a mask. Add two flat pieces to define the holes he tore for eye holes. Just indicate the basic mass of the mustache at this point, because the finer hairs on the mustache and eyebrows will be added when we apply the paper mache.

4. Smooth out the clay and use a tool to emphasize details, like the gap between the lips, to make sure they won't be lost under the paper mache layers.

CHAPTER

11

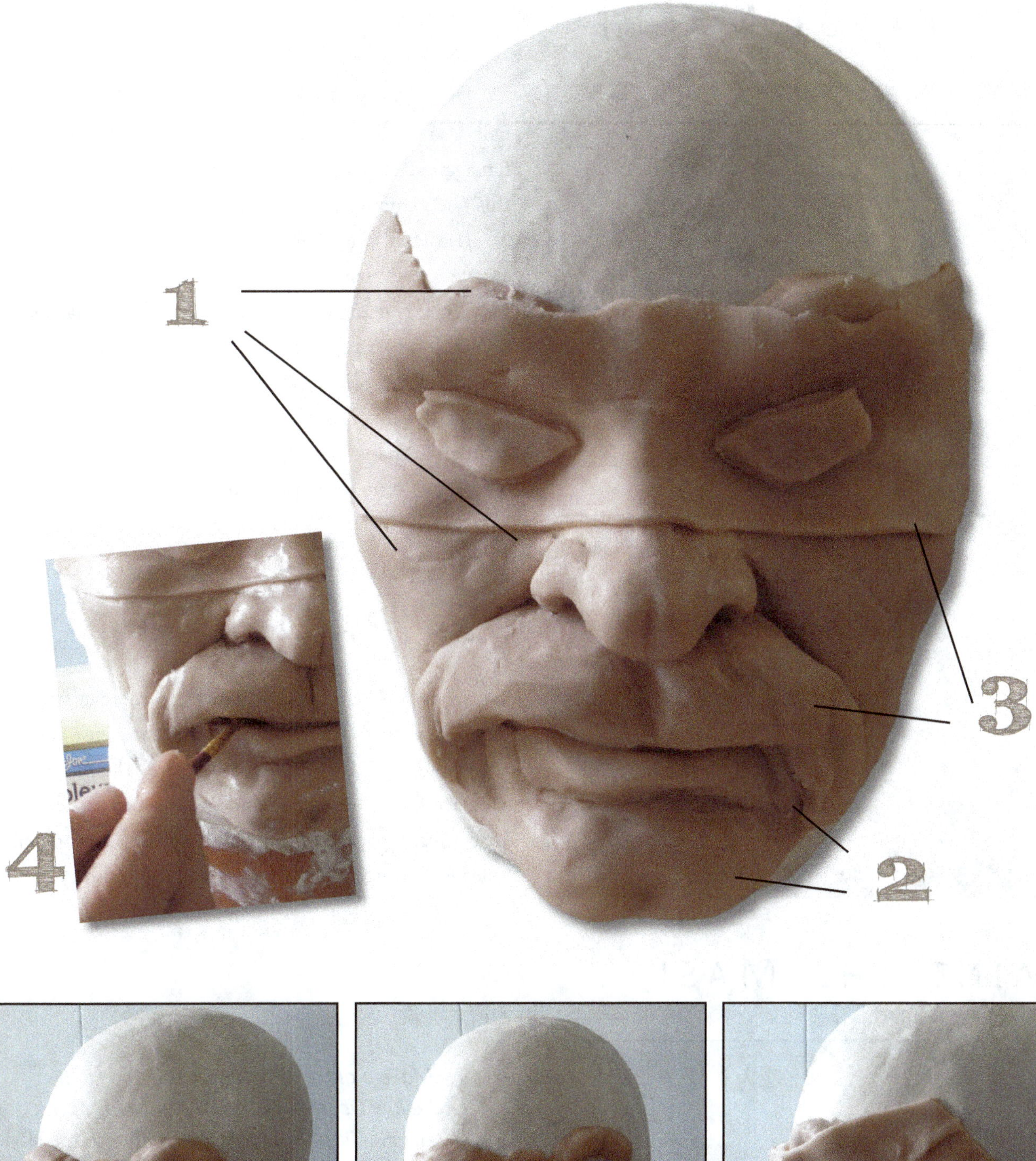

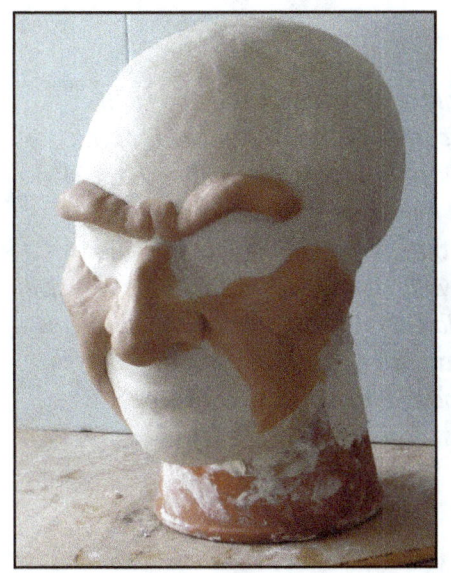
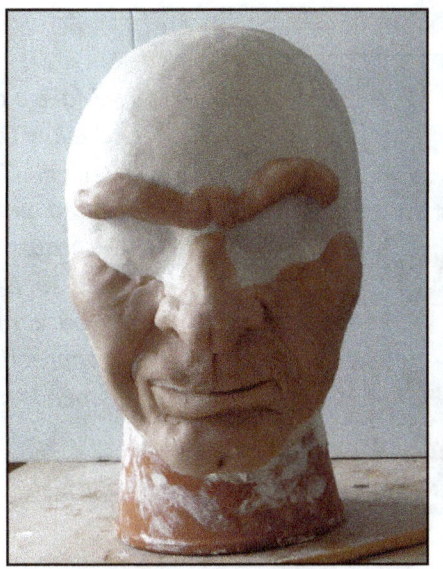
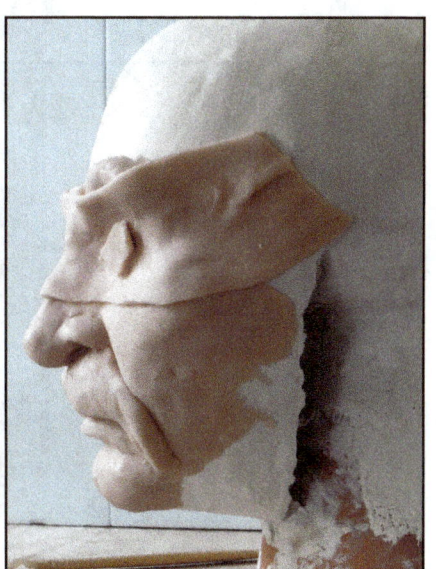

ADD PAPER MACHE

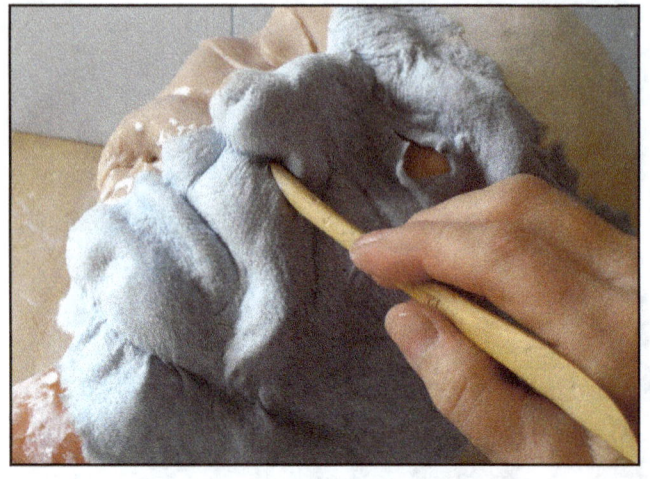

Dampen two Scott Paper Towels and tear them in half. Use smaller pieces, if needed, to get the paper to lie flat against our mold. You'll need to make a lot of tears for this fairly complicated shape, so take your time.

Use a tool to push the damp paper and paste deep into any details, like the nostrils and the line between the lips.

When you add the second layer of paper mache, tear several long strips. They should be about as wide as the mustache. Put paste on both sides of the paper, then lay it over the mustache area. Use your tool to push and scrunch the paper together, to create hair-like ridges. You can do the same for the eyebrows if you want.

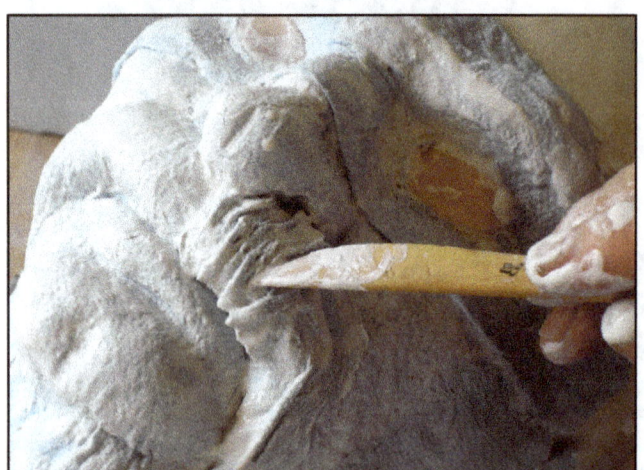

PREPARE THE MASK FOR PAINTING

When the mask is dry enough to remove from the mold, cut away the extra paper around the edges. Sand the edges, punch or cut a hole for the cord (I used a leather shoelace for this mask) and add a layer or two of Plaster Based Gesso, page 7. Wet-polish the gesso, but remember to leave plenty of texture on the mustache and eyebrows.

PAINT THE MASK

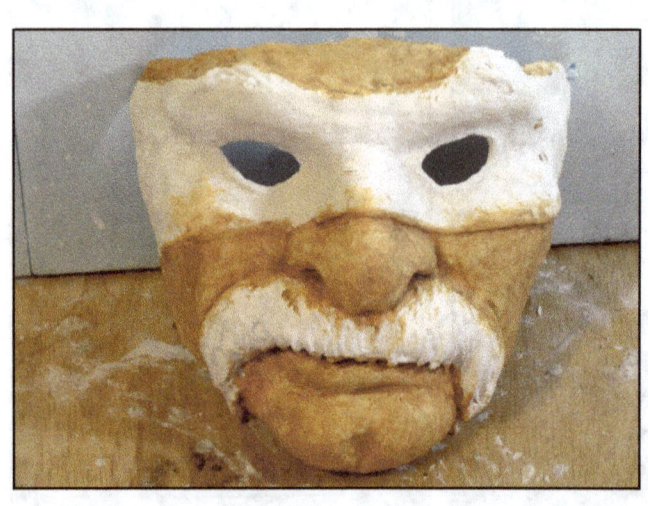

Make a glaze using Cadmium Red Light, Yellow Ochre, Raw Sienna and White with Acrylic Glazing Liquid. Brush it on to the skin area and then wipe it off immediately. Because the glaze is going over unsealed gesso, it will not wipe off evenly. This will give your outlaw a fairly rough look, which seems appropriate for a tough guy like this who spends many hours in the Texas sun.

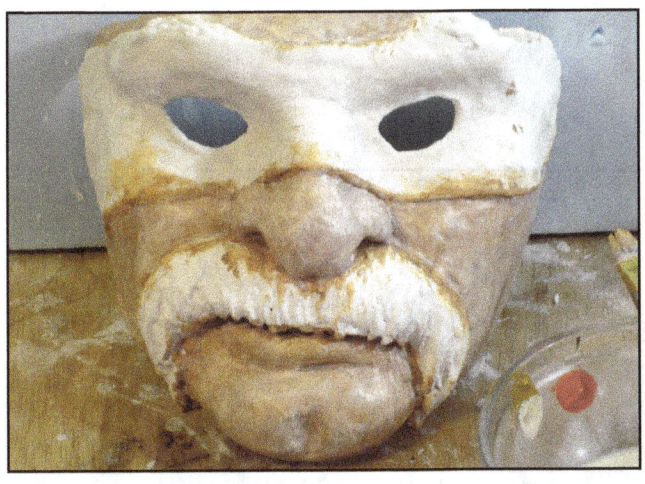

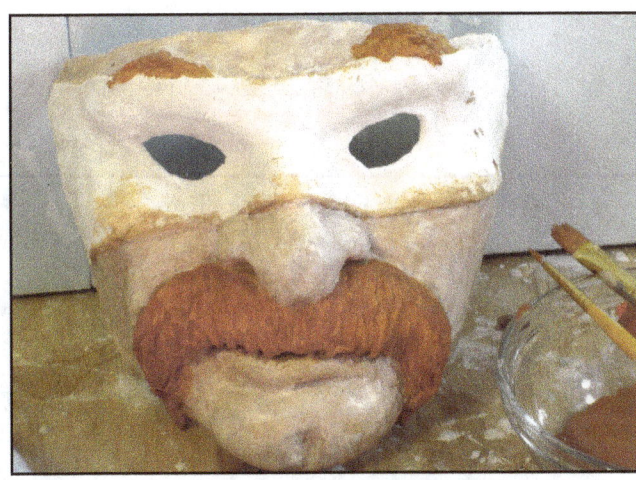

2 *Allow the previous glaze to dry completely. Then mix up a small amount of Cadmium Red Light and Yellow with Matte Acrylic Varnish. Lightly brush it over the previous layer.*

3 *Mix Cadmium Red Light with Raw Sienna for the mustache and eyebrows. Red hair isn't really this red, so you may want to tone it down with Yellow Ochre for a more realistic look. Paint it onto the mustache and wipe off a little on the top of the ridges for lighter highlights.*

4 *Mix Black and Burnt Umber with a bit of water and brush it over the Outlaw's mask. Use Yellow Ochre and an almost dry brush to add highlights to the mustache and eyebrows.*

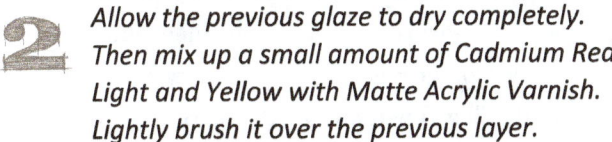

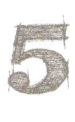

5 *When all the paint is dry, mix Burnt Umber with Acrylic Glazing Liquid. Brush it over the mask and wipe it off with a dry paper towel (see page 30). Wipe almost all of it off the skin area, but leave the dark color in the shadows of the mustache, mouth and nose. Allow to dry, finish with Matte Acrylic Varnish, and tie on the cord.*

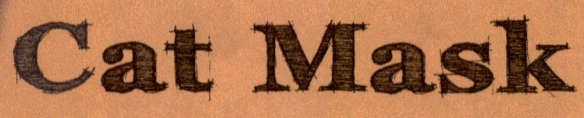

Cat Mask

Bᴀᴄᴋ ᴡʜᴇɴ ɪᴛ was common for people in Vienna to wear masks in public, the cat mask was often worn by young noblemen who wanted to do something slightly naughty (or perhaps slightly illegal) without anyone knowing who they were. Now, of course, we just wear them for fun.

The clay mold for this mask can be made in either one stage or two, depending on whether or not you wish to make a ruff around your cat's cheeks, like I did. Your cat's expression will depend on the top shape of the eye, and the position of the ears. (I made mine a bit irritated, since that's my own cat's normal expression.) To finish your mask you'll need Acrylic Paint, Acrylic Glazing Liquid, and Matte Acrylic Varnish.

MAKE THE MOLD

1 *Model the forehead first. See the small photos for details about how this area shapes the top of the eye. Add clay on the side of the form's nose to flatten it.*

2 *Add the cheeks, which also define the bottom shape of the eye, and add two oval disks for the pupils. Define the lower inner corners of the eyes with a modeling tool.*

3 *Add two pear-shaped balls at the lower end of the form's nose, and add the cat's nose between the balls. The nose is shaped like the letter T.*

4 *Use strips of clay to define the top edge of the mask, and the strap where the ribbon will be attached. Also add two C-shaped noodles of clay where the cardboard ears will be added.*

5 *Cut two triangular ears out of light card stock. The cardboard used to make cereal boxes is good for ears.*

Cʜᴀᴘᴛᴇʀ

12

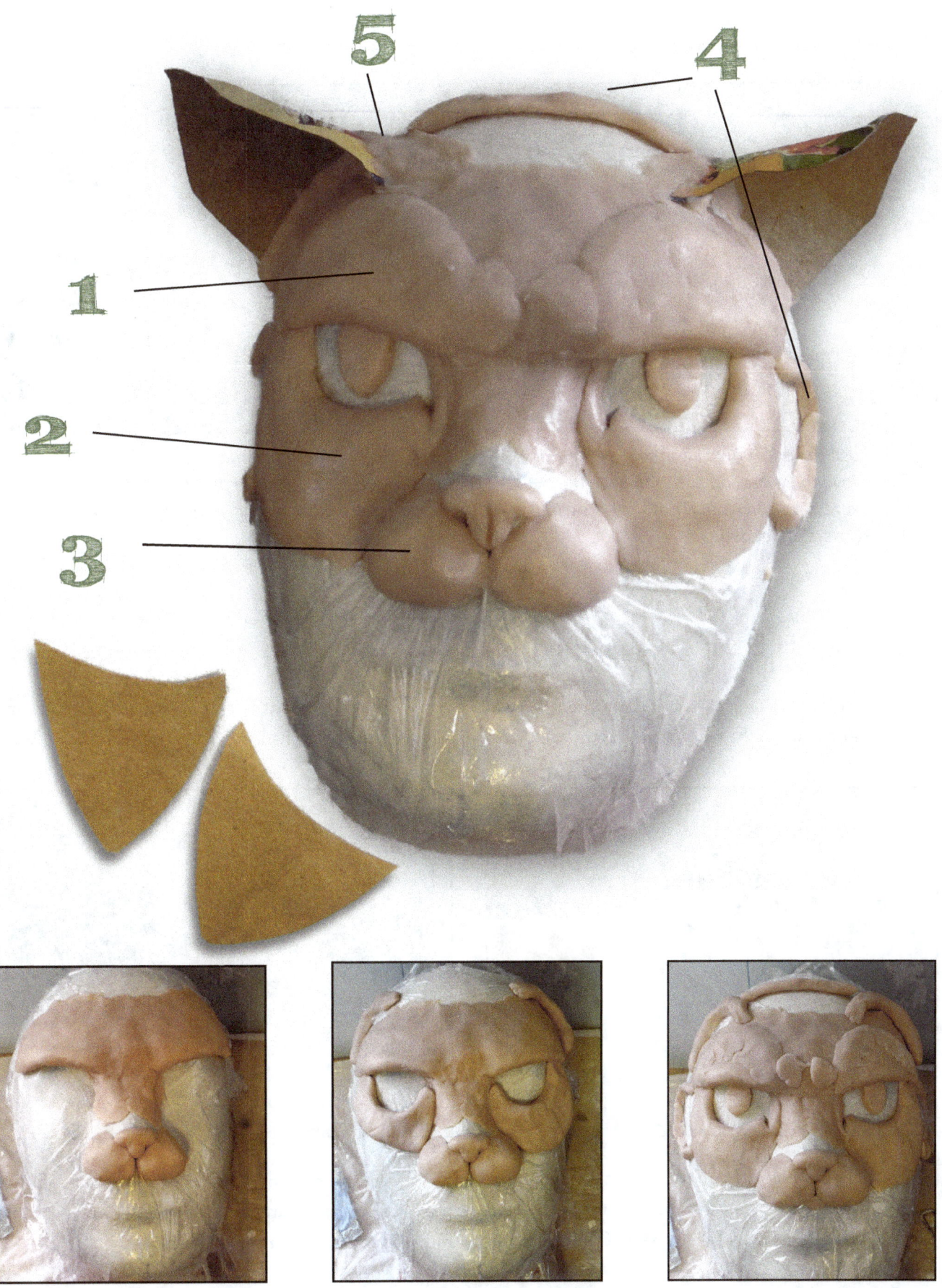

59

EARS

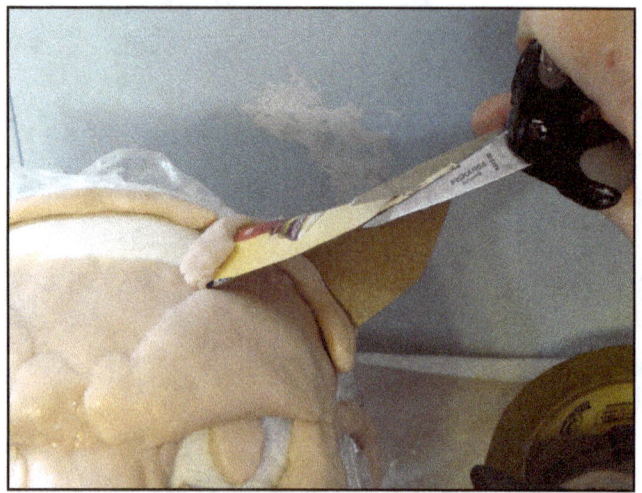

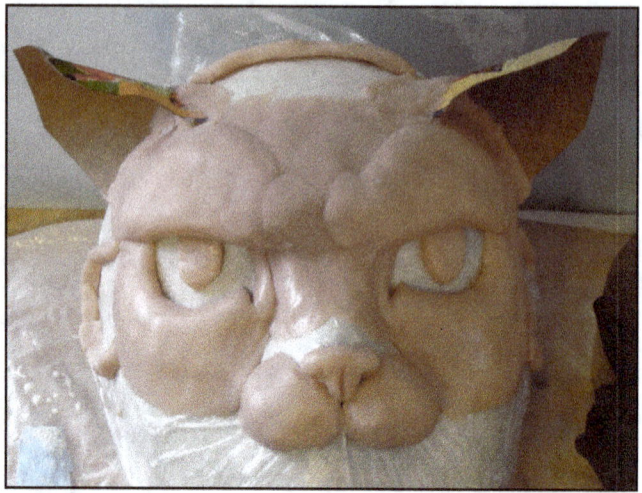

 Push the ears down into the C-shaped clay. Move them around until you have the expression you want. Trim the ears with scissors, if needed.

7 Blend the clay under the ears into the forehead. Smooth out all the clay, using petroleum jelly on your fingers if needed.

ADD THE PAPER MACHE

Apply two layers of paper mache. Use a tool to push the paper deep into the cat's nostrils. Remember to add one extra piece of paper to the tab to reinforce the area where the ribbon will be attached.

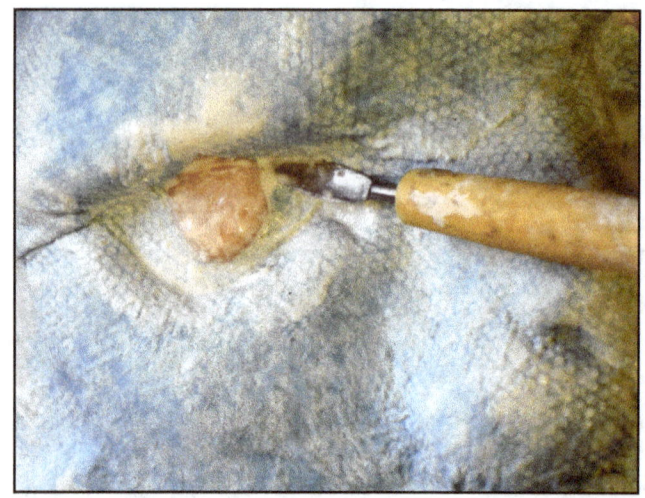

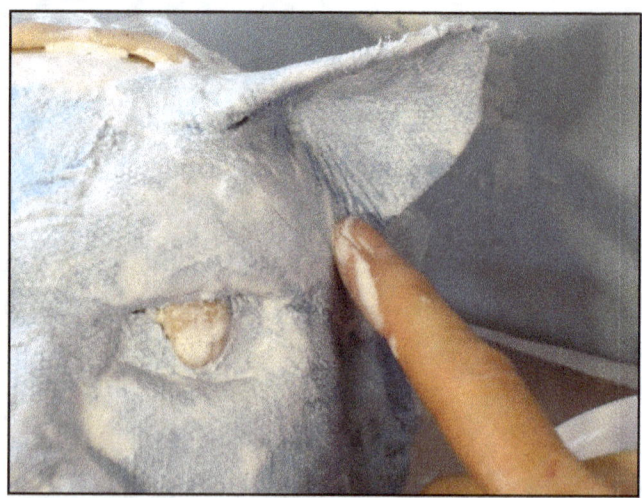

To make the holes so you can see out, use a knife or modeling tool to tear an opening for the pupil, and carefully smooth the flaps over the rest of the eye.

Cover both sides of the cardboard ears with smaller pieces of paper. Be sure to overlap these pieces onto the forehead to create a strong connection.

ADD THE RUFF AROUND THE CHEEKS

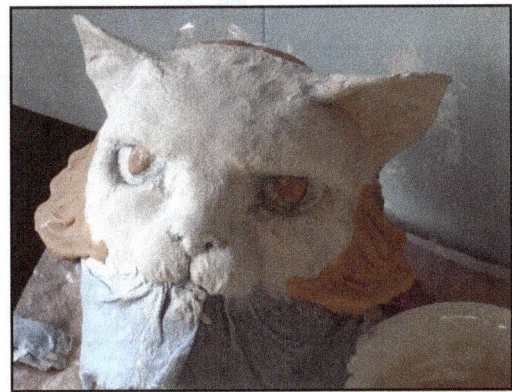

When you're finished adding the paper mache to the mold, allow it to dry in front of a fan or in a warm place until it is hard enough to handle. Then use some modeling clay to put a nice fringe of fur around the kitty's cheeks, as shown. You may skip this step if you prefer a short-haired cat.

Cover the ruff with two layers of paper mache, smoothing the new edges over the previous dried layers. Allow your cat mask to dry again before lifting it from the mold.

Use a sharp pair of scissors to trim away the extra paper around the edge. The inside of your mask will look like this:

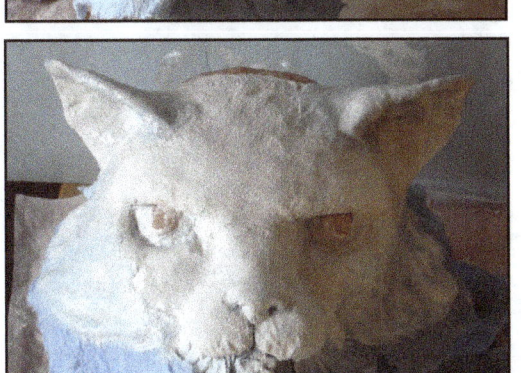

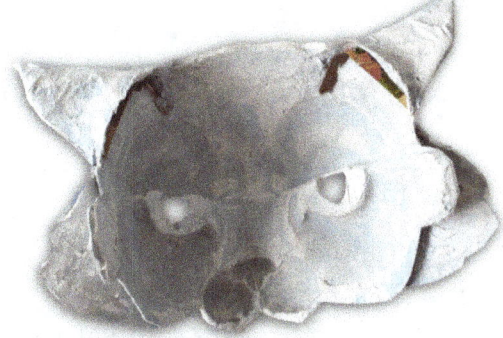

PREPARE THE MASK FOR PAINTING

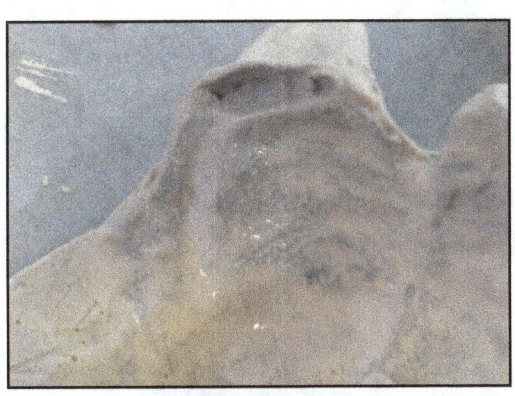

The cardboard inside the ears will show on the back of the mask. Mix up a batch of plaster-based gesso, and use it as paste to add two small pieces of paper mache over the inside of the ears.

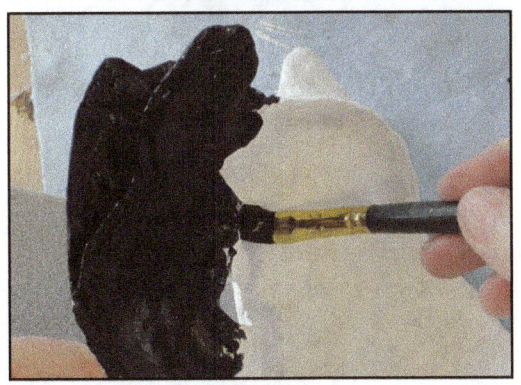

Use the rest of the gesso to smooth out the back of the mask. When the gesso is dry, paint the back of the mask and the front of the tab you made for the ribbon with black paint.

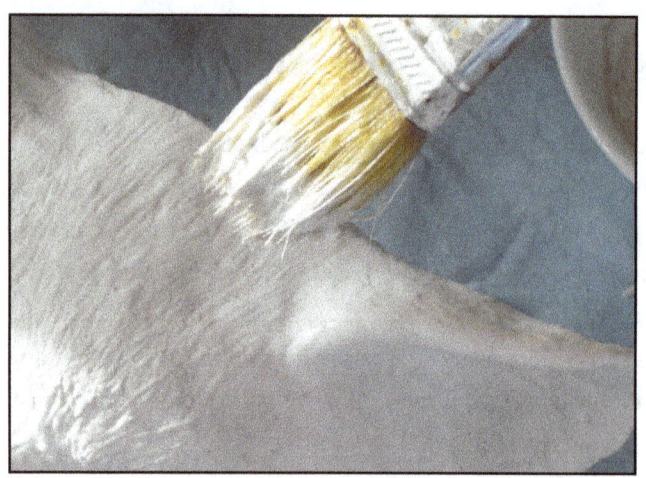

3 Apply a coat of Plaster-Based Gesso to the front of the mask with a stiff brush to make "fur."

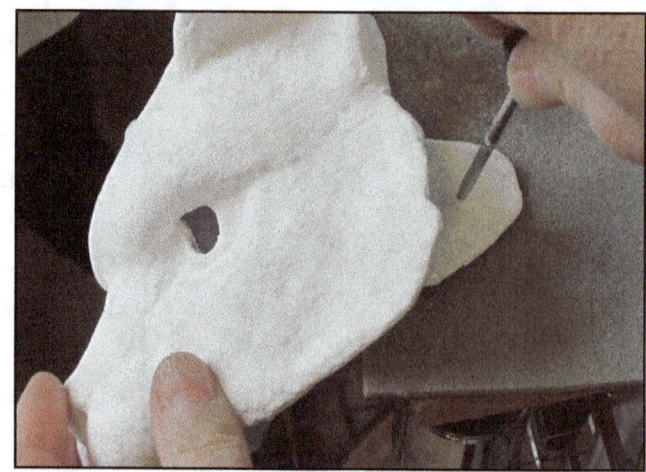

4 When dry, punch or drill a hole for the ribbon or cord.

FINISH YOUR MASK

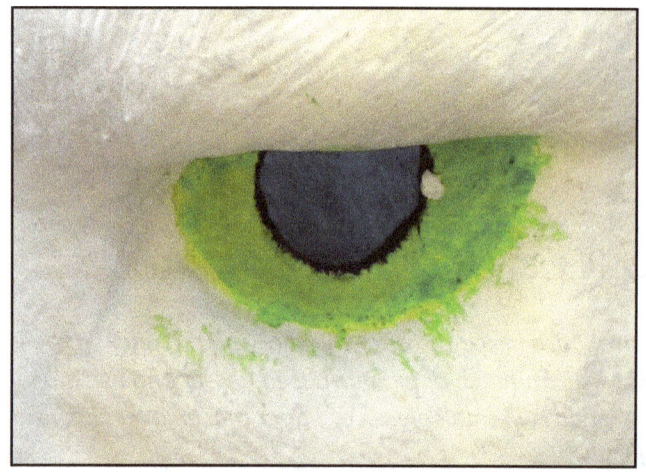

1 Paint the eyes green. Paint the inside rim of the hole black, and add a small white reflection spot.

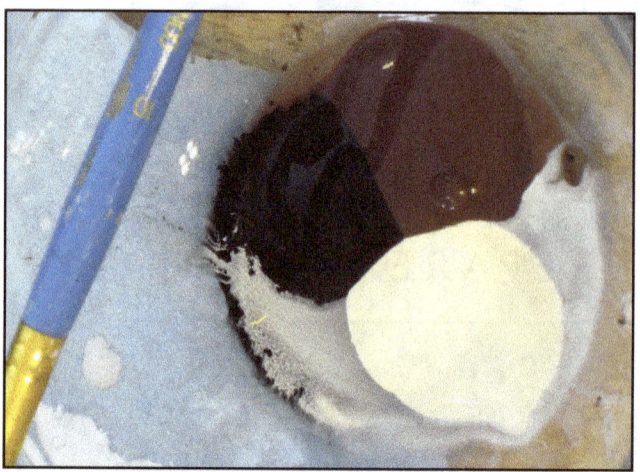

2 Mix a light, warm gray using Black, White and Burnt Umber.

3 Cover the front of the mask with this gray paint and allow to dry.

4 Define the edges of the eyes with black paint.

5 Mix Black with Acrylic Glazing Liquid. It should be transparent, so some of the light gray will show through.

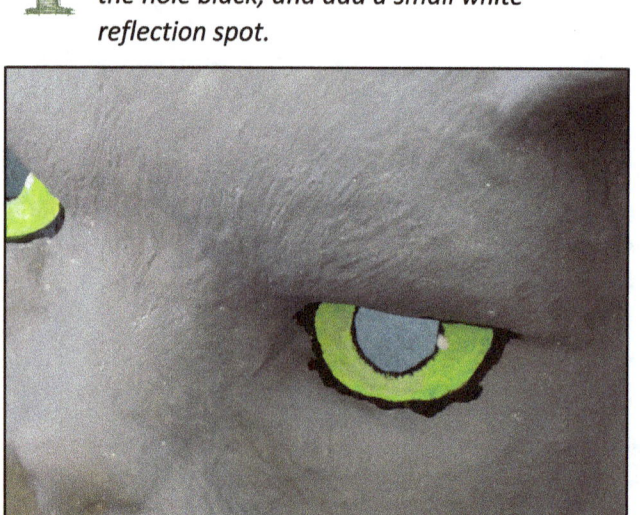

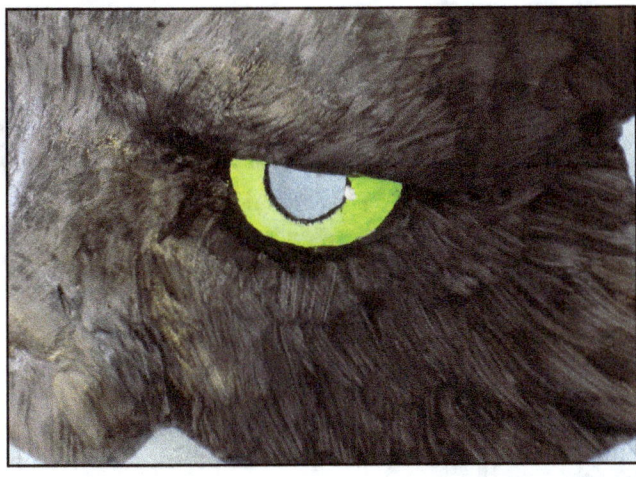

6 Apply the black glaze in two steps. The first coat will leave brush marks and much of the gray will show through. Allow the glaze to dry completely.

7 The second coat will even out the brush marks, leaving a subtle texture on the fur, as shown below.

8 When the final coat of black glaze is dry, you can add the white spots, if desired. For Halloween, you may prefer to leave your cat all black.

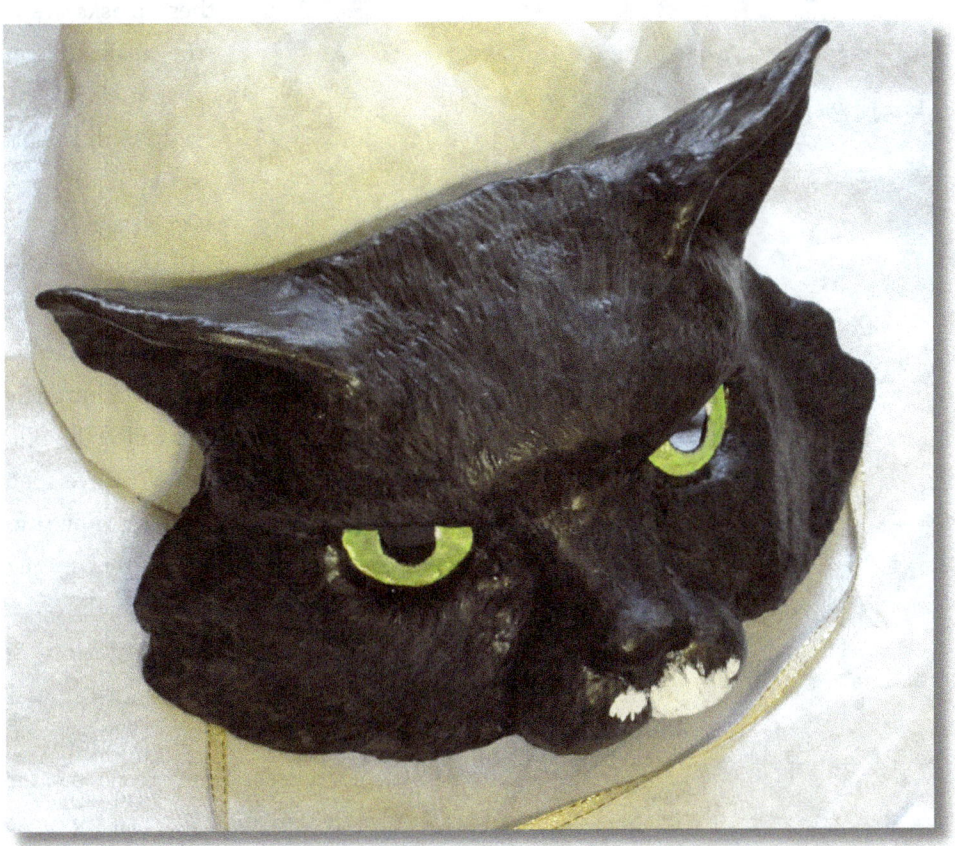

I had some metallic paint on hand, so I mixed up a drop of Metallic Gold, a drop of Metallic Silver, and water. I washed this over the green in the eyes, which added just a hint of color and a bit of sparkle.

When the paint is dry, finish with a matte acrylic varnish and add your ribbon or cord.

I chose to paint my mask in the colors and pattern of a tuxedo cat so it would look equally appropriate at both a Halloween party or a masquerade ball. If you prefer, you could paint your cat as a Siamese, a calico, a tabby, or whatever colors you prefer. If your own cat is nicer than mine, she might be willing to pose for you.

Butterfly

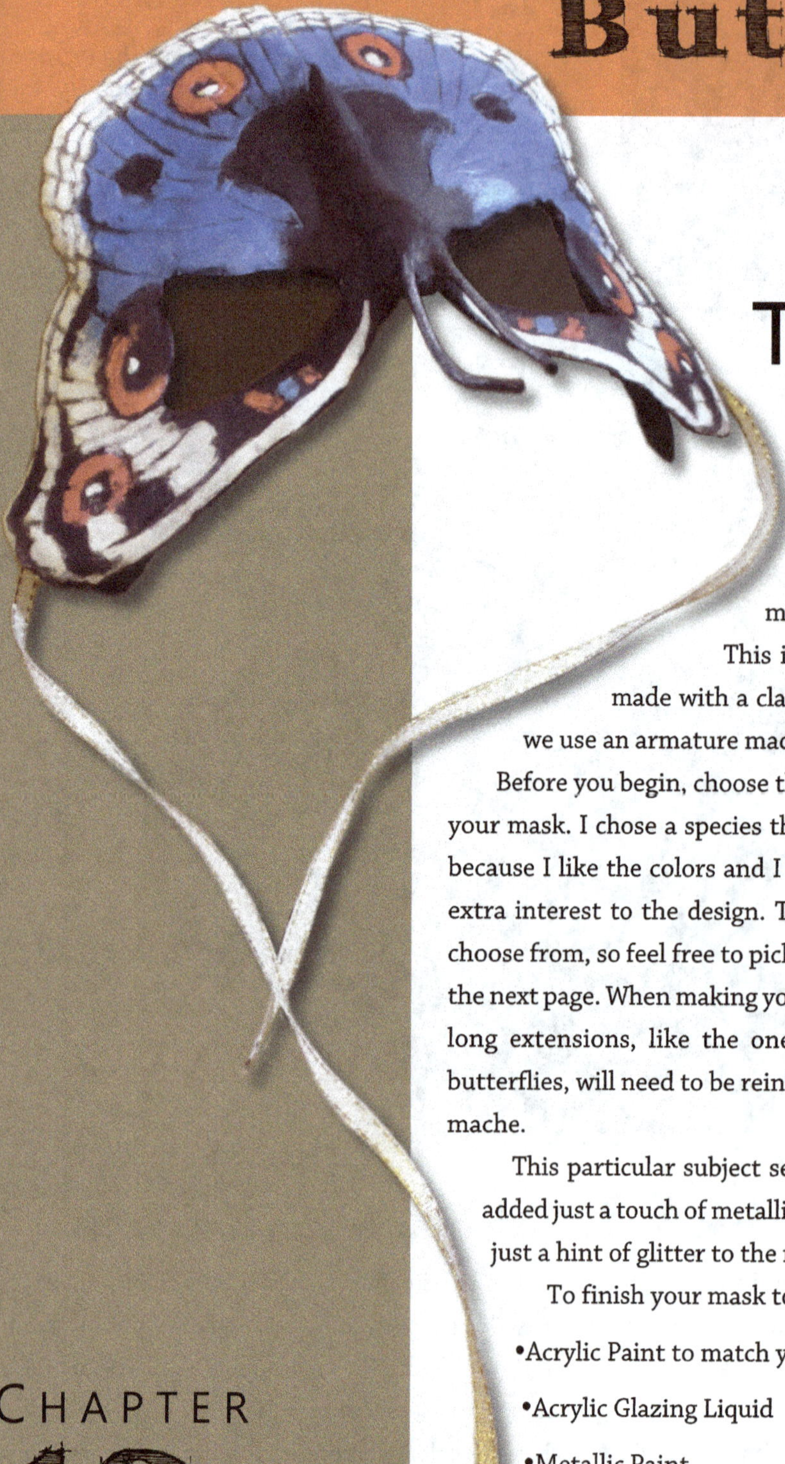

T HE BUTTERFLY IS a popular subject for
carnival masks, and for good reason—
these masks are colorful and elegant, and
they make the wearer seem intriguing (and
even a bit mysterious). Your mask can be
worn with ribbons, as shown here, or you
can attach it to a stick, like the owl half-
mask on page 70.

This is the only mask in this book that was not
made with a clay mold. To bring the wings up off the face,
we use an armature made with light cardboard.

Before you begin, choose the type of butterfly that you wish to use for
your mask. I chose a species that's called the Blue Pansy (or Eyed Pansy),
because I like the colors and I think the eye spots on the mask add some
extra interest to the design. There are thousands of other butterflies to
choose from, so feel free to pick a different species, or copy the drawing on
the next page. When making your choice, the one thing to remember is that
long extensions, like the ones you find on some of the Swallowtail
butterflies, will need to be reinforced with at least one extra layer of paper
mache.

This particular subject seems to cry out for a shimmery finish, so I
added just a touch of metallic paint to my acrylic craft paint, which gives
just a hint of glitter to the mask.

To finish your mask to look like the one in the photo, you'll need:

•Acrylic Paint to match your butterfly

•Acrylic Glazing Liquid

•Metallic Paint

•Matte Acrylic Varnish

•Joint Compound (optional)

CHAPTER

13

64

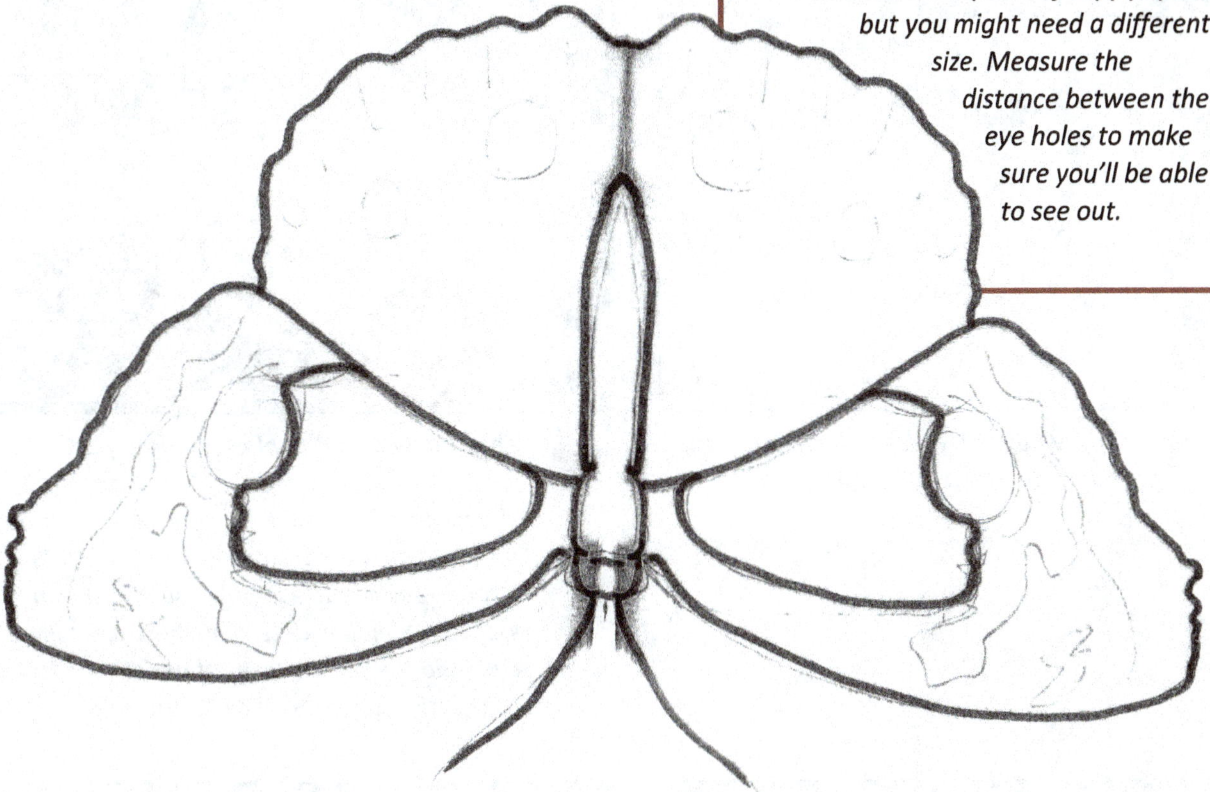

1 Draw your butterfly on a piece of paper. I made mine almost as wide as a standard piece of copy paper, but you might need a different size. Measure the distance between the eye holes to make sure you'll be able to see out.

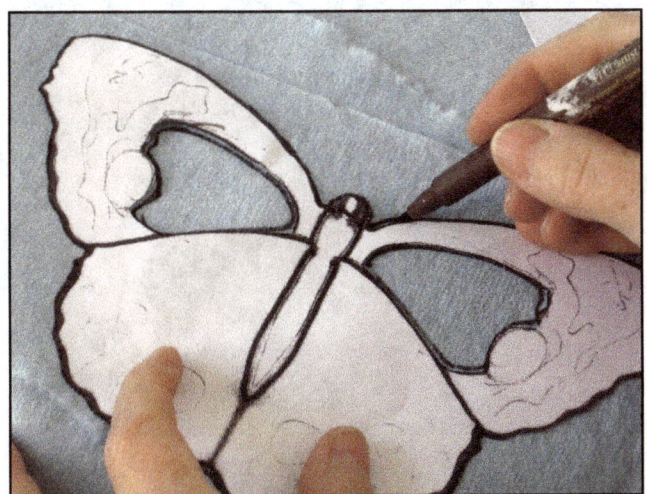

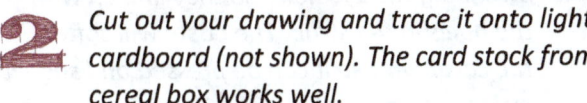

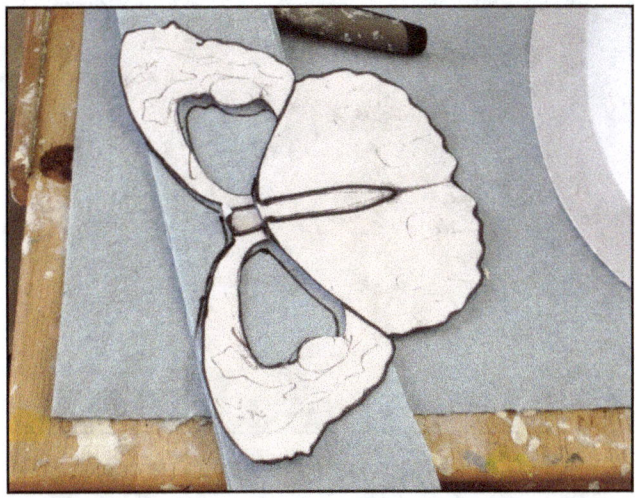

2 Cut out your drawing and trace it onto light cardboard (not shown). The card stock from a cereal box works well.

Tear a sheet of Scott Shop Towels in half, stack them together, and trace the butterfly on the top towel.

3 Tear a second towel into two strips, about 2 1/2 inches wide. This will become the strap that the ribbon or cord is attached to. Set your drawing on the strips as shown, and trace the eye holes on the towels. Cut out the design on your cardboard and paper towels.

ADD THE PAPER MACHE

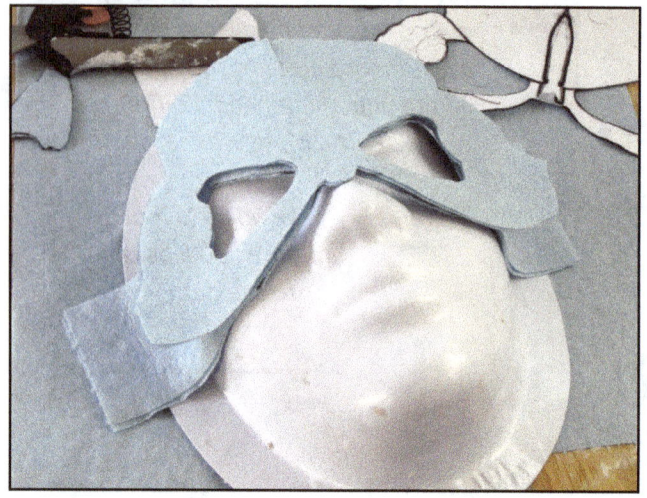

1 Lay your dry paper towels on the mask form, to get a feel for where to brush on the paste.

Cover your mask form with plastic wrap (see page 19).

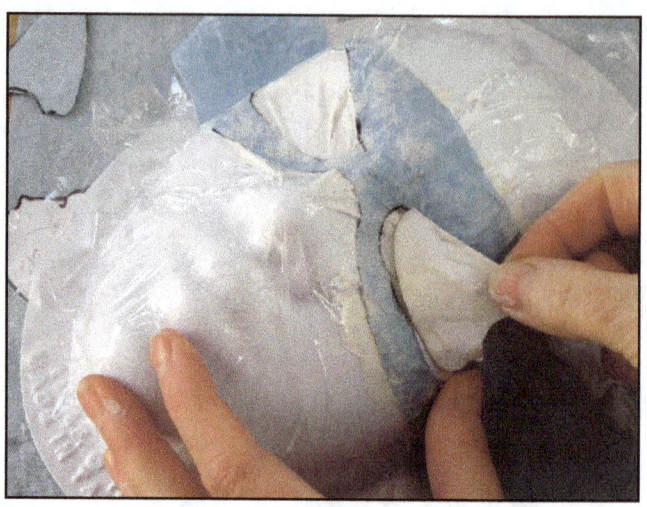

2 Then apply a coat of plaster-based paste where you determined that the ribbon strap should go. Place one of the pieces you cut out for the strap over the paste. The towel will stretch, so use the eye hole you saved from step 1 to help you determine how to shape the eye. Add the second layer of paper mache. Put the mask in a warm place to dry.

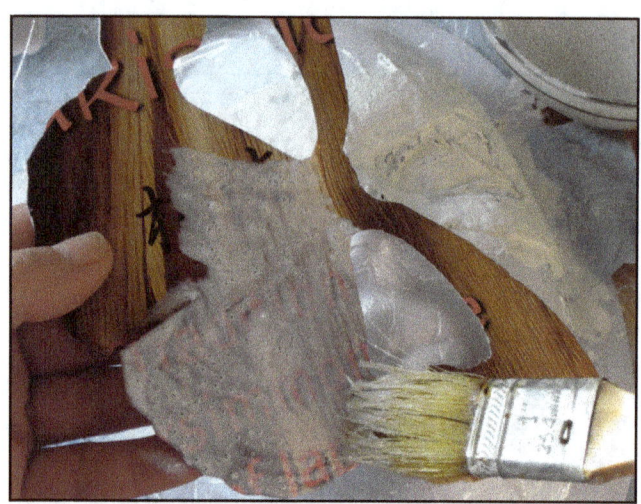

3 When the strap is dry, brush paste over the back of the light cardboard butterfly shape you made in step 1.

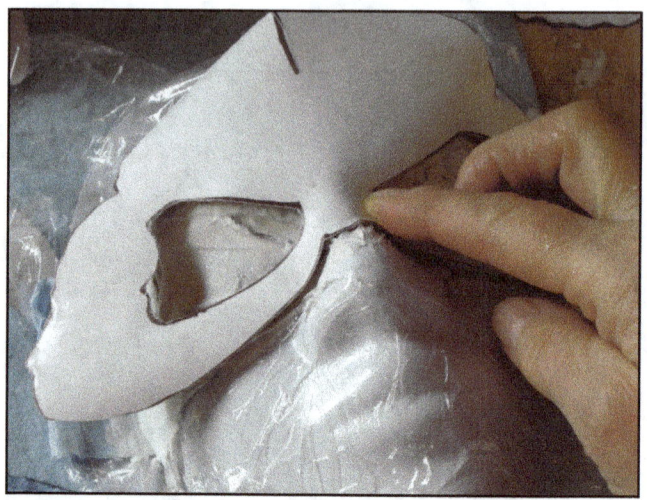

4 Place the cardboard over the mask form, arranging the eye holes so they line up with the holes in the strap. The paste will soften the cardboard so it can be pressed and shaped over the form. Make sure it is pasted down all around the eye, to get a solid connection. If the card is not soft enough, brush some water over it with a soft brush.

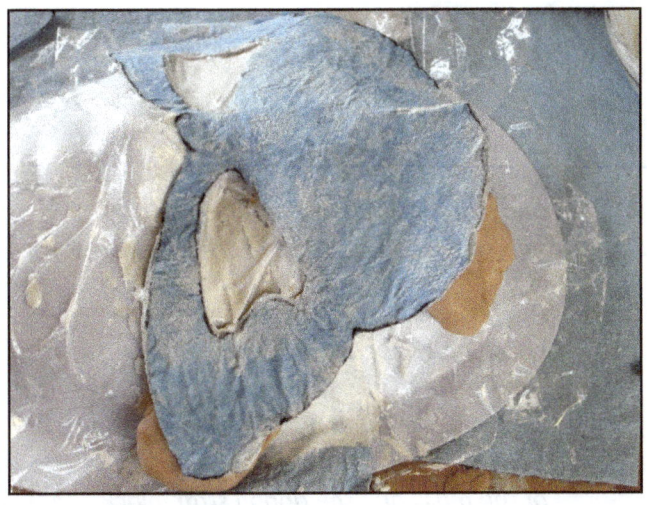

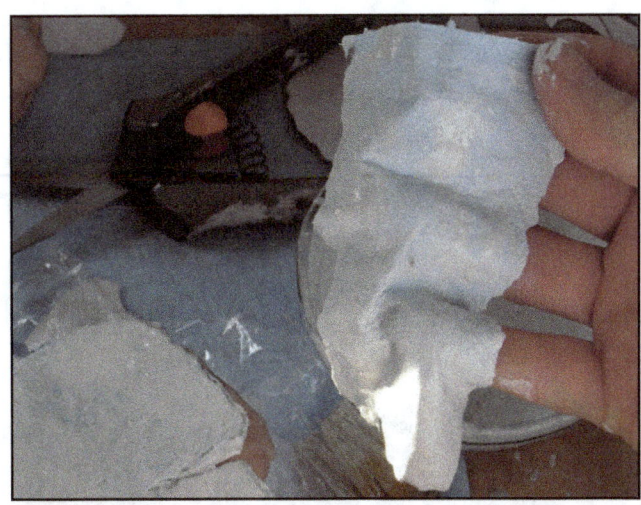

5 Add paste to the cardboard butterfly, and apply two layers of paper mache, using the paper towels you cut out previously. The wings will sag, so arrange the curve of the wings in a way that you find pleasing, and prop them up with small bits of clay (or anything you have handy that won't stick to the paste).

6 For the body, tear off a small strip of towel and cover it with paste. Roll it up into a body-shaped cylinder, and press it down over mask. The tail end is pointy, and the head end is blunt (see next photo).

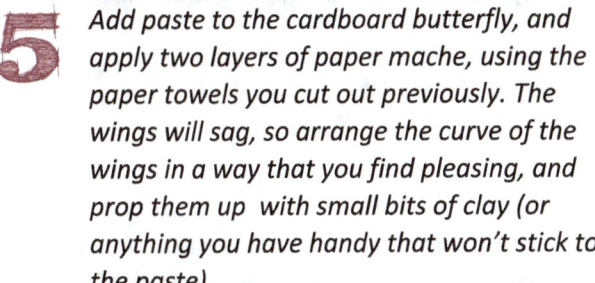

7 Cut two pieces of cord, (or use embroidery floss or cotton string). Lay them over the top of the head, and prop up the ends on a piece of clay, as shown. Paste a small piece of paper towel over the ends to attach them to the butterfly.

If you use soft string that won't hold it's shape on it's own, dip it in paste before attaching it to the head. This will stiffen the string when it dries. Hold the antennae up high enough so they won't tickle your nose when you wear the mask.

Place the mask in a nice warm spot or in front of a fan, and allow it to dry before lifting it from the mask form.

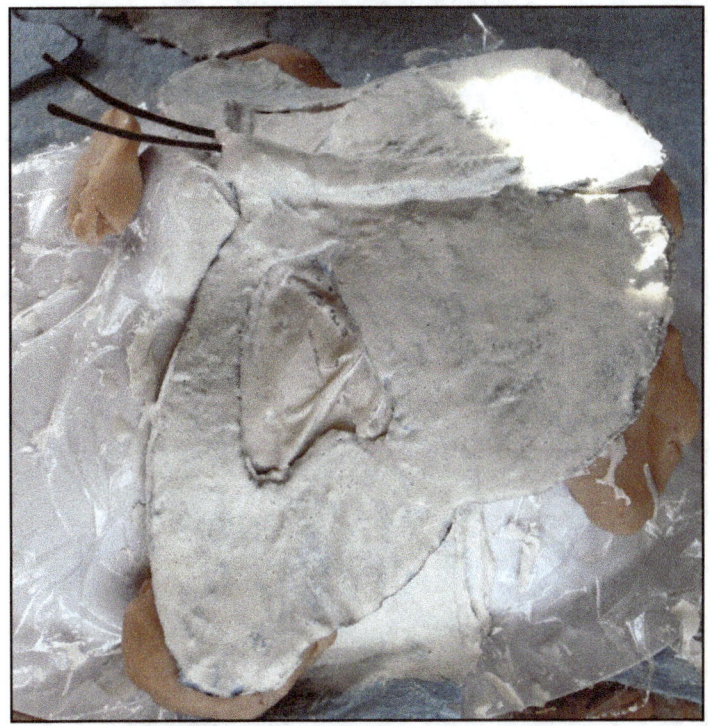

PREPARE THE MASK FOR PAINTING

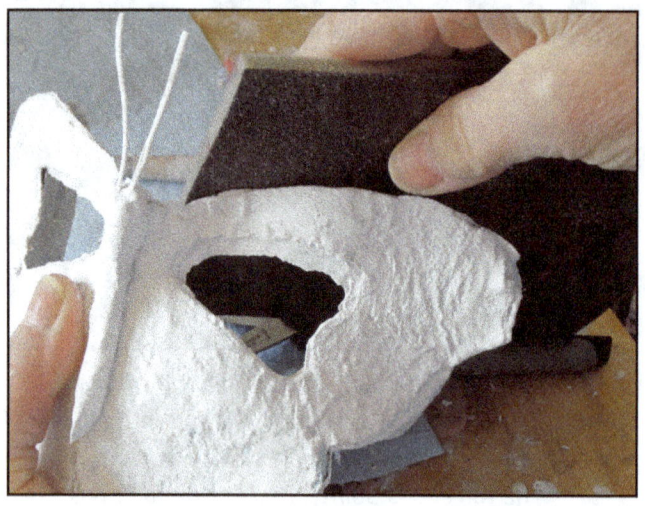

1 When the mask is dry, lift it off the mask form and trim the ends of the ribbon strap with a pair of scissors. Sand the edges of the mask.

Apply one or two layers of gesso, wet-polishing between coats. The surface doesn't need to be perfectly smooth, because the next step will even out any irregularities. Punch or cut a hole for the ribbon, and paint the back of the mask and the ribbon strap black.

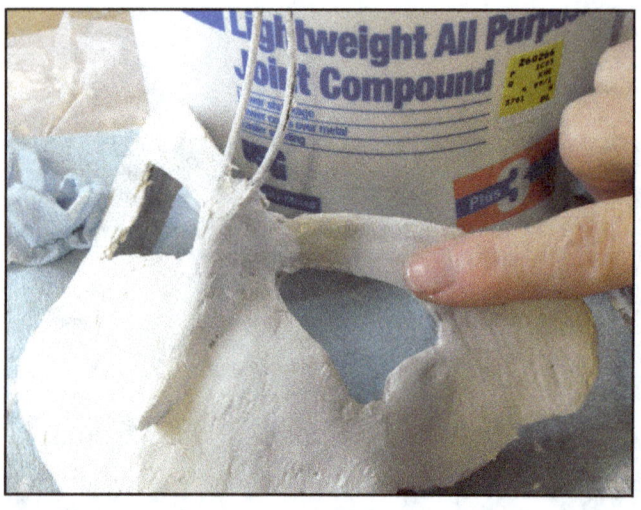

2 Use your finger or a knife to spread joint compound over the wings and body. Allow the joint compound to dry completely.

If you don't have any joint compound, just give your butterfly a few coats of plaster-based gesso. Then continue to step 3.

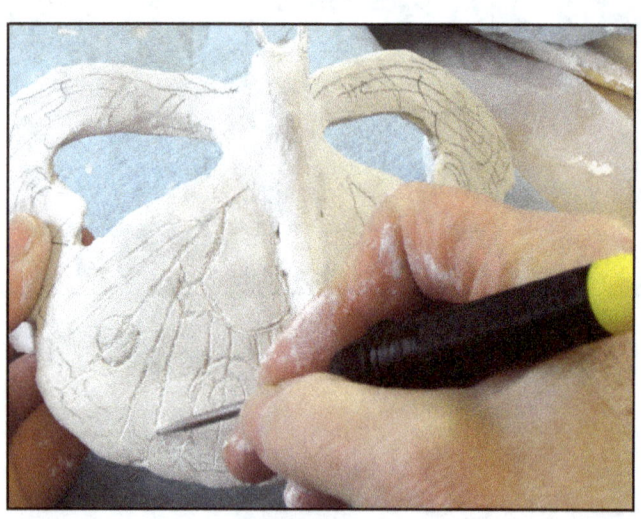

3 Wet-polish the joint compound after it dries. Then draw the butterfly's veins and color patterns onto the surface with a pencil, and incise the lines with a sharp tool. In the photo you can see that I rushed things a little, and didn't allow the joint compound to dry completely—it's easier to make lines in slightly damp joint compound, but you have much more control if you wait for it to dry.

If using gesso for this step, incise your lines while the gesso is still a little damp.

FINISH YOUR MASK

1 *Mix acrylic craft paint and just a touch of Metallic paint to give it a nice shimmer. Brush the paint over your butterfly, following the color patterns of whichever species you chose for your mask.*

2 *When the paint is dry, you may want to seal the butterfly with spray varnish. I used Krylon Matte Finish because it dries quickly. Be sure to spray the varnish in a well-ventilated room, or outside. You could brush on Matte Acrylic Varnish instead.*

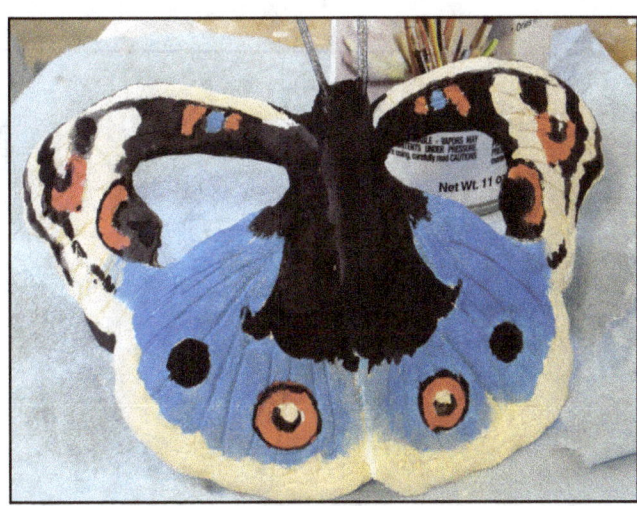

3 *Mix a glaze using Black craft paint and Acrylic Glazing Liquid. Dampen a paper towel, and then brush the glaze over the butterfly, rubbing off most of the glaze with the towel before it dries. This will leave the dark glaze in the veins you cut into the joint compound. (See photo below).*

4 *When the glaze is dry, go back over the mask with your colors in any area that got too dark.*

Finish with matte varnish and attach your ribbon to the strap.

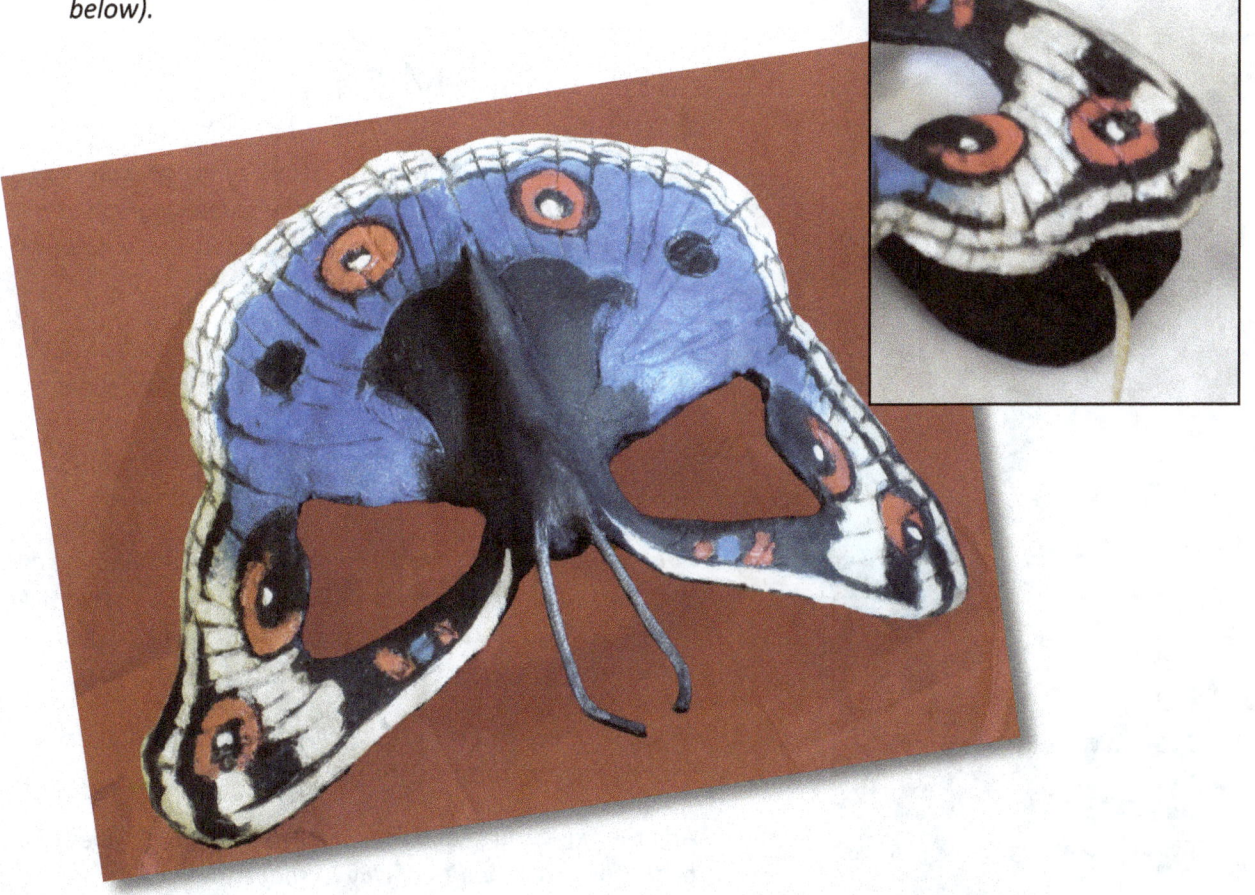

Owl

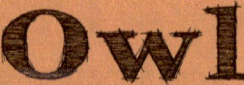

OWLS ARE A popular subject for masquerade masks, perhaps because they play such an important role in so many fables and folk tales. In some cultural traditions, the owl is a harbinger of doom, while in other places it's seen as a sign of great impending prosperity. For that reason, this mask will be creepy or delightful, depending on where it's worn.

This mask is held up with a stick, but if you prefer to wear it with ribbon ties, just add clay noodles at the sides to make ribbon tabs, as shown on the cat mold on page 59. I made a pattern for my mask, but you can sculpt yours freehand, if you prefer.

MAKE THE MOLD

1 To make a pattern, draw out your owl's face on a piece of copy paper, using the drawing on the following page as a guide. Be sure to measure the distance between your owl's pupils so you'll be able to see out.

2 Apply petroleum jelly to your mask form, and then stick your cut-out drawing onto the form. Apply more petroleum jelly over the drawing and stick a thin sheet of plastic over the form. You should be able to see the drawing through the plastic.

3 Put two large rounded disks over the eyes. Surround the eyes with a noodle of clay, and then flatten them, as shown. Add the eyelids and the two disks for the pupils, which will become the openings for your eyes.

4 Sculpt the beak out of clay. It will hook over the human-shaped nose on the mask form.

5 Add the "eyebrows" and the ridges of clay on the sides of the beak. Then use noodles of clay to shape the edges.

CHAPTER

14

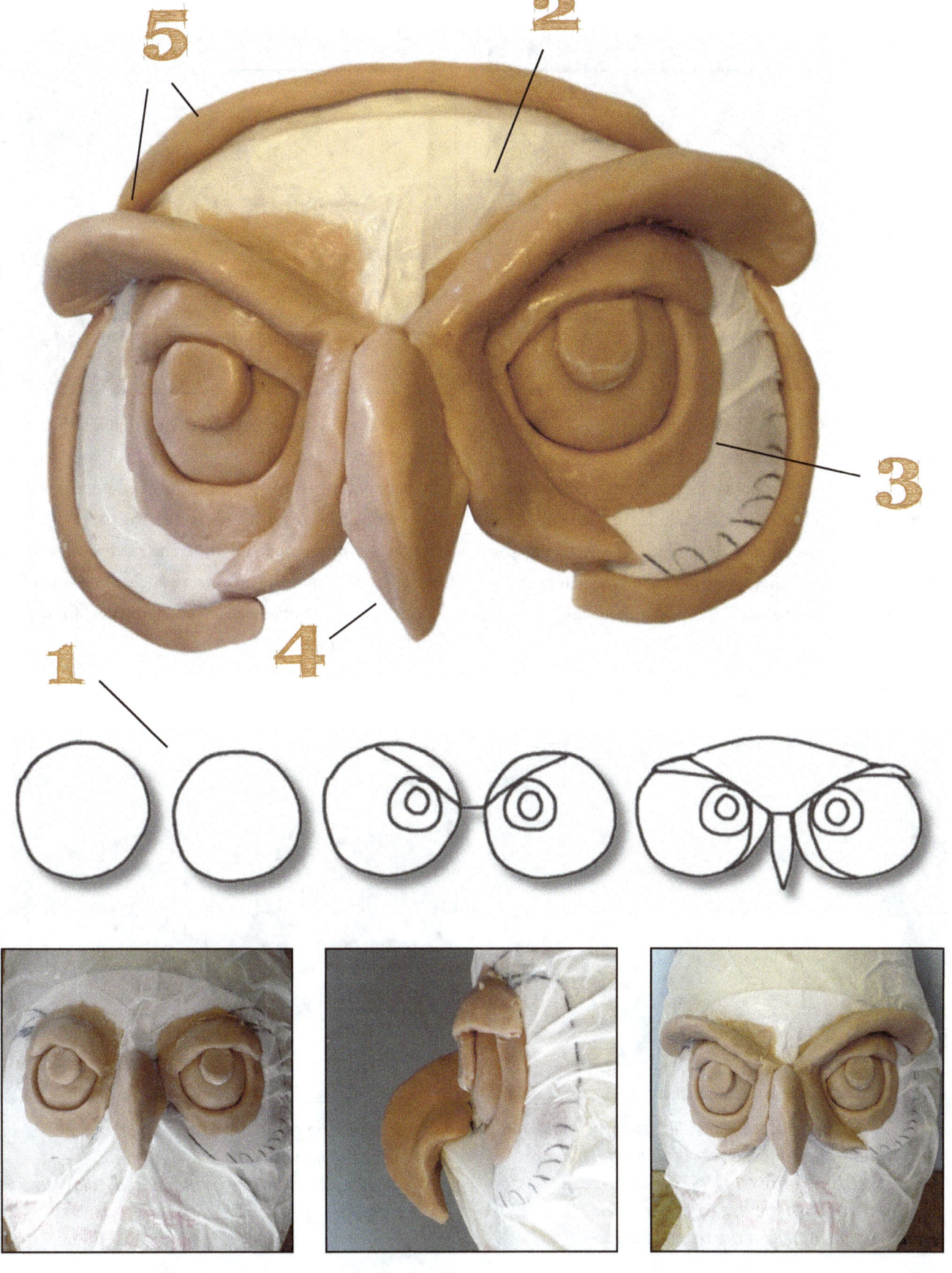

ADD PAPER MACHE

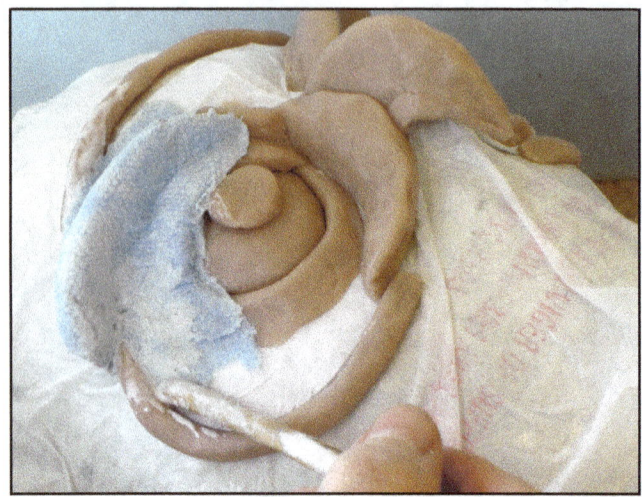

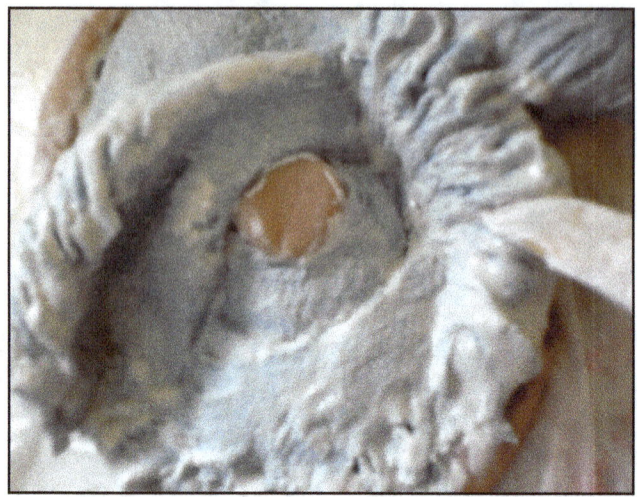

There are a lot of weird shapes on the owl's face, so you will probably want to use smaller pieces of paper towel than usual. Be sure to press the paper mache down into all the curves and valleys, using a knife or modeling tool. We'll make some ruffles around the beak, along the outside edge of the cheek, and on the outside ends of the eyebrows, with the second layer of paper mache.

To make the deep random ridges that define these feathered areas, put paste on both sides of a long narrow strip of paper towel. Lay it over the area where the ruffles are needed, and then push and scrunch the paper together into pleats, using a modeling tool. The ruffles will rest on the clay noodle around the outside edges. Use small flat pieces to cover the inside edges of the ruffles, to make a smooth transition.

FINISH THE MASK

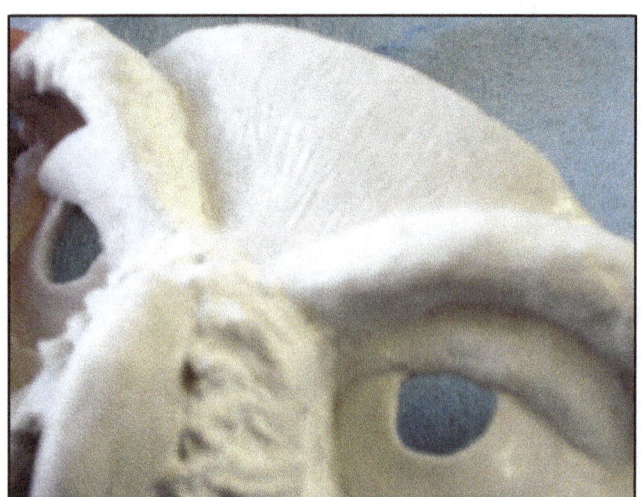

1 *When the mask is dry, lift from the mold and sand the edges. Cover both inside and out with one or two layers of plaster-based gesso. Wet-polish the eyes and beak, and leave brush marks on the rest of the face.*

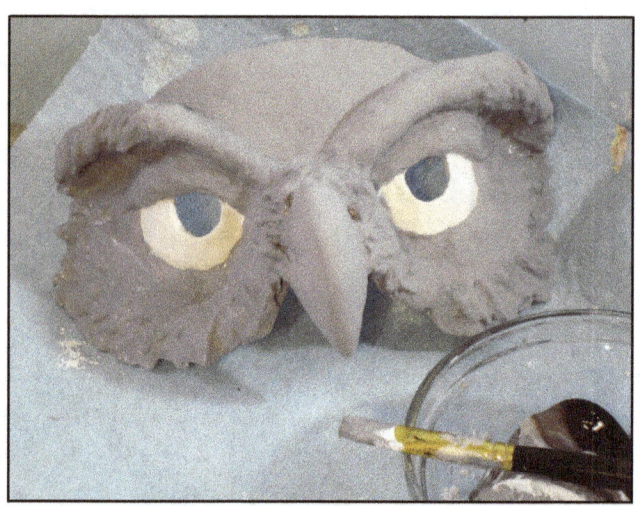

2 *When the gesso is dry, give the owl a base coat of light gray (black, burnt umber and white). Leave the eyes unpainted. Allow to dry.*

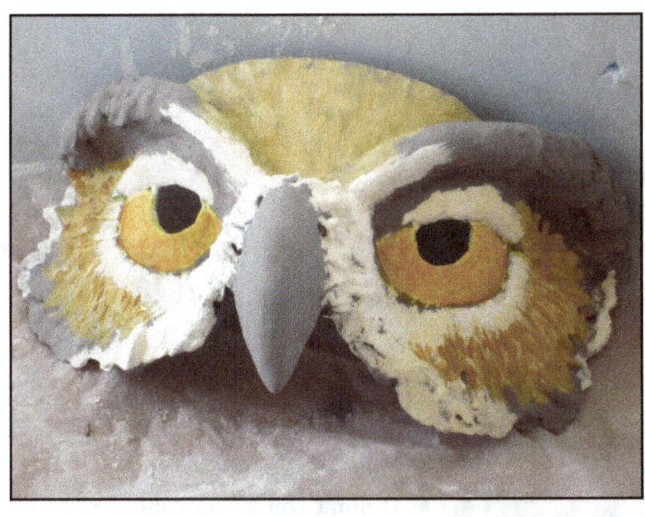

3 *Mix golden brown craft paint with antique white, and paint the cheeks and forehead. Go back over these areas with a dry brush and slightly lighter and slightly darker paint, to give these areas a feathery look. End with very light strokes using almost pure golden brown on the cheeks, as shown.*

4 *Paint the white parts with antique white, and then go back over them with pure white, using an almost dry brush.*

5 *Paint the eyes yellow, and allow to dry. Then mix a small amount of Cadmium red light or orange craft paint with water, and paint this watery mix over the eyes so the yellow shows through.*

6 *Paint the black areas. To highlight the big feathers on the eyebrows, wipe off just a bit of the black along the top of the ridges. The gray will then show through. Use random strokes on the forehead for the brindle pattern of feathers. Paint the edges of the eye holes black, and add a small white reflection spot.*

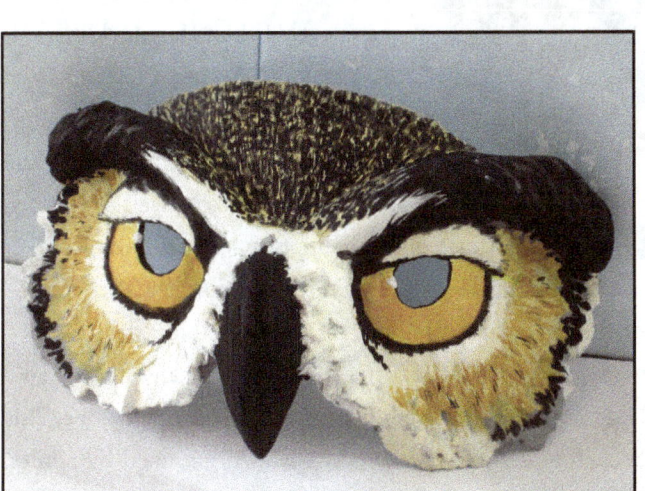

7 *When all the paint is dry, seal the mask if needed, using spray finish or Matte Acrylic Varnish. Allow to dry.*

8 *Dampen a paper towel, and then mix a dark glaze, using black, burnt umber and Acrylic Glazing Liquid. Spread this glaze over the owl and wipe it off with the towel. The dark color will bring out the ruffled texture of the feathers around the beak and cheeks.*

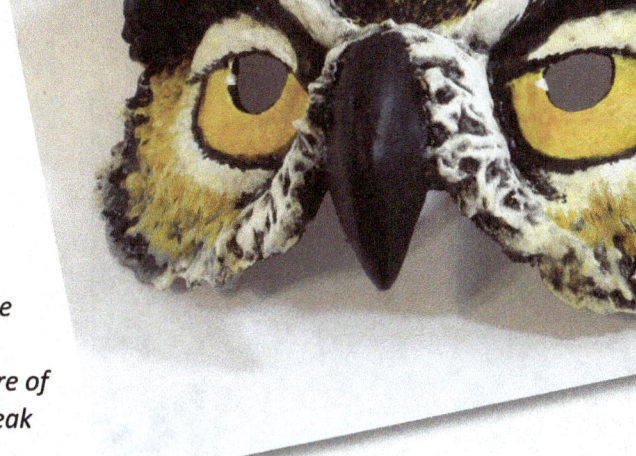

Allow the mask to dry, finish with acrylic vanish, and attach the stick (see page 31), or ribbons.

Duckling Hat

FOR A CHILD'S trick-or-treat costume, I don't think you could get much more adorable than this duckling hat. It sits on top of the head, so there's no need for eye holes.

When you make your mold, the weight of the bill needs to be well-supported if you use a full helmet-style form, like I did. It would be much easier to use a form that is just the shape of the top of the head, so the bill can rest on the table.

I made my mask bigger than the form. When the mask was finished I used foam padding made for bicycle helmets to make it the right size. This is a good idea even for helmet-style masks that will be used by adults, because it makes the mask more comfortable to wear.

To finish your mask you'll need Acrylic Paint, Acrylic Glazing Liquid and Matte Acrylic Varnish.

MAKE THE MOLD

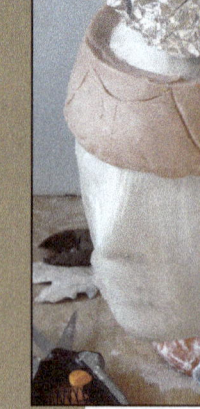

1 Put a layer of clay around the mask form to make the hat slightly larger than the child's head. I used a layer of clay about ½ inch thick and about 2 ½ inches wide. This forms the cheek area on the duckling. Wad up some aluminum foil into a flattened ball, and use it as padding for the upper portion of the head (see small photo on next page for shape).

C H A P T E R
15

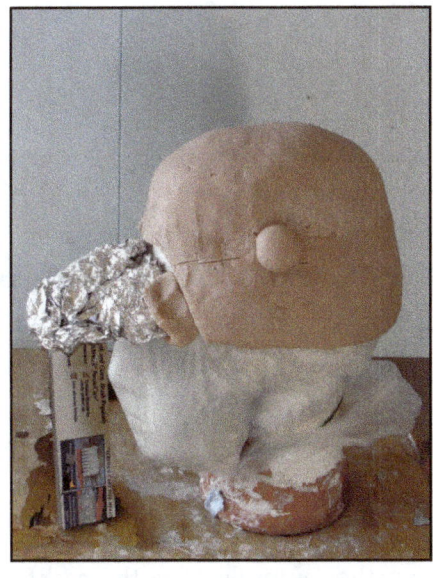 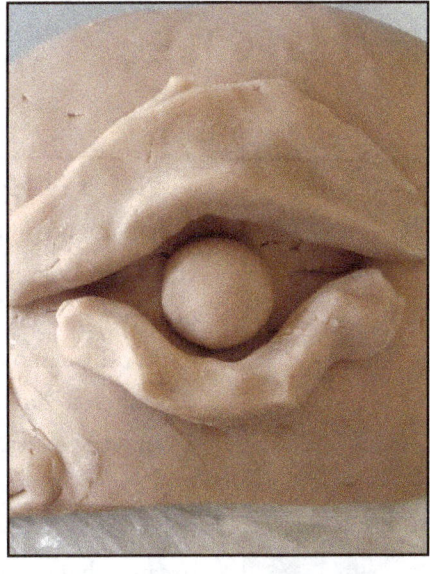 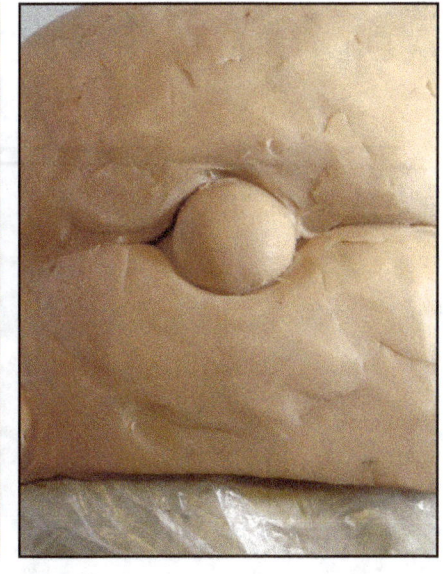

2 Cover the foil with a skin of clay, and add a large ball of clay for the eye where the cheek and top meet. Crumple some foil for the beak and hold it on to the form with a few bits of clay. Support it underneath. I used a cut-down toothpaste carton.

3 Surround the eyeball with two large noodles of clay, as shown.

4 Smooth out the clay around the eyes, leaving a horizontal valley in front of and in back of the eye.

5 Add a thin layer of clay over the foil to sculpt the bill, as shown. Cover just the top of the bill with clay, and leave the bottom open. Ducks don't really have smile muscles, but I gave my duckling a smile, anyway.

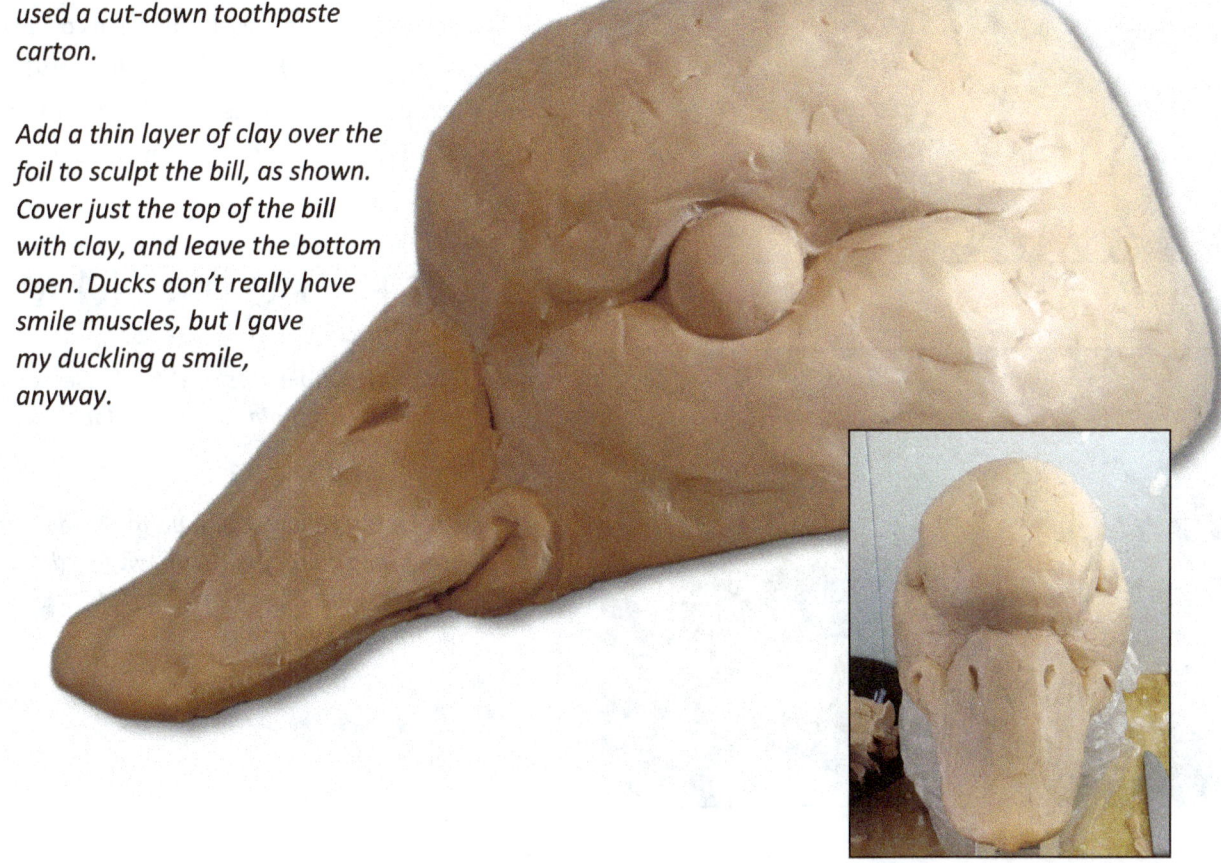

ADD THE PAPER MACHE

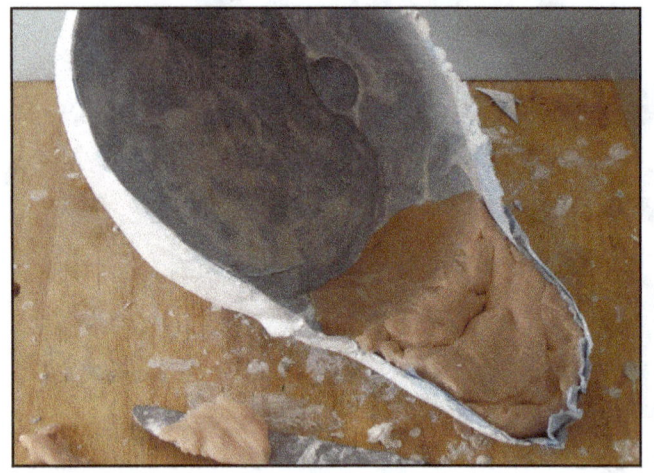

This is a fairly easy shape to cover with paper mache. I recommend doing it in two stages. For the first stage, cover the mold in the usual way with two or three layers of paper mache. Allow the paper mache to dry, lift the mask off the mold, and pull out all of the clay except the clay and foil that forms the bill. Cut away the excess paper around the edges.

Then add a layer of paper mache to complete the inside curve of the hat. Don't cover the bottom of the bill, because that would trap the clay inside. Allow the mask to dry completely, and then remove the clay. This will help the hat fit the head better.

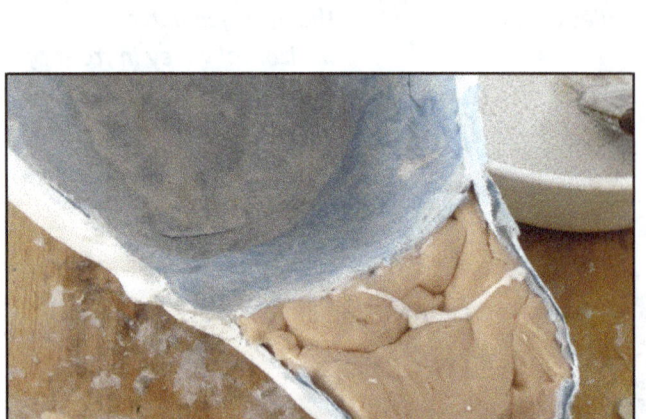

PREPARE THE MASK FOR PAINTING

Sand the edges of the mask, and then cover with one or two layers of Plaster-Based Gesso. Use a stiff brush to create a feather texture on the head (like the cat fur at the top of page 62). Sand or wet-polish the bill to make it smooth.

FINISH YOUR MASK

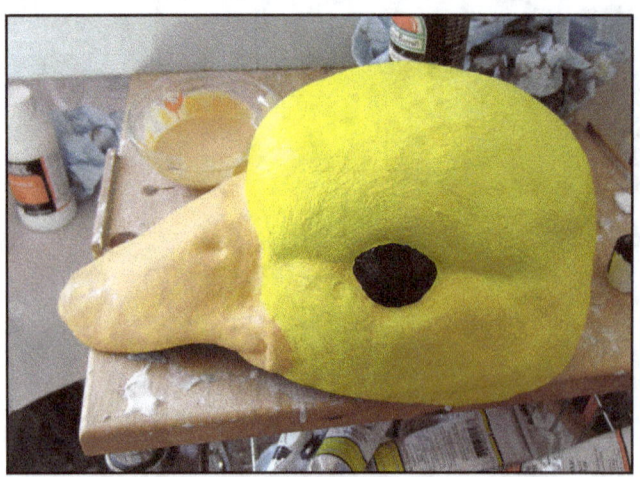

1 *Paint the whole mask yellow (I used Cadmium Yellow Light). Paint the eyes black.*

2 *When the yellow is dry, paint the bill with a soft pinkish orange, made with Cadmium Yellow Light, Cadmium Red Light, Yellow Ochre and White.*

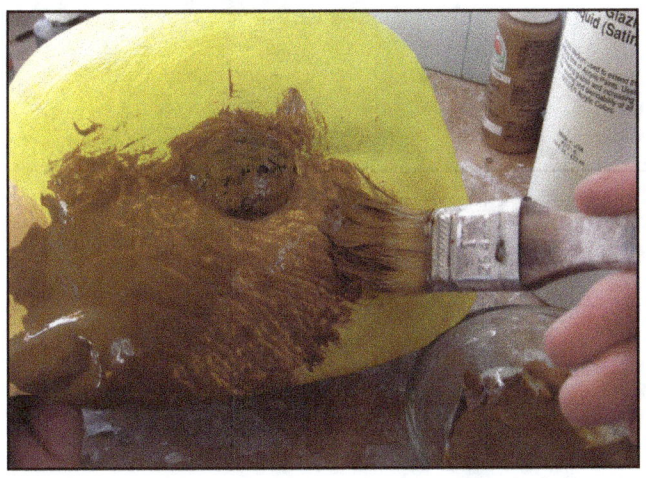

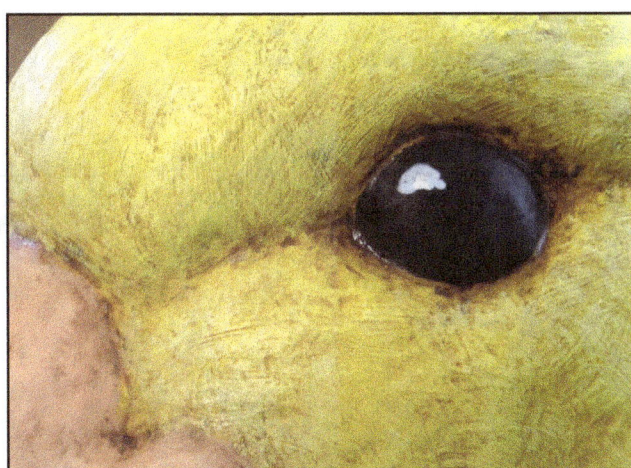

3 Brush on a glaze made with a mixture of Raw Sienna, Burnt Umber, and Acrylic Glazing Liquid. Immediately rub off most of the glaze with a paper towel. This will bring out the feather texture you made with the gesso.

4 Mix a very Light Blue and paint a reflection spot in each eye.

5 To bring all the colors together, I used one last glaze, made with Cadmium Yellow Light and a touch of Cadmium Red Light, mixed with White. I added enough Acrylic Glazing Liquid to make the mixture very transparent. This was brushed over the entire mask, except the eyes.

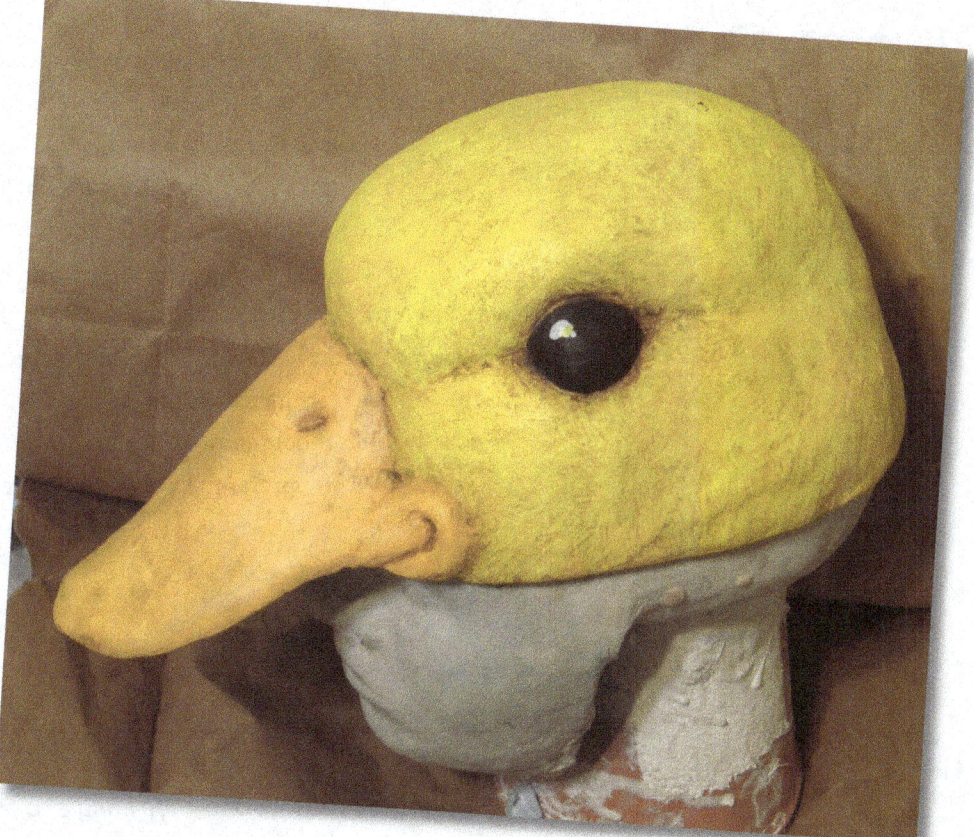

When all the paint is dry, add foam strips to the inside of the mask, (see page 31) to make it fit comfortably.

Celtic Helmet

T HIS ANCIENT IRON helmet could be part of a costume for role-playing games, or it could be displayed on a stand if you're interested in military history. For inspiration, I used a photo of a helmet that is now housed in the collection of the Naturhistoiches Museum in Vienna. The original was first worn sometime in the first century BCE, and was found in Yugoslavia (now Slovenia). I admit that I changed the design on the cheek guards, (just because I felt like it). If you're a military arts or history buff, you'll probably want to do more research and follow the original design more carefully.

For the finish I used products called Instant Iron and Instant Rust, purchased online from DickBlick.com. They created a very realistic rusty iron surface on my helmet. If you decide to purchase these products, be sure to read all the warning labels and keep the products locked up away from kids. It wouldn't look quite as authentic, but you can use dark gray and orange paint if you prefer to work with non-toxic art materials.

MAKE THE MOLD

1 *Use aluminum foil to make the top of the mask form rounder, as we did for the duck, page 74. Lay a "skin" of modeling clay over the form and foil. Add the brim and rivets.*

2 *I used the side of a knife handle to beat my helmet smooth. It doesn't have to be too smooth, though, since it's bound to get a little beat up during battle.*

3 *Make the cheek guards separately. Cut out the shape you want on a piece of paper, and use it as a pattern to make both guards the same. Add a slightly raised Celtic pattern. I chose one from the Book of Kells.*

CHAPTER
16

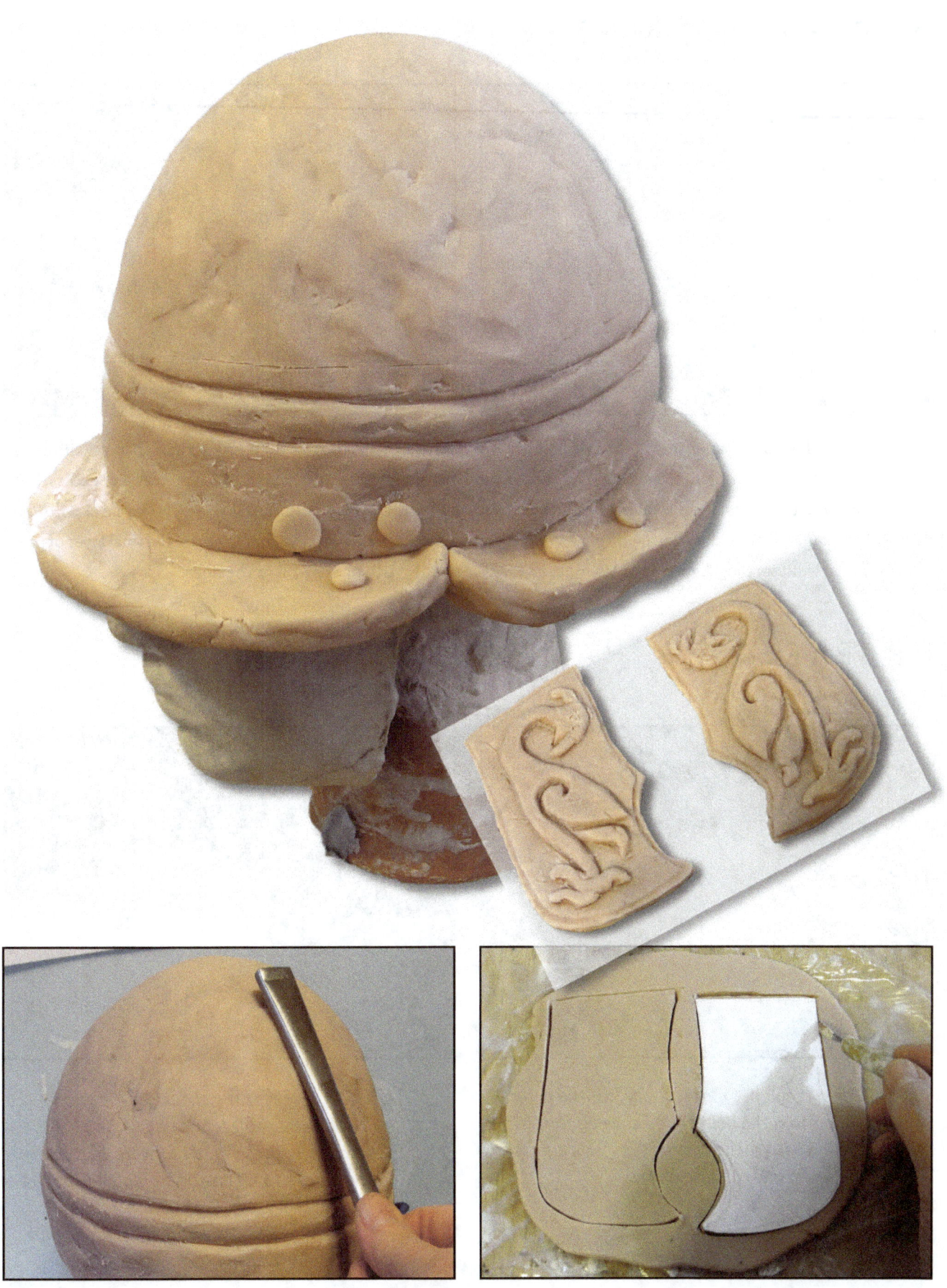

ADD PAPER MACHE

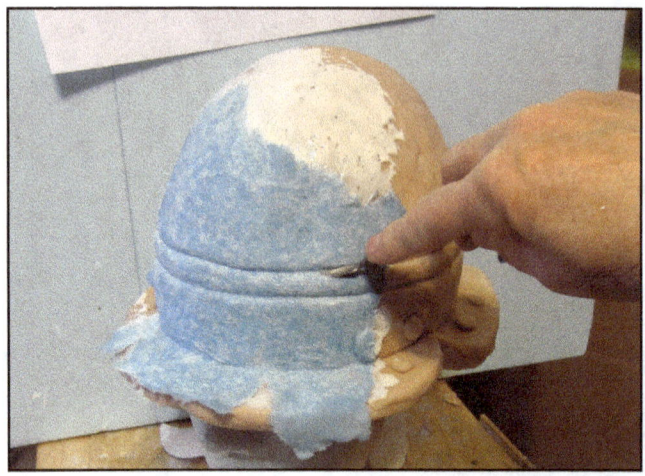 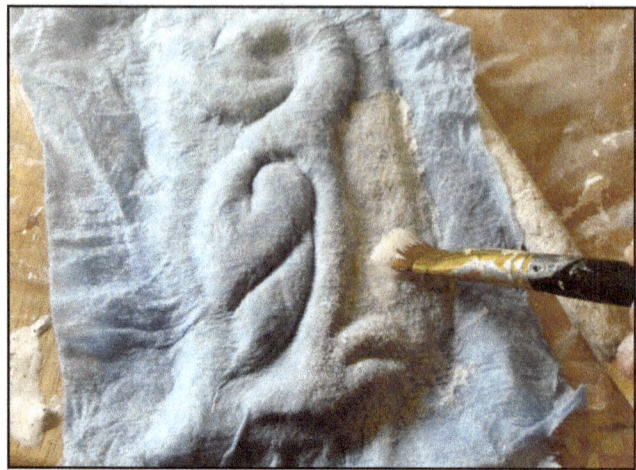

Apply two layers of paper mache to the helmet and both cheek guards. Use a tool to push the paper into the lines and around the rivets, if your helmet design has these details. The paper mache doesn't have to be completely smooth if you want an old, slightly beat-up look.

Use your tool to keep the details crisp on the cheek guards, and be sure to push all air bubbles and excess paste out of the valleys of the design. The second layer will go on much easier. Use a small brush to add the final layer of paste so the paste doesn't fill in the lines.

PREPARE FOR PAINTING

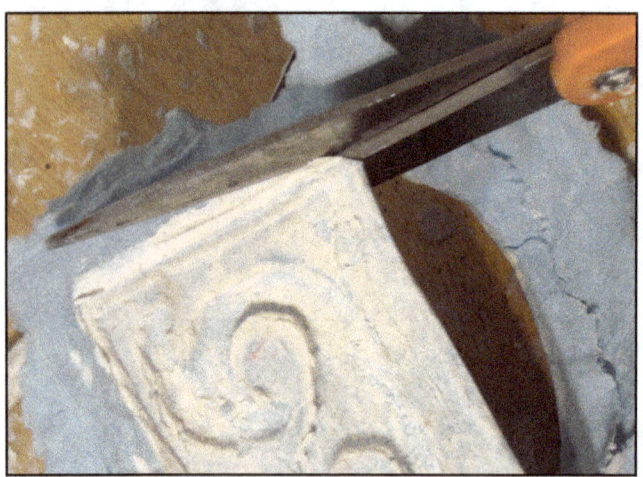 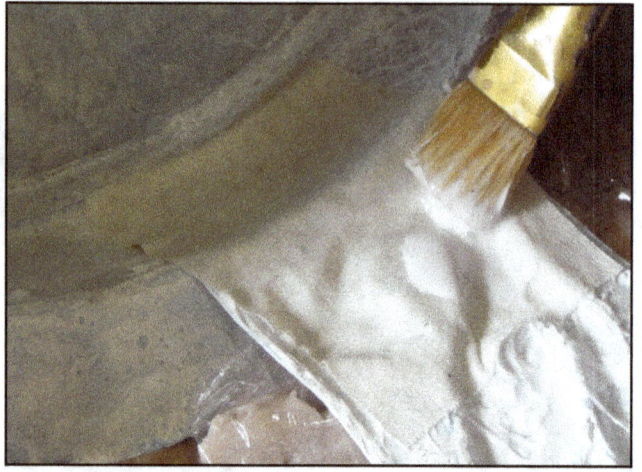

1 *When the paper mache is dry, cut the excess paper from the helmet and cheek guards. The cutting line will be easy to see if you cut from the underside of these pieces.*

2 *Create a hinge for the cheek guards using muslin or other soft fabric and white glue. Attach the guards slightly forward of center— you will need to let one dry completely before doing the other one. Prop up the guards to hold them in the right position while the glue dries.*

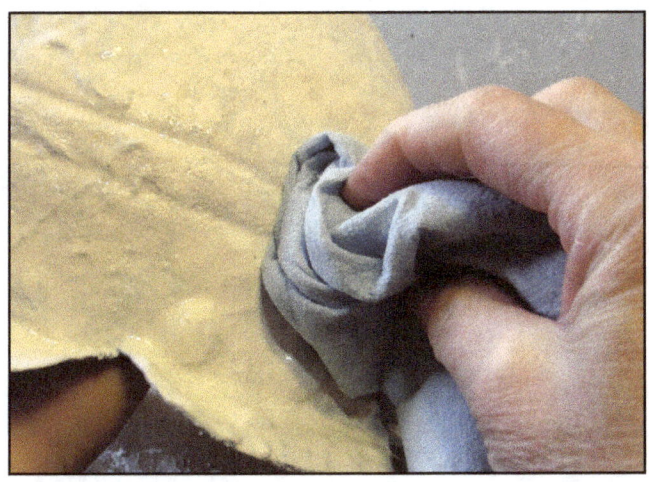

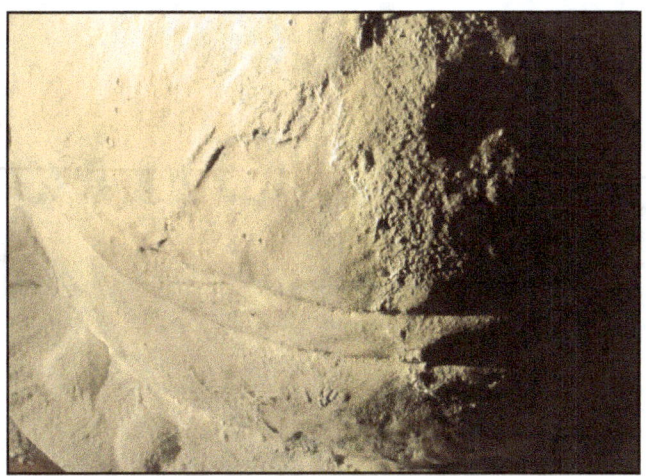

3 Apply one coat of Really Smooth Gesso mix, page 8. If you want the helmet to look like it was buried in a field for several thousand years, you can rough up the gesso by dabbing a few places with a dry paper towel, as shown

As you can see, I left my helmet quite rough. The paint and Instant Iron will smooth it out a bit, but still leave nice raised parts for interesting shadows.

FINISH THE HELMET

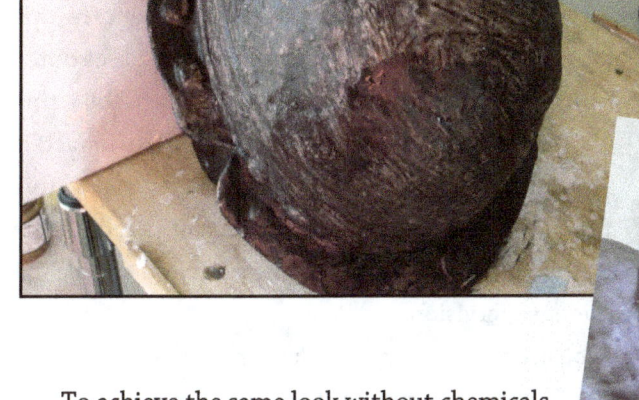

1 Give the helmet a base coat of Burnt Umber mixed with water. Allow to dry.

2 Apply the Instant Iron and Instant Rust according to package directions. Be sure to read all the warning labels, and work in a well-ventilated space.

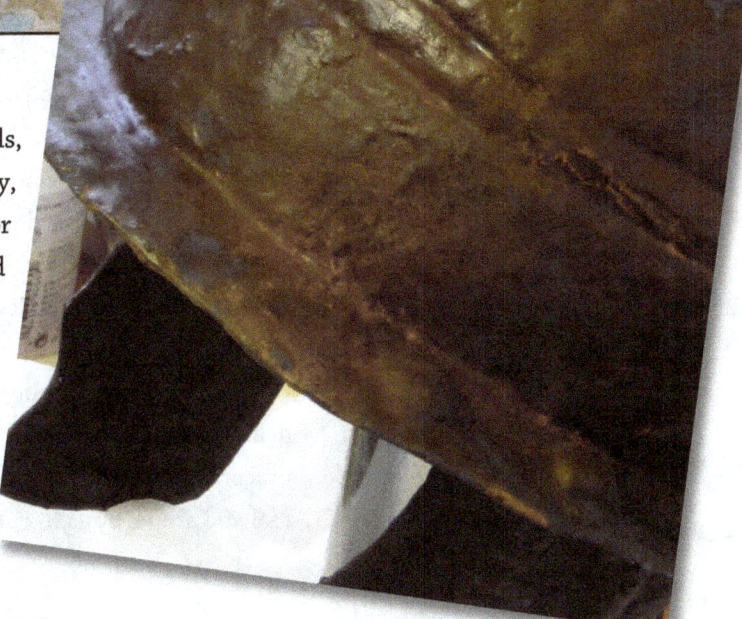

To achieve the same look without chemicals, paint the helmet a flat dark gray. Allow to dry, and then sponge on a glaze using Raw Sienna for the rust. A series of glazes will give the mottled look of natural rust.

Add a final coat of Matte Acrylic Varnish, or use Marine Varnish if the helmet will be worn in the rain.

Unicorn

O̲UR PEARLY WHITE unicorn is wearing a decorative silver ornament on his forehead that was given to him by Boudica, the Celtic warrior queen. The ornament has magic powers from a spell cast by the queen's Druid priest. (The magic, in this case, allows the person wearing the mask to see out.)

Any mask can be used as wall art, but this particular mask seems perfect for that role. In fact, it would be a wonderful gift for anyone devoted to this fabled beast. Since the horn would make a formidable weapon, this mask should not be worn by a small child without supervision.

If you use a helmet-type mask form for the base of your mold, like I did, be sure to support the muzzle, and prop up the sculpture so it can't become unbalanced and fall on the floor.

I used an Arabian horse for my model, because the dish-shaped face fits onto a human mask form better than other breeds. The Arabian also has more of a woodland look, which seems to be a good fit for the unicorn legends.

To help reduce the weight on the front of the Unicorn mask, I deliberately shortened the muzzle. This works for a mythical beast like the unicorn, but if you make a horse mask instead you may want to use more realistic proportions.

CHAPTER

17

MAKE YOUR MOLD

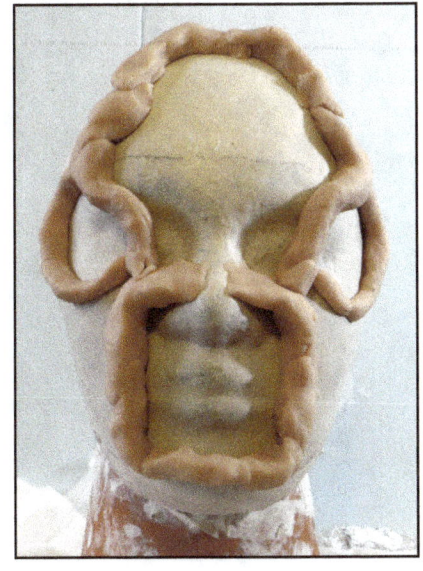

1 Use thick noodles of clay to outline the eye sockets, the forehead, and the muzzle. This will help you place the features over the human face on your form.

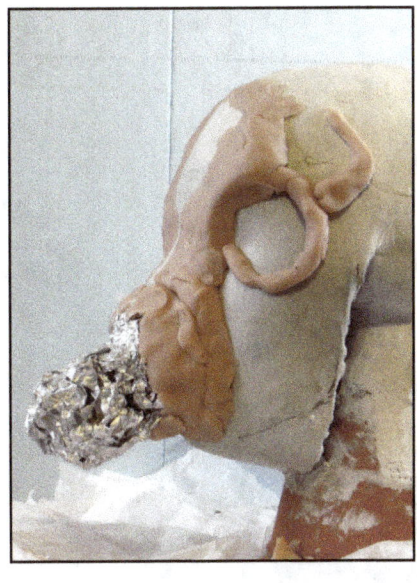

2 Crumple some aluminum foil into a snout-shaped cylinder, and use pieces of clay to hold it onto the mask form. Add clay to level off the forehead and between the eyes.

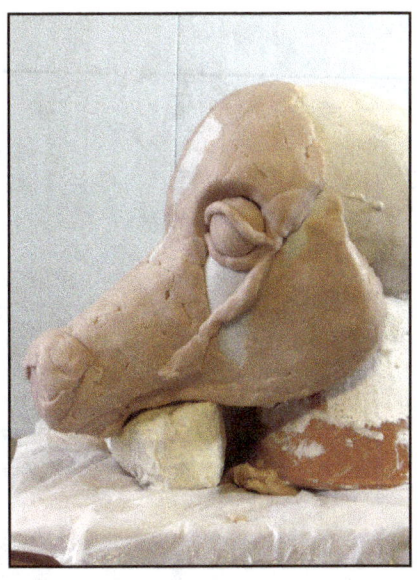

3 Put a thin skin of clay over the muzzle, and add clay to shape the cheeks. Put a ball of clay in each eye socket, and outline the upper eyelids with noodles of clay.

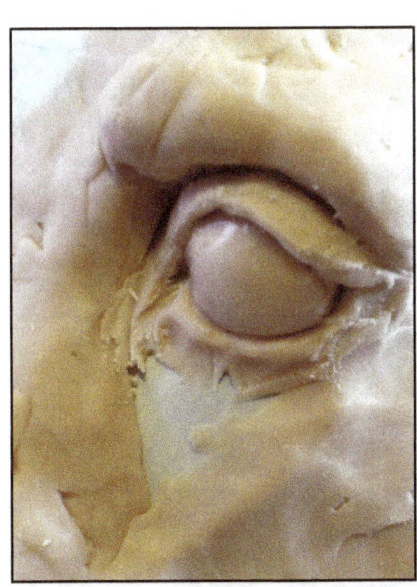

4 Add clay above the eye to fill in the eyebrow muscles. Use a modeling tool to define the eye, as shown.

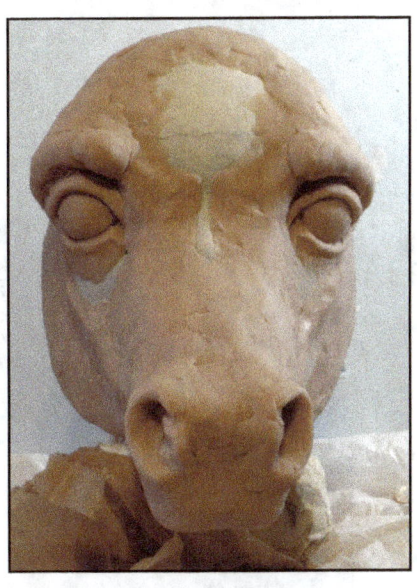

5 Pad the upper corners of the snout where the nose will be, and sculpt deep nostrils.

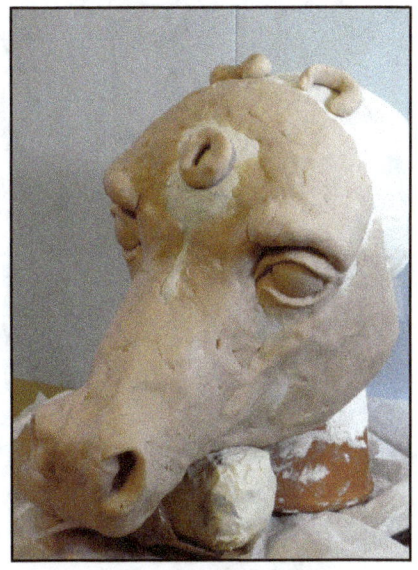

6 Add two noodles of clay where the ears will be attached, above the forehead. Put a circle of clay where the horn will go.

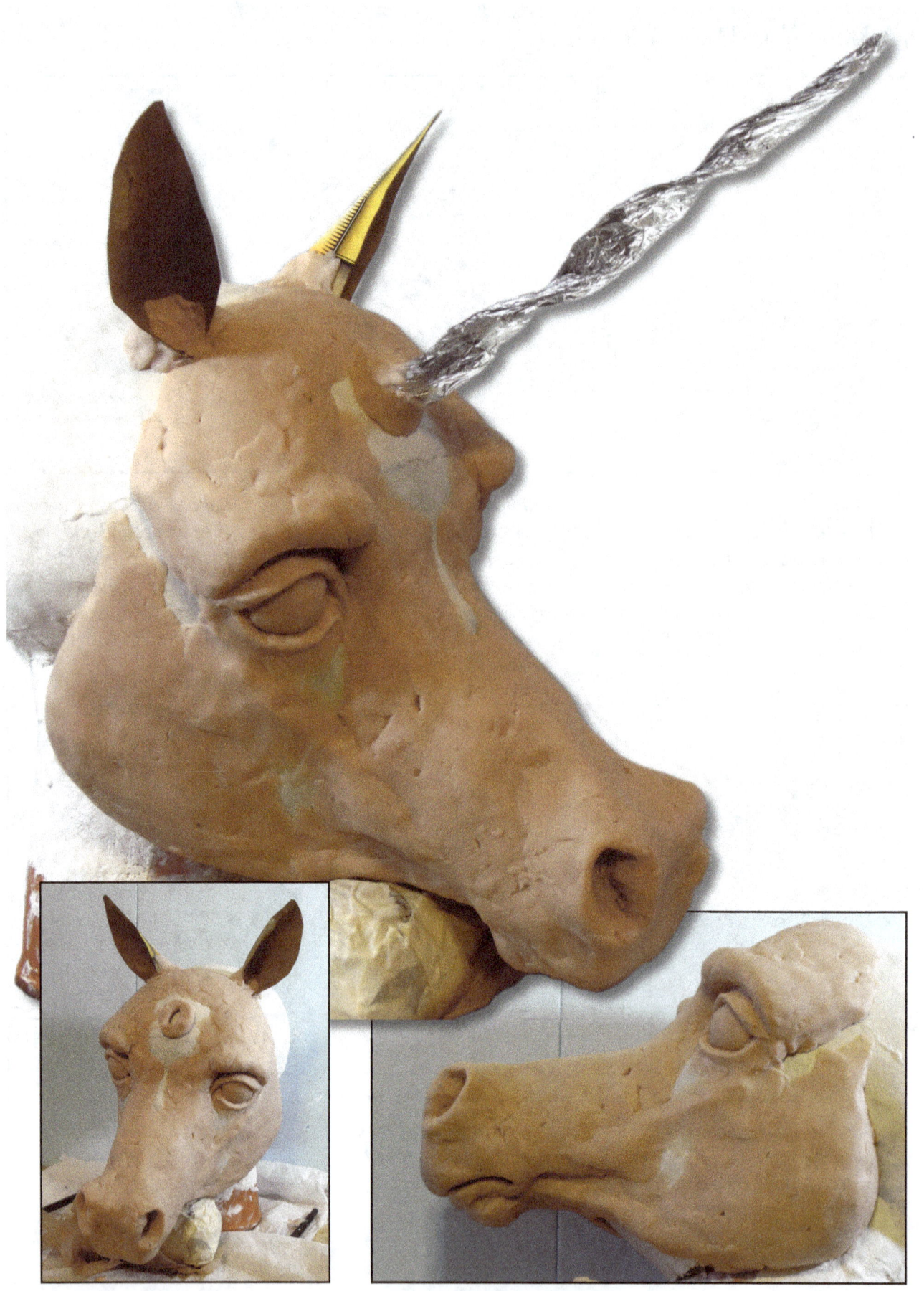

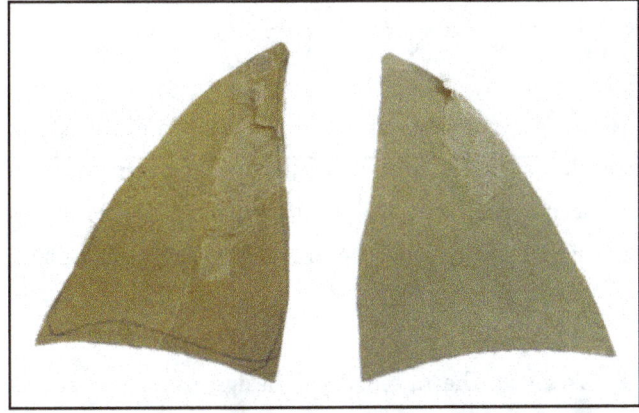

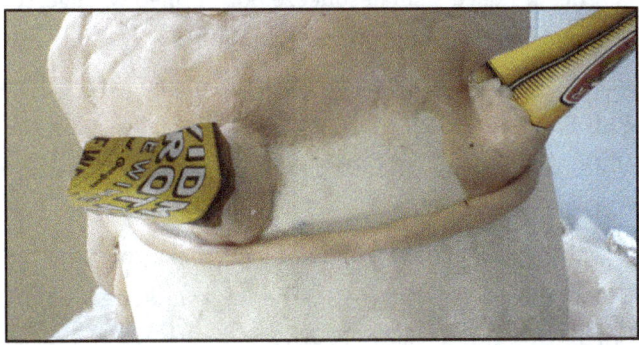

7 *Sculpt the lips and chin of the unicorn, as shown in the photo on the opposite page.*

8 *Cut two ears out of light cardboard. A cereal box works well. Press the ears into the two C-shaped clay noodles above the forehead, and then press the clay up against the ears to create a smooth transition.*

9 *Tear off a piece of aluminum foil about 18 inches long, fold it to about 8" long, and then crumple and twist it into a horn. Press the horn into the circle of clay on the forehead.*

10 *Run a noodle of clay behind the ears to outline the top edge of the mask.*

Check the sculpture from all angles to make sure it's symmetrical. Smooth the clay, as shown on page 21.

ADD THE PAPER MACHE

This is a challenging shape to cover with paper mache, so take your time. Stretch and shape the damp paper towels over the mold, tearing wherever needed. You may need to use smaller pieces than usual, which will result in more edges. Because the mask is quite large, have at least four damp paper towels ready before you begin.

If possible, avoid making a seam across the eyes. Tear the paper, as shown below, to prevent the extra paper from folding up behind the eyes. Don't cover the underside of the snout with paper mache, because you need access to this area when the paper mache is dry.

When the paste gets too thick in your bowl or on your brush, throw it out and make another batch.

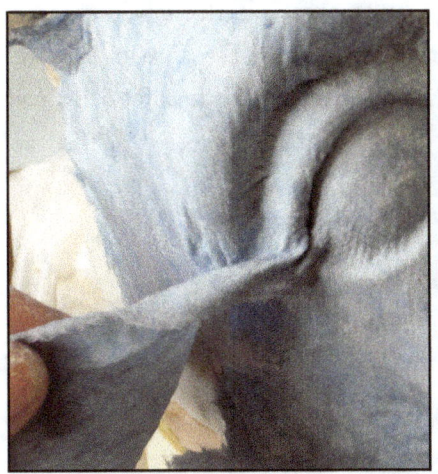
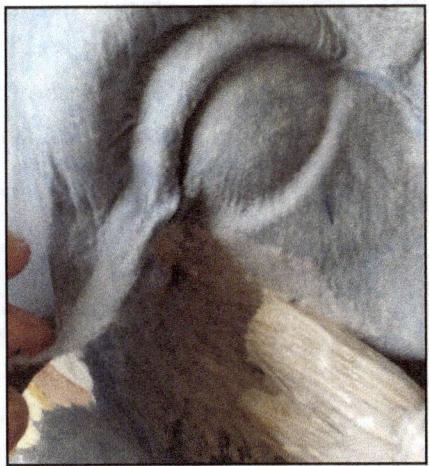
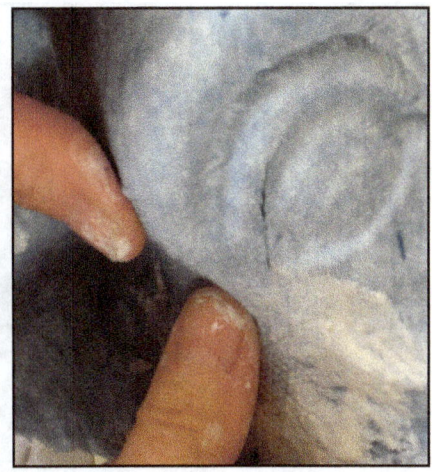

PREPARE THE MASK FOR PAINTING

When the mask is hard enough to lift off the mold, trim away the extra paper around the edges. Sand the edges. The cardboard ears and foil horn will show on the inside of the mask. Use small bits of paper to cover these areas, using gesso as paste. Then give your mask one or more coats of Plaster-Based Gesso, using a large stiff brush to leave fur marks on the surface (see page 62). If you think it would be easier, you can cut the eye holes before adding the raised design, instead of doing it last, as I did.

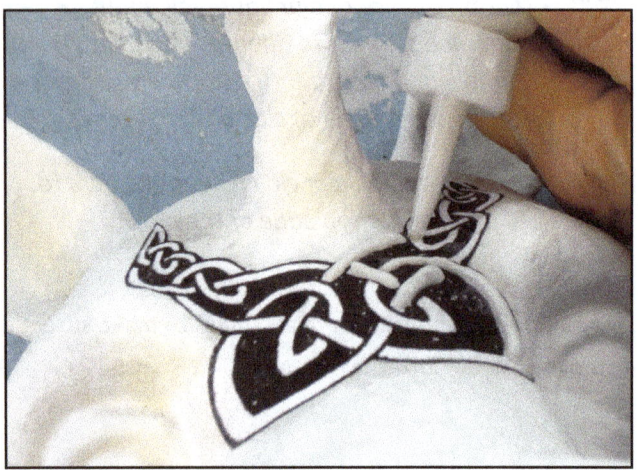

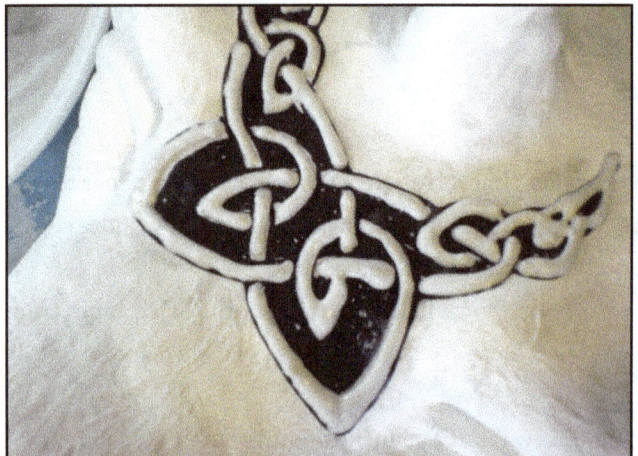

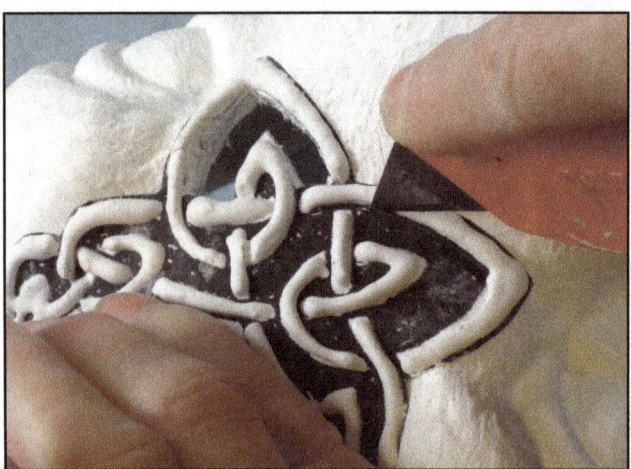

To make the raised Celtic design on the unicorn's forehead, I used a small squeeze bottle filled with gesso. If the gesso seems too runny to hold it's shape, you can use less water. The gesso is easier to sand and carve than Puff Paint, which I used for the gilded lace design on the Volto mask, page 36, but the thicker gesso was more difficult to apply. You can use whichever one you prefer.

Draw a design on a piece of copy paper, or trace the design on the opposite page. The large dark areas at the bottom of the design will become your eye holes, so measure your design to make sure you will be able to see out when you wear the mask.

Cut out your paper design and then dampen the back of the copy paper with a sponge to soften it. Paste it onto the unicorn with gesso. The bottom corners should be where your eyes will be when the mask is worn. (If you intend to use this as a display mask, you don't need to worry about the placement).

Squeeze the gesso or Puff Paint onto the design, leaving little gaps where the silver strands will cross under each other.

When the raised design is dry, use a craft knife to cut out the two large black areas on the lower corners. Support the paper mache with a piece of foam or wood from underneath, and use all the knife safety tips you learned from your scout master.

This knotted Celtic design was adapted from an illustration I found in the wonderful book *Celtic Art: The Methods of Construction*, by George Bain.

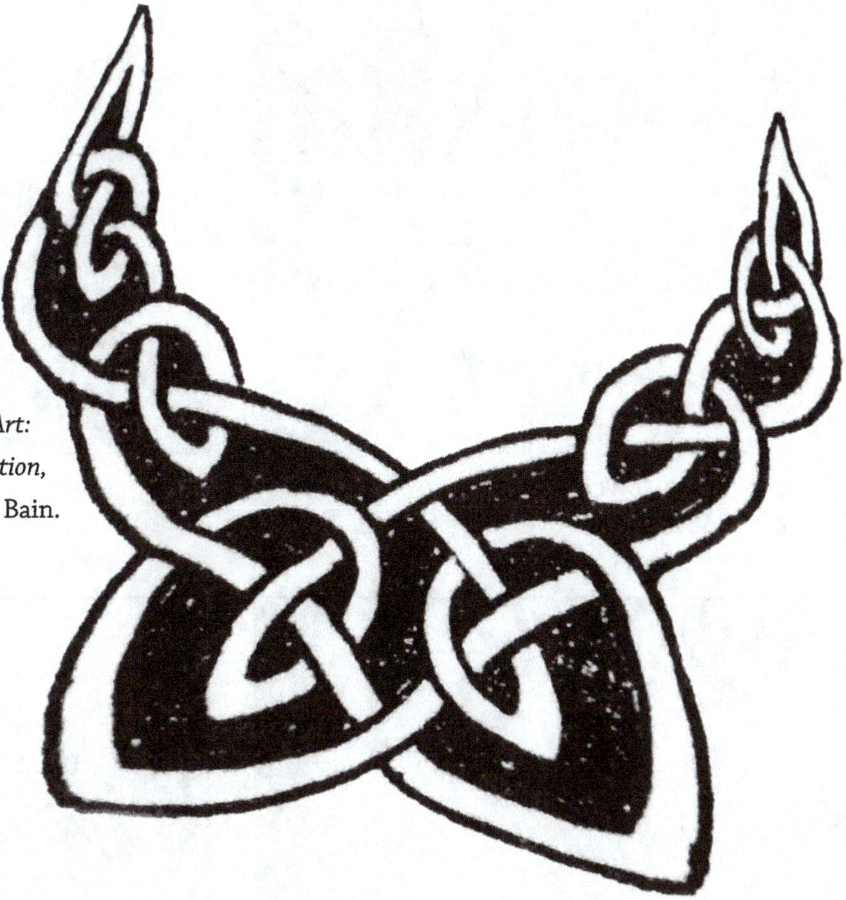

FINISH YOUR MASK

Sand the inside edges of the eye holes you just cut out, and sand the raised design, if needed. If the gesso or paint ran together, repair the design with a sharp craft knife.

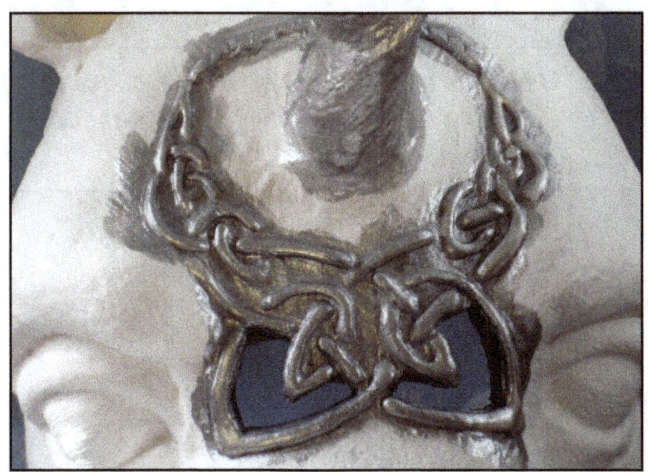

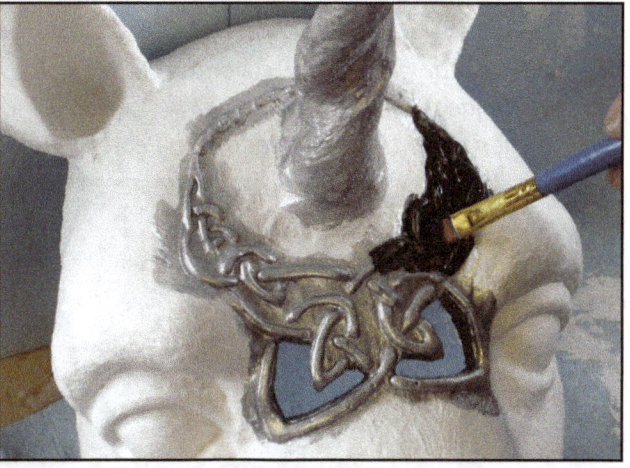

1 *Paint the ornament and the horn with Metallic Silver paint.*

Before moving to the next step, make sure you have two paper towels handy. One should be dry, and the other one should be slightly damp.

2 *Mix Acrylic Glazing Liquid with a small amount of Black and a drop of Metallic Silver. Brush over the raised design. Also cover the silver on the horn.*

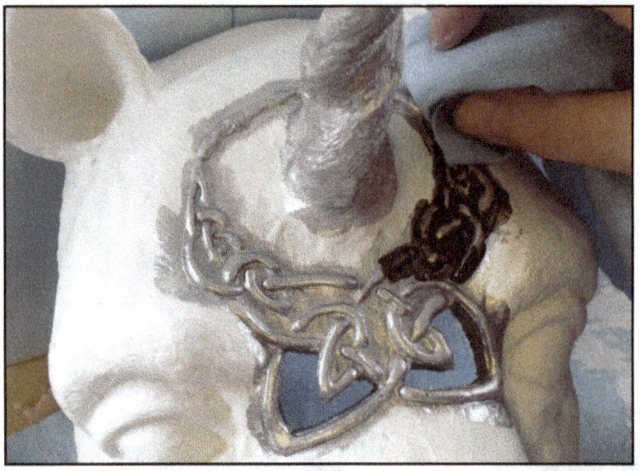

3 Use the dry towel to remove the excess black glaze. Save the left-over glaze for step 7.

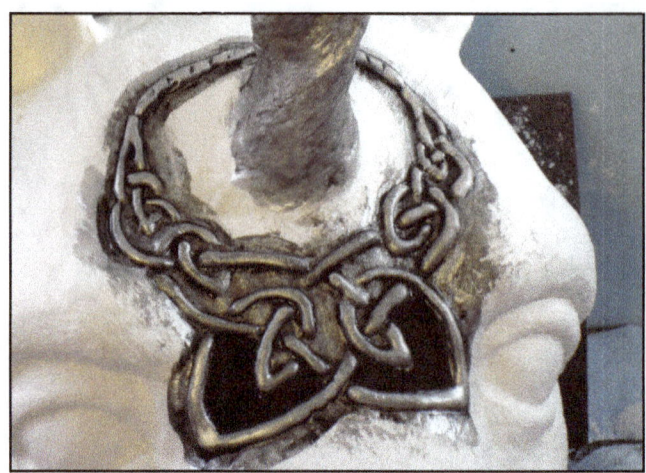

4 Leave enough of the glaze to make the silver look antiqued, and to help define the knot pattern.

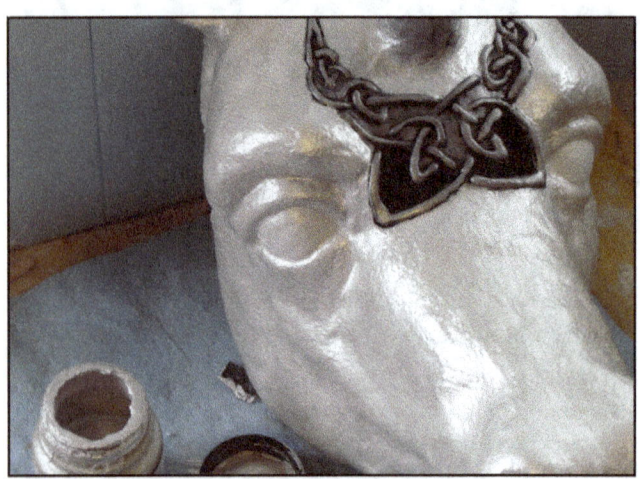

5 When the glaze is dry, cover the extra black outside the raised design with white paint. Then cover the entire head with Pearl White.

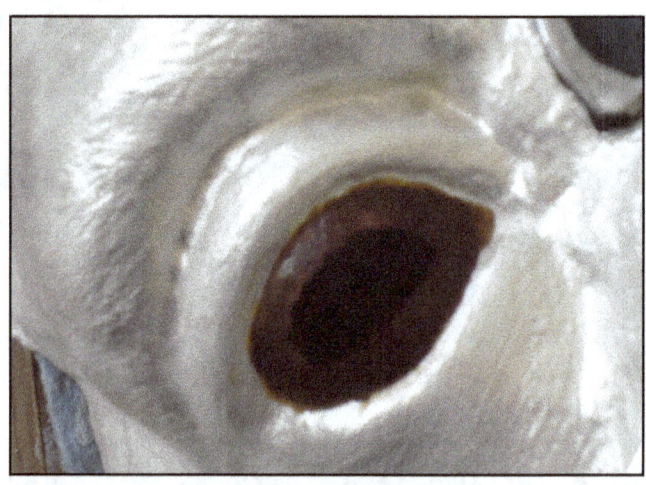

6 Paint the eye with Reddish Brown, and allow the paint to dry. Then paint the oval-shaped pupil Black.

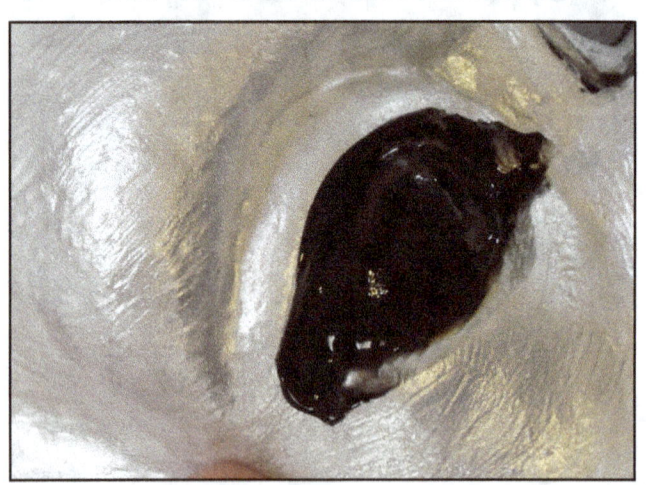

7 Use your black glaze to cover the eye.

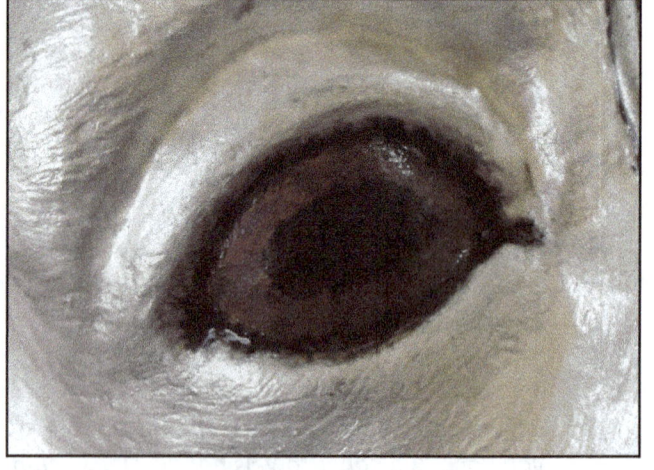

8 Wipe off the glaze, leaving a soft black outline. Do the same for the upper eyelid.

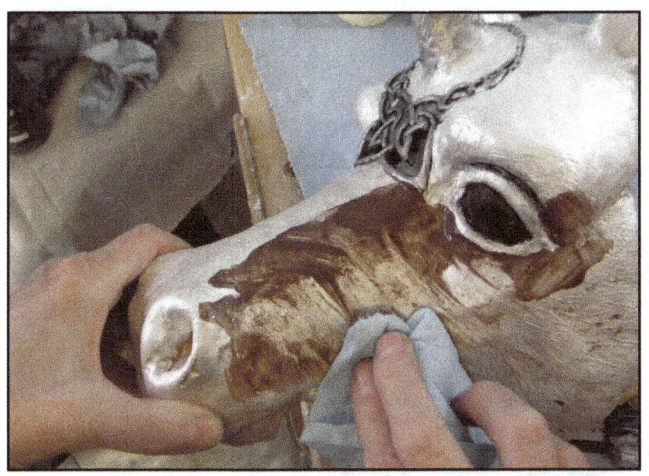

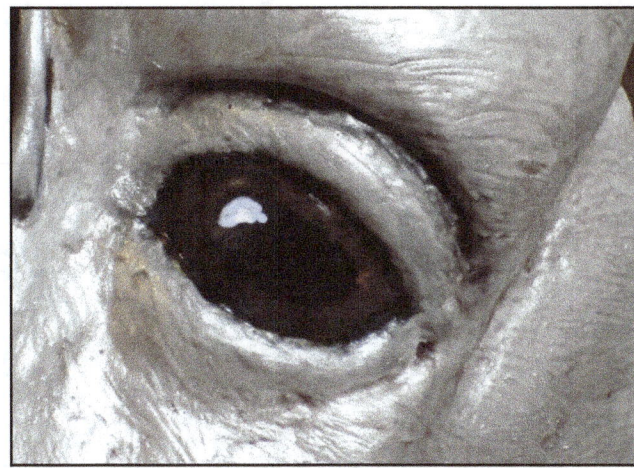

9 *Mix Acrylic Glazing Liquid with Burn Umber, and brush this over the white unicorn. Wipe most of it off with a paper towel, leaving just enough to leave traces in the fur pattern you created with the gesso, and to define the mouth.*

10 *Mix a very light Blue, and give the eyes a spot of reflected light.*

When all the paint is dry, finish your unicorn with Acrylic Varnish. Attach a cord or ribbon, or, if you wish to use your mask as wall art, attach a hanger to the back (see page 31).

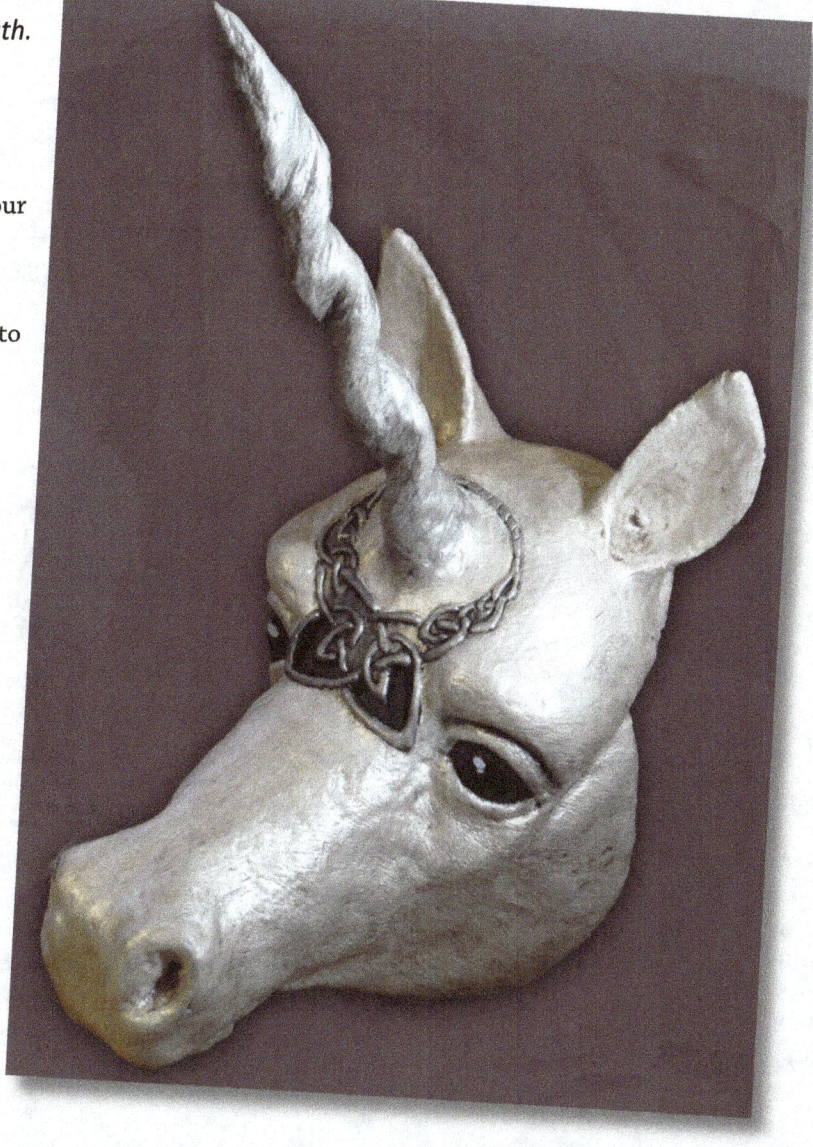

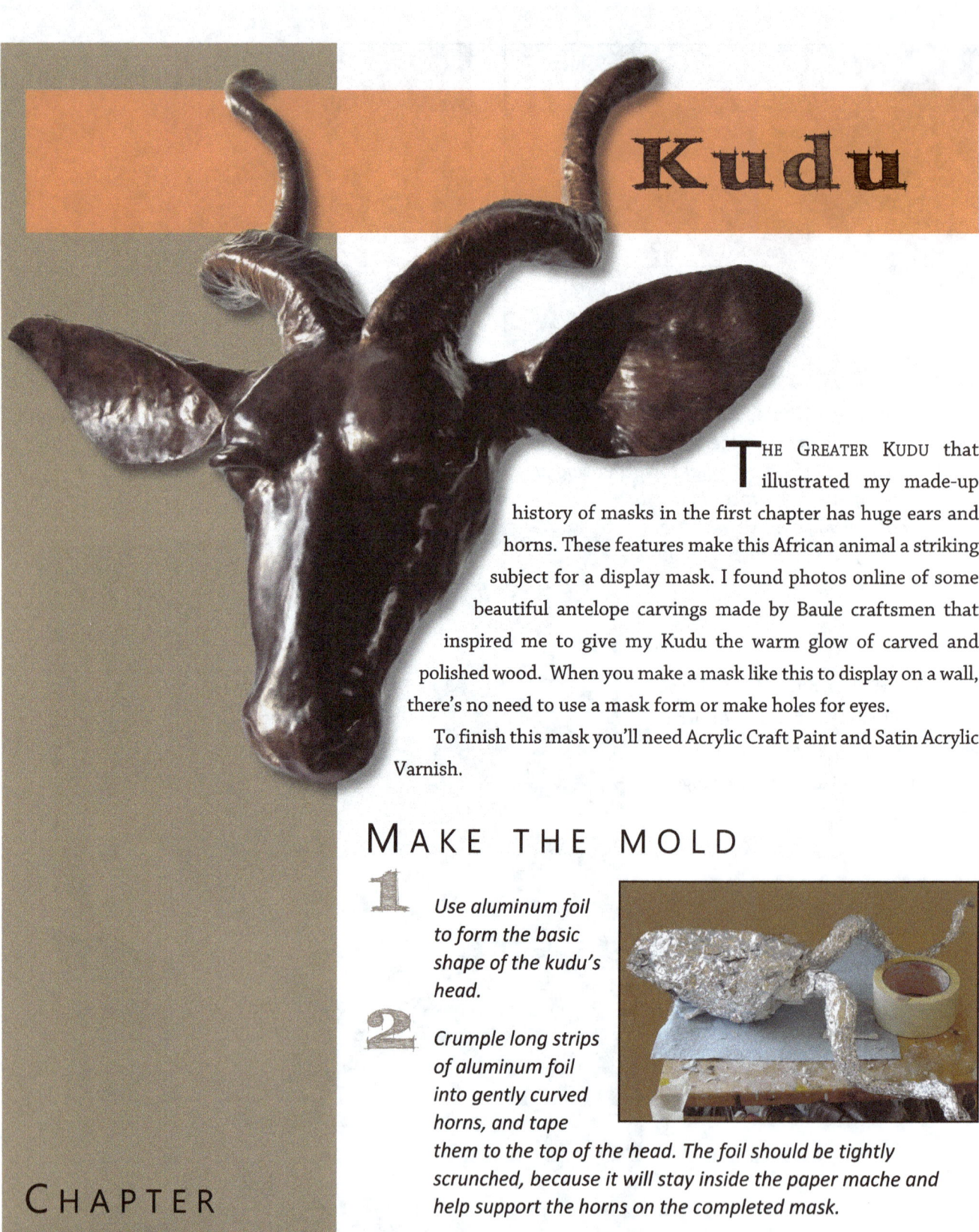

Kudu

THE GREATER KUDU that illustrated my made-up history of masks in the first chapter has huge ears and horns. These features make this African animal a striking subject for a display mask. I found photos online of some beautiful antelope carvings made by Baule craftsmen that inspired me to give my Kudu the warm glow of carved and polished wood. When you make a mask like this to display on a wall, there's no need to use a mask form or make holes for eyes.

To finish this mask you'll need Acrylic Craft Paint and Satin Acrylic Varnish.

MAKE THE MOLD

1 *Use aluminum foil to form the basic shape of the kudu's head.*

2 *Crumple long strips of aluminum foil into gently curved horns, and tape them to the top of the head. The foil should be tightly scrunched, because it will stay inside the paper mache and help support the horns on the completed mask.*

3 *Cover the head, (but not the horns), with a skin of modeling clay. Sculpt the eyes and nose, add a ridge down the middle of the muzzle, and add a lump of clay below each horn to hold the ears.*

CHAPTER

18

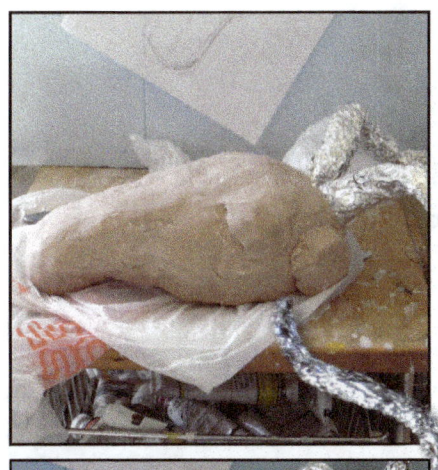

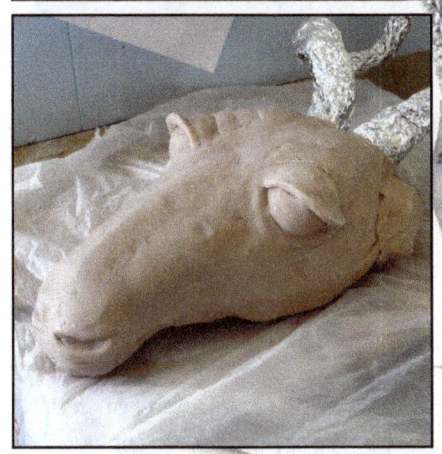

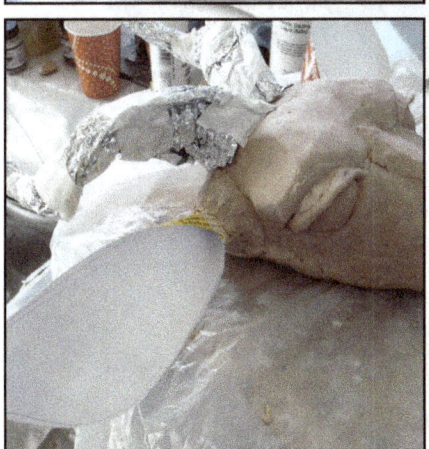

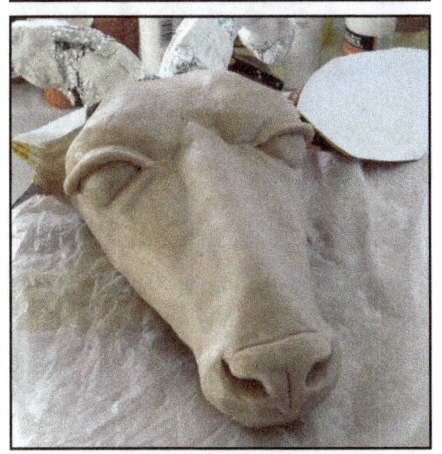

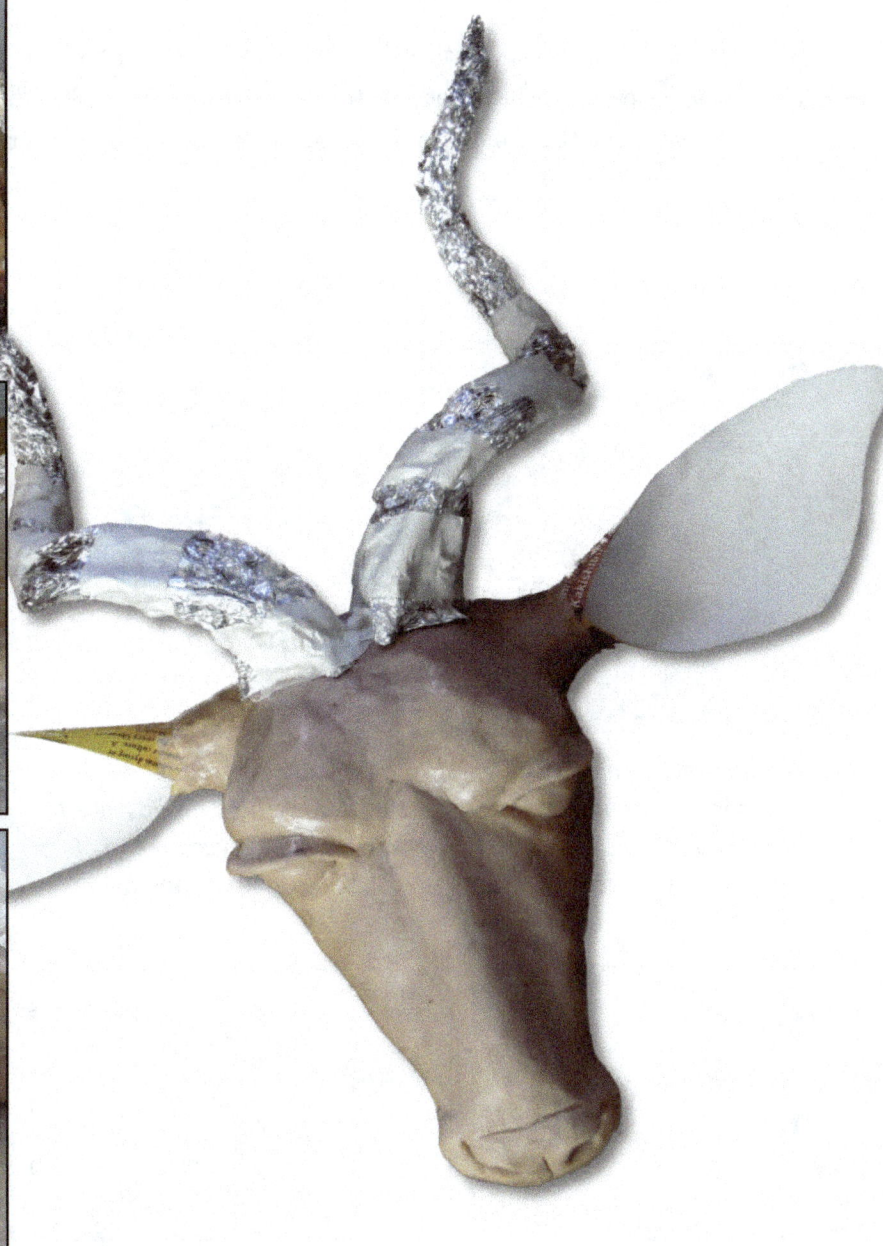

4 Roll up a long piece of foil and tape it to the front of the horns to make ridges that almost meet at the bottom of the horns where they're attached to the forehead. The ridges then wind around the horns, as shown above.

5 Cut two ears out of light cardboard, like the kind used to make cereal boxes. Kudus have very large ears

6 Roll up the bottom end of the ears and tape the corners together. Put them in position and pull the clay up around the ears to hold them in place.

APPLY THE PAPER MACHE

You will want to apply your paper mache in several stages, allowing each stage to dry and harden before continuing. This will let you apply paper mache to both the front and back of the mask without damaging the mold.

Apply two layers to the mask, and a third layer along the top edge to reinforce it.

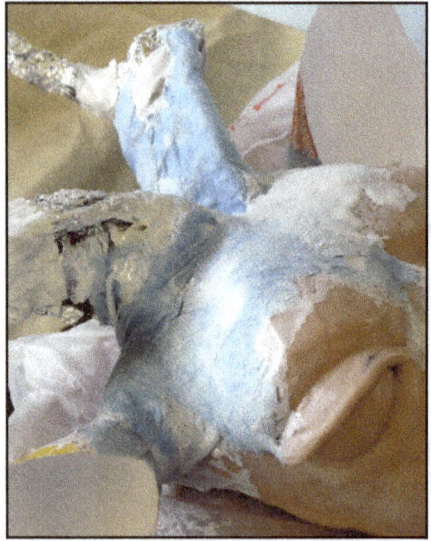

1 First, cover the areas where the horns and ears are attached so they'll be secure. Then cover the rest of the face.

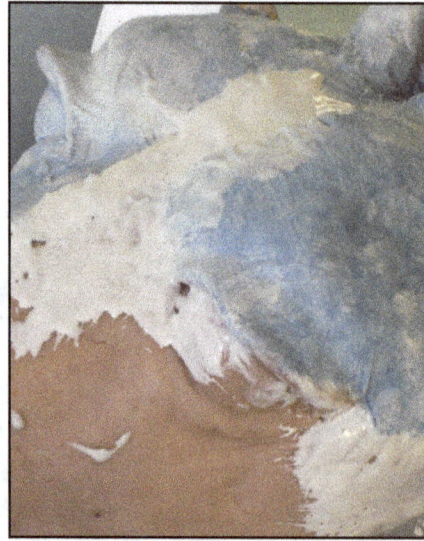

2 If you gave your kudu exaggerated eyelids, like I did, first cover the top of the eyelid, as shown.

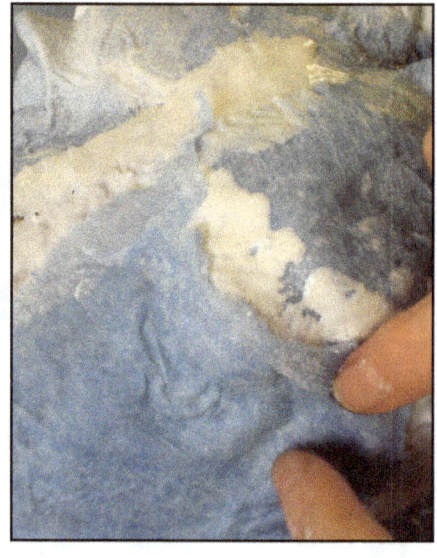

3 Then tear another strip of paper and cover the eye. The seam will be along the top of the eyelid, leaving the eye smooth.

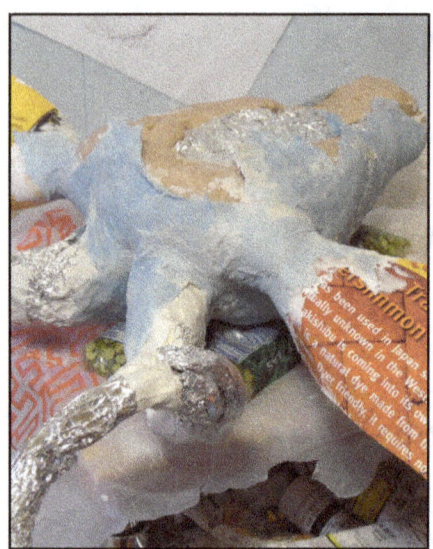

4 Allow the paper mache on the front of the face to harden before turning the mask over.

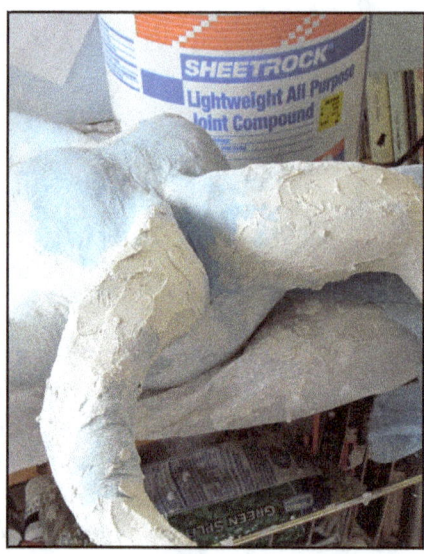

5 If the horns are not as smooth as you would like, you can fix this with joint compound (see page 29).

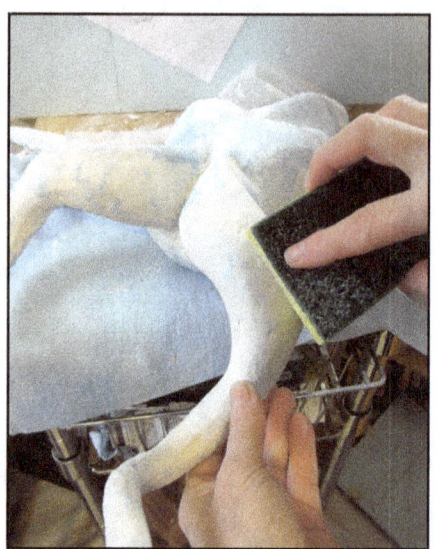

6 After the joint compound is dry, wet-polish it with a scrubby sponge.

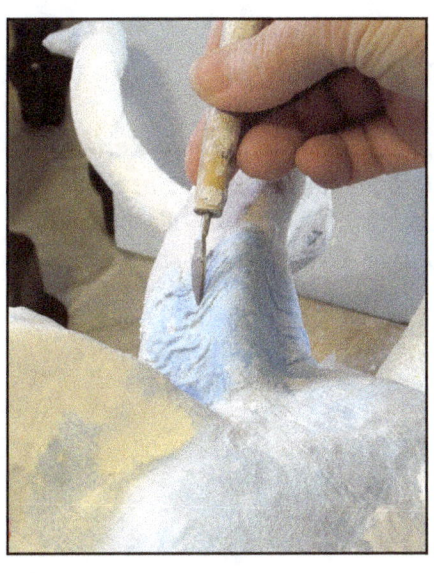

 You can make the distinctive waves on the kudu's horns when you apply the last layer of paper mache. Use fairly small pieces of paper towel. While the paste is still wet, use a tool to push the paper into small waves along the sides of the large central ridge. The waves are less distinct towards the top of the horns.

If you used joint compound to smooth out the horns, be sure to cover all of it with this layer of paper mache. The horns will remain slightly flexible, and the joint compound could crack when the mask is handled if it's not protected by paper mache.

PREPARE THE MASK FOR PAINTING

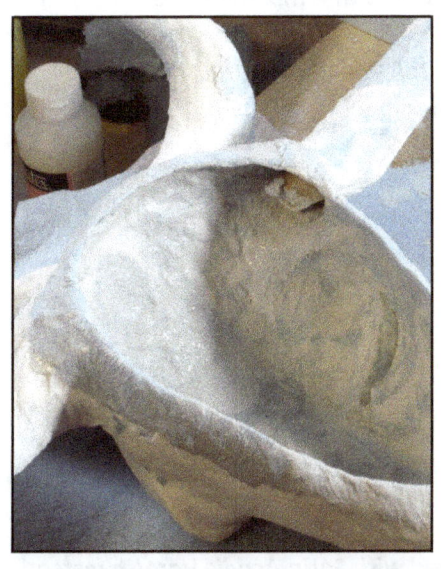

When the paper mache is dry, lift the mask from the mold and cut away the extra paper around the edges.

Mix a double recipe of plaster-based gesso (unless you made your kudu a lot smaller than I did). You can use the gesso as paste and cover the aluminum foil at the bottom of the horns and the cardboard at the bottom of the ears with paper mache. I also added small pieces of paper mache to give the edges a nice neat finish. Use the rest of the gesso for the back portion of the mask that you can see.

When the back of the mask is dry, turn it over and give the front a coat of gesso. To get a smooth surface, use one layer of the Plaster-Based Gesso recipe on page 7, wet-polish the gesso when it's dry, and apply a final layer using a double recipe of the Really Smooth Gesso recipe on page 8. If the mask is still not as smooth as you would like, you can wet-polish again and give it another coat. Don't completely cover the waves you made along the horns.

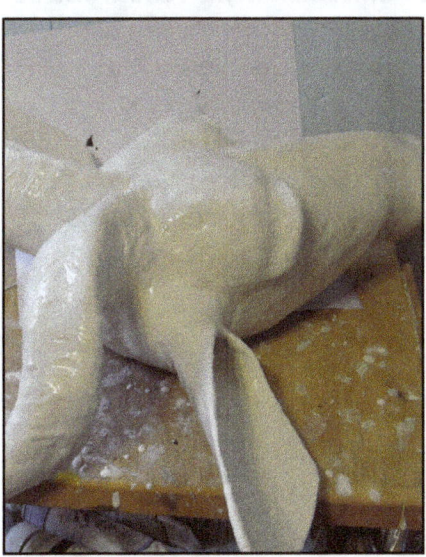

FINISH YOUR MASK

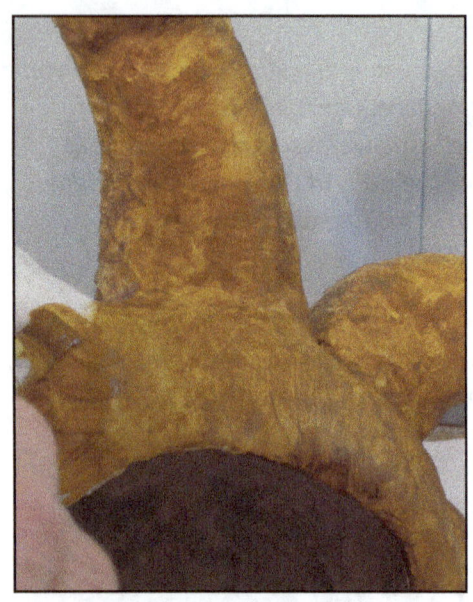

 Mix Golden Brown craft paint (or Raw Sienna acrylic artists' paint) with a bit of water. Use a small brush to paint this over the gesso. The paint will not cover the gesso evenly, but this is OK—the finish will get smoother as more layers are applied.

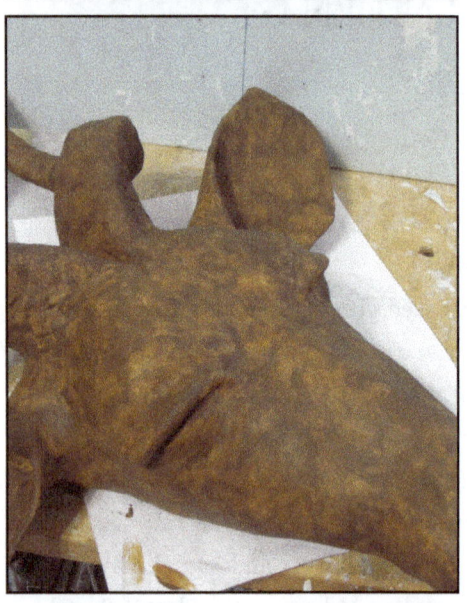

 When the first coat is completely dry, mix the same color you used before with a little bit of Burnt Umber to darken it, plus a little water. Paint this over the first coat. At this point, it will start to look a bit like leather.

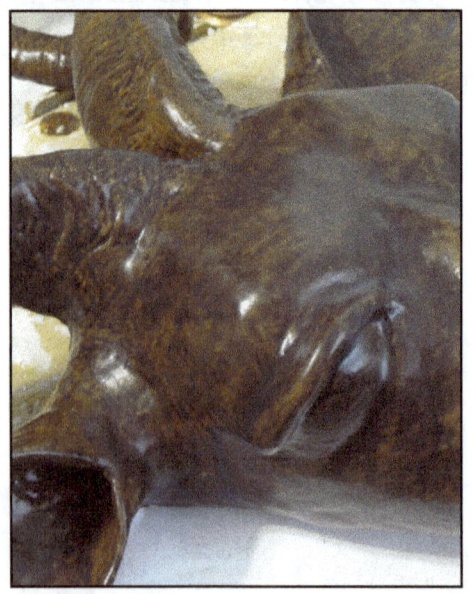

 The last two coats are mixed with Satin Acrylic Varnish instead of water. Use Burnt Umber and Black to make a very dark brown. Use enough varnish to make a transparent mixture. Wash this over the mask, using a wide soft brush. Don't put too much paint on your brush, or it will run. The pigments you mixed into the varnish will settle into the depressions on the surface of the mask, and will show off the waves in the horns.

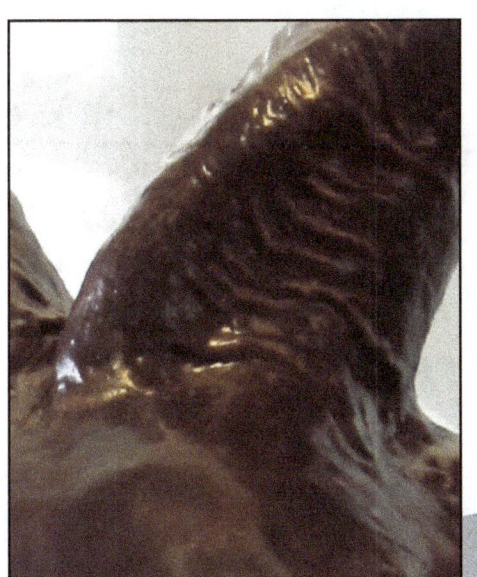

4 *Allow the varnish to dry overnight, and then give your mask one final coat of the dark brown varnish mixture. This last coat will smooth out the colors, but the first layers of golden brown will still show through, giving a warm, wood-like glow.*

If you want to go even darker to look like ebony, you can add a third layer of paint and varnish, with more black in the mix.

When the varnish is dry you can attach a hanger to the back (see page 31). If you want, you can use a final coat of paste wax to soften the shine and make the mask seem more like polished wood. Then hang him on your wall, and enjoy!

95

Gallery

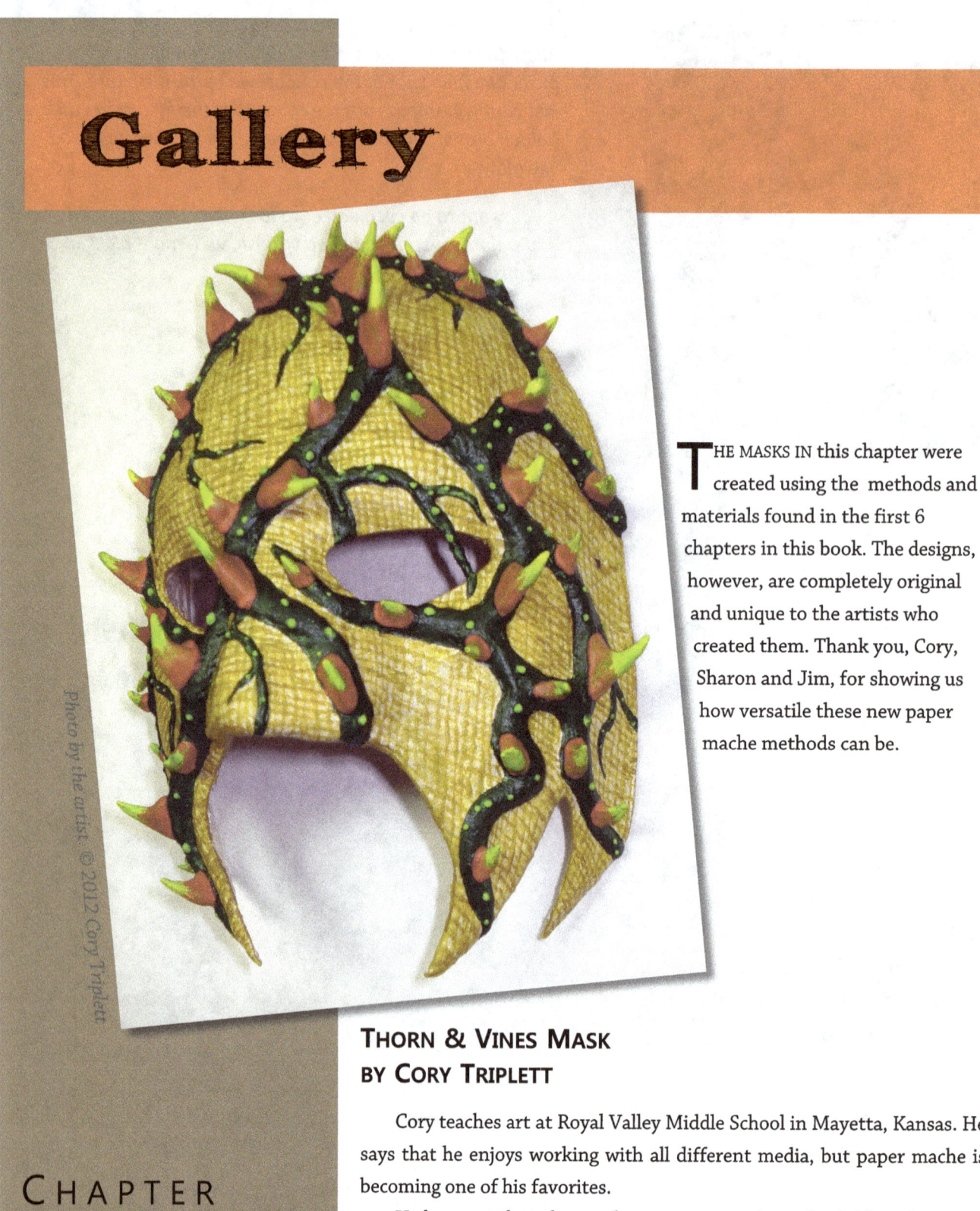

THE MASKS IN this chapter were created using the methods and materials found in the first 6 chapters in this book. The designs, however, are completely original and unique to the artists who created them. Thank you, Cory, Sharon and Jim, for showing us how versatile these new paper mache methods can be.

THORN & VINES MASK
BY CORY TRIPLETT

Cory teaches art at Royal Valley Middle School in Mayetta, Kansas. He says that he enjoys working with all different media, but paper mache is becoming one of his favorites.

He has contributed several guest posts on the author's blog, showing off masks, theater props, and even a life-sized panther—all created by Cory and his students with paper mache. You can see read his posts at UltimatePaperMache.com (just type his name in the search bar).

CHAPTER
19

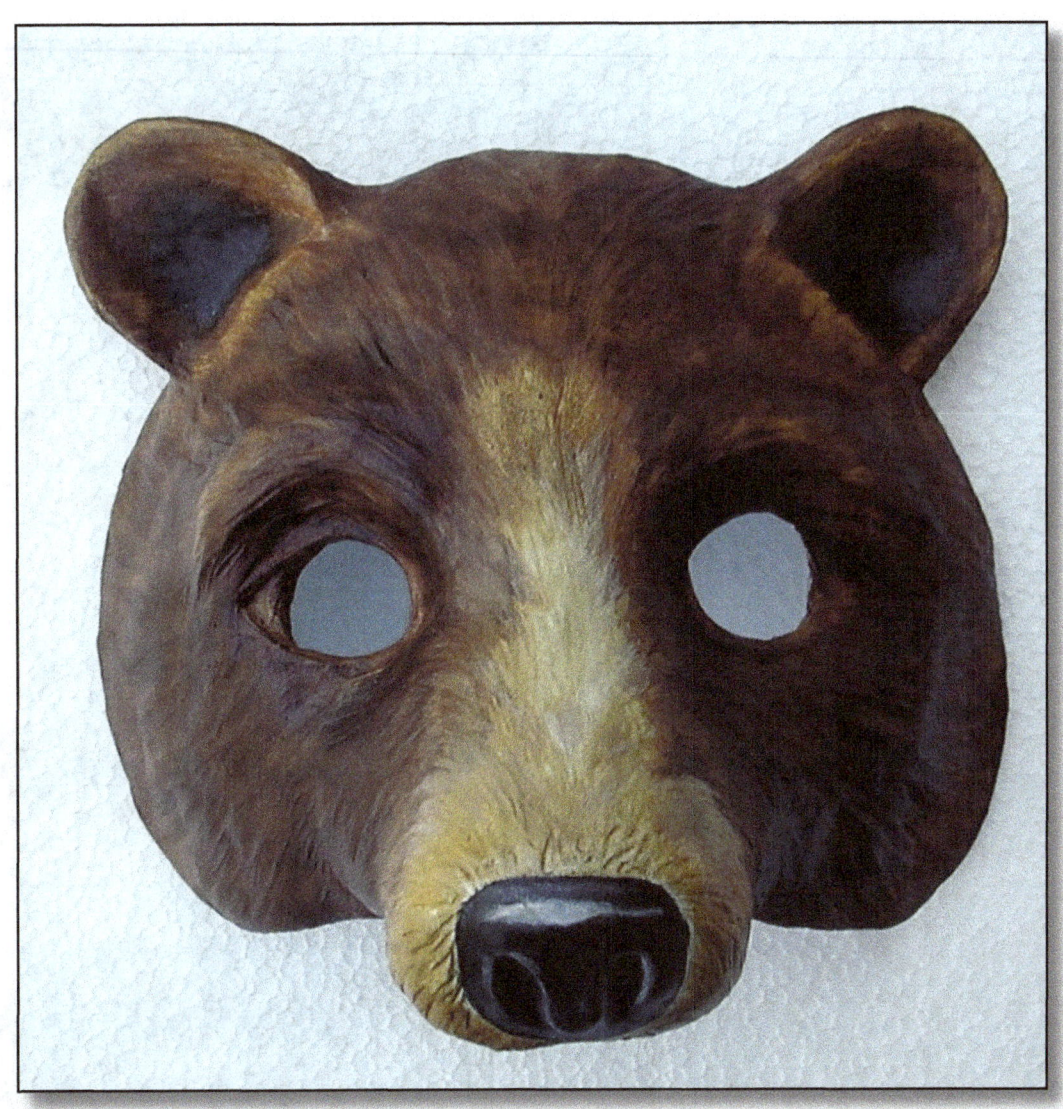

BEAR MASK
BY SHARON OMAN MORENO

Sharon's drive to express her creative force has covered many genres through the years. Winning Honorable Mention at an early age at a local museum exhibition, followed by numerous Blue Ribbons of her wildlife art at the County Fair, cemented her drive to create with any medium that took her fancy.

For the past few years working in paper mache has been her main focus. Bringing her visions to life through her sculpting and painting has fulfilled her love for a good challenge. With paper mache she has also found a way to address her sense of personal responsibility regarding the overwhelming waste issue. Through her art, she is able to reuse and recycle much of her household paper waste into transformations of whimsical creations.

You can see some of her art at http://www.etsy.com/shop/thepaintedladys where she occasionally lists when she isn't working on her recently acquired run down, falling apart, fixer-upper house.

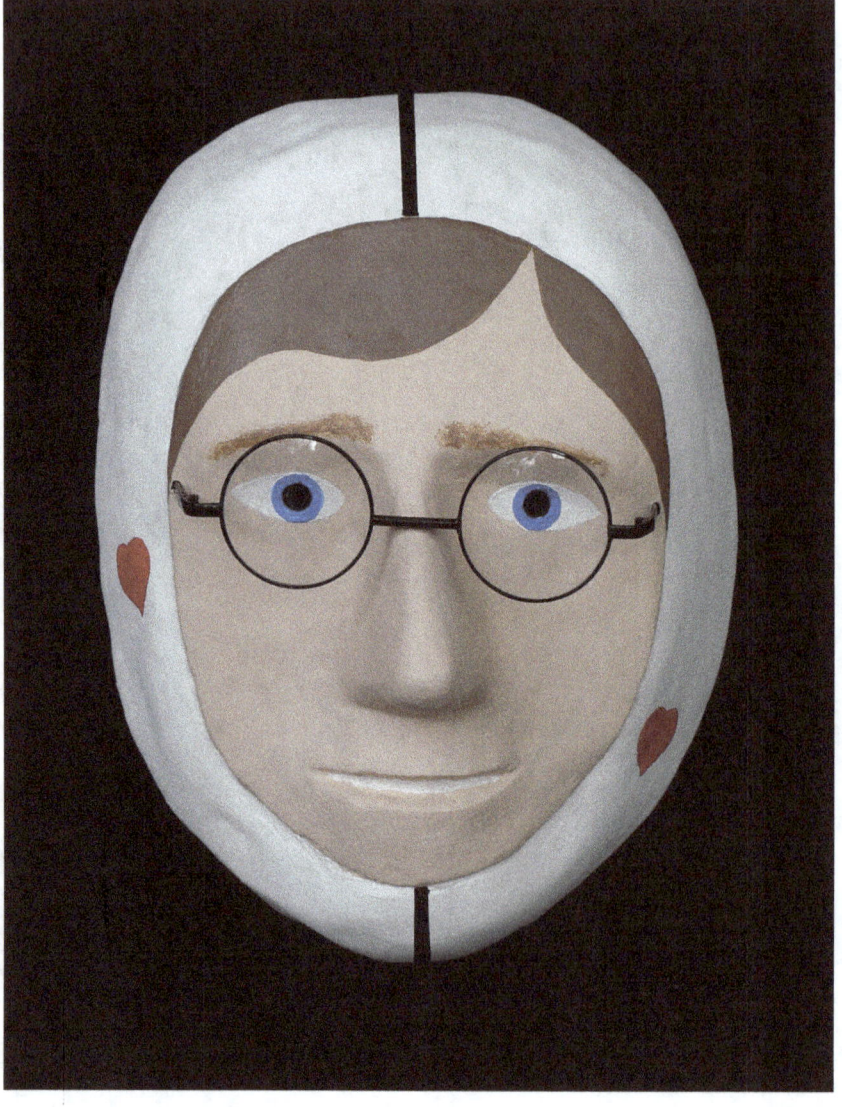

TWO-FACED MIME MASK
BY JIM KRANSBERGER

Jim says "my motto (words to live by) comes from a very famous artist, Norman Rockwell: 'If an image doesn't work, put a dog in it. If the dog doesn't work, put a bandage on the dog.' And, don't take yourself too seriously . . . nobody else does."

Jim is a sculptor working in basswood, papier-mâché and mixed media. He is primarily known for his humorous mechanical sculptures, which have been shown in a number of fine art galleries and shows, including the 2012 Humor in Craft Invitational in Pittsburgh, PA.

Jim's work was featured in the September/October 2011 issue of ARTsee magazine and will appear in the book *Humor in Crafts* by Brigitte Martin. He lives in Asheville, NC .

You can see some of Jim's sculptures and learn more about him by visiting his website, at http://www.JimKransberger.com

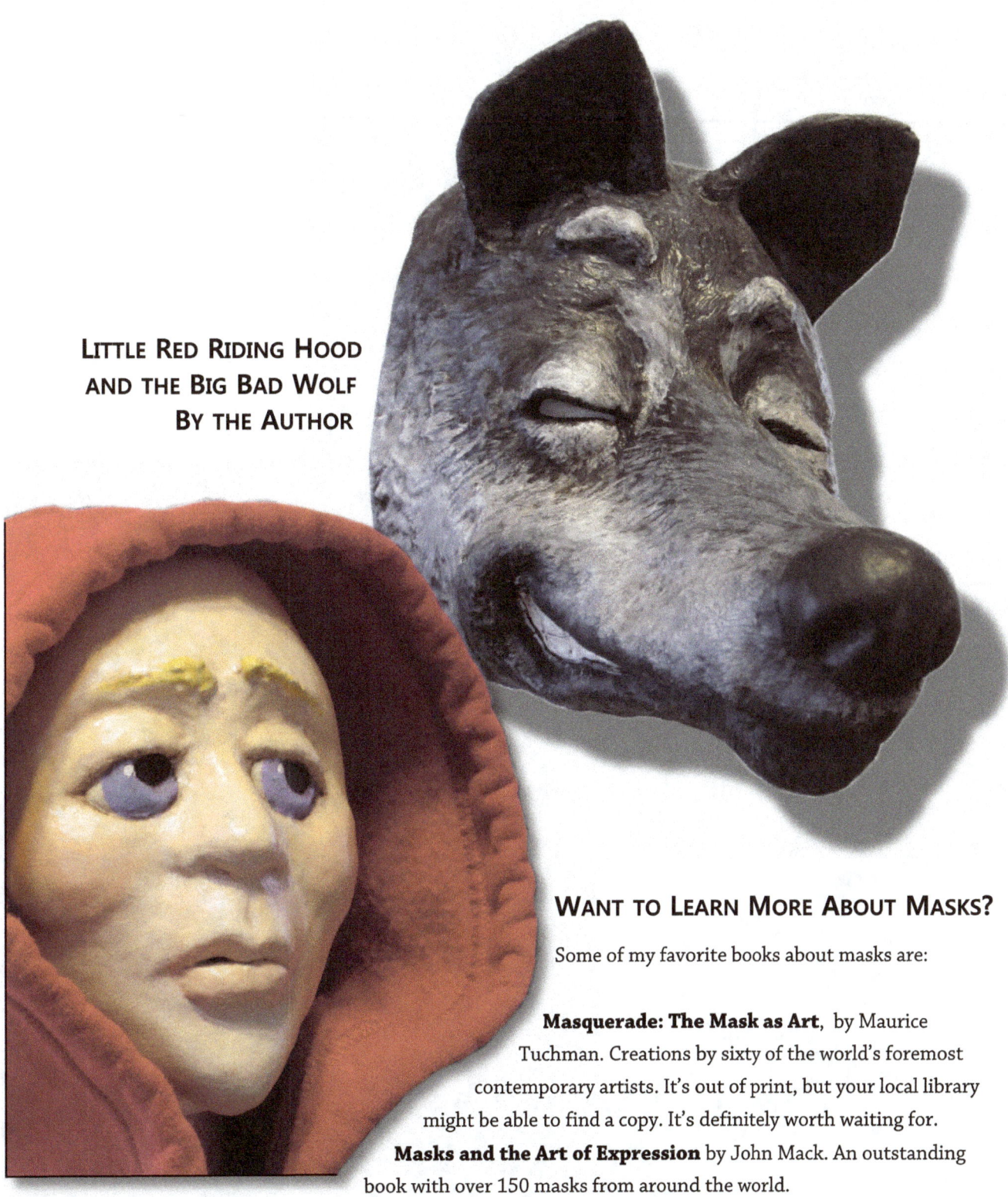

LITTLE RED RIDING HOOD
AND THE BIG BAD WOLF
BY THE AUTHOR

WANT TO LEARN MORE ABOUT MASKS?

Some of my favorite books about masks are:

Masquerade: The Mask as Art, by Maurice Tuchman. Creations by sixty of the world's foremost contemporary artists. It's out of print, but your local library might be able to find a copy. It's definitely worth waiting for.

Masks and the Art of Expression by John Mack. An outstanding book with over 150 masks from around the world.

Faces of Your Soul: Rituals in Art, Maskmaking, and Guided Imagery with Ancestors, Spirit Guides, and Totem Animals by Kaleo Ching and Elise Dirlam Ching. The use of art in self-expression, meditation, and healing.

Please tell the world if you like this book by leaving a Customer Review on Amazon.com

www.ingramcontent.com/pod-product-compliance
Lightning Source LLC
Chambersburg PA
CBHW081008170526

45158CB00010B/2962